T0116159

Survival

GLOBAL POLITICS AND STRATEGY

Volume 65 Number 6 | December 2023–January 2024

'It is fair to say that the tone and regularity of Medvedev's comments, the lack of follow-through and frequent rumours about his sobriety meant that these statements were taken less seriously than he might have wished.'

Lawrence Freedman, The Russo-Ukrainian War and the Durability of Deterrence, p. 17.

'The genocidal character of Hamas's attack on Israel was the living embodiment of the latter's deepest national nightmare: that its enemies' true objective was the annihilation of Jews, as Jews, and ultimately the destruction of the state of Israel.'

Chuck Freilich, Israel and the Palestinians: The Day After, p. 68.

'When it comes to burden-sharing in NATO, old habits die hard. Instead of working toward the investment target, some allies, such as Canada, instead spent 2022–23 lobbying to broaden the definition of what counts as defence spending.'

Sara Bjerg Moller, NATO at 75: The Perils of Empty Promises, p. 105.

Survival

GLOBAL POLITICS AND STRATEGY

Volume 65 Number 6 | December 2023–January 2024

Contents

Survival

GLOBAL POLITICS AND STRATEGY

The International Institute for Strategic Studies

2121 K Street, NW | Suite 600 | Washington DC 20037 | USA
Tel +1 202 659 1490   Fax +1 202 659 1499   E-mail survival@iiss.org   Web www.iiss.org

Arundel House | 6 Temple Place | London | WC2R 2PG | UK
Tel +44 (0)20 7379 7676   Fax +44 (0)20 7836 3108   E-mail iiss@iiss.org

14th Floor, GFH Tower | Bahrain Financial Harbour | Manama | Kingdom of Bahrain
Tel +973 1718 1155   Fax +973 1710 0155   E-mail iiss-middleeast@iiss.org

9 Raffles Place | #49-01 Republic Plaza | Singapore 048619
Tel +65 6499 0055   Fax +65 6499 0059   E-mail iiss-asia@iiss.org

Pariser Platz 6A | 10117 Berlin | Germany
Tel +49 30 311 99 300   E-mail iiss-europe@iiss.org

Survival Online www.tandfonline.com/survival and www.iiss.org/publications/survival

Aims and Scope *Survival* is one of the world's leading forums for analysis and debate of international and strategic affairs. Shaped by its editors to be both timely and forward thinking, the journal encourages writers to challenge conventional wisdom and bring fresh, often controversial, perspectives to bear on the strategic issues of the moment. With a diverse range of authors, *Survival* aims to be scholarly in depth while vivid, well written and policy-relevant in approach. Through commentary, analytical articles, case studies, forums, review essays, reviews and letters to the editor, the journal promotes lively, critical debate on issues of international politics and strategy.

Editor **Dana Allin**
Managing Editor **Jonathan Stevenson**
Associate Editor **Carolyn West**
Editorial Assistant **Conor Hodges**
Production and Cartography **Alessandra Beluffi, Ravi Gopar, Jade Panganiban, James Parker, Kelly Verity**

Contributing Editors

William Alberque	**Chester A. Crocker**	**Melissa K. Griffith**	**Irene Mia**	**Karen Smith**
Målfrid Braut-Hegghammer	**Bill Emmott**	**Emile Hokayem**	**Meia Nouwens**	**Angela Stent**
	Franz-Stefan Gady	**Nigel Inkster**	**Benjamin Rhode**	**Robert Ward**
Aaron Connelly	**Bastian Giegerich**	**Jeffrey Mazo**	**Ben Schreer**	**Marcus Willett**
James Crabtree	**Nigel Gould-Davies**	**Fenella McGerty**	**Maria Shagina**	**Lanxin Xiang**

Published for the IISS by
Routledge Journals, an imprint of Taylor & Francis, an Informa business.

ISBN 978-1-032-53714-6 paperback / 978-1-003-42939-5 ebook

About the IISS The IISS, a registered charity with offices in Washington, London, Manama, Singapore and Berlin, is the world's leading authority on political–military conflict. It is the primary independent source of accurate, objective information on international strategic issues. Publications include *The Military Balance*, an annual reference work on each nation's defence capabilities; *Survival*, a bimonthly journal on international affairs; *Strategic Comments*, an online analysis of topical issues in international affairs; and the *Adelphi* series of books on issues of international security.

SUBMISSIONS

To submit an article, authors are advised to follow these guidelines:

- *Survival* articles are around 4,000–10,000 words long including endnotes. A word count should be included with a draft.
- All text, including endnotes, should be double-spaced with wide margins.
- Any tables or artwork should be supplied in separate files, ideally not embedded in the document or linked to text around it.
- All *Survival* articles are expected to include endnote references. These should be complete and include first and last names of authors, titles of articles (even from newspapers), place of publication, publisher, exact publication dates, volume and issue number (if from a journal) and page numbers. Web sources should include complete URLs and DOIs if available.
- A summary of up to 150 words should be included with the article. The summary should state the main argument clearly and concisely, not simply say what the article is about.

- A short author's biography of one or two lines should also be included. This information will appear at the foot of the first page of the article.

Please note that *Survival* has a strict policy of listing multiple authors in alphabetical order.

Submissions should be made by email, in Microsoft Word format, to survival@iiss.org. Alternatively, hard copies may be sent to *Survival*, IISS–US, 2121 K Street NW, Suite 801, Washington, DC 20037, USA.

The editorial review process can take up to three months. *Survival*'s acceptance rate for unsolicited manuscripts is less than 20%. *Survival* does not normally provide referees' comments in the event of rejection. Authors are permitted to submit simultaneously elsewhere so long as this is consistent with the policy of the other publication and the Editors of *Survival* are informed of the dual submission.

Readers are encouraged to comment on articles from the previous issue. Letters should be concise, no longer than 750 words and relate directly to the argument or points made in the original article.

Survival: Global Politics and Strategy (Print ISSN 0039-6338, Online ISSN 1468-2699) is published bimonthly for a total of 6 issues per year by Taylor & Francis Group, 4 Park Square, Milton Park, Abingdon, Oxon, OX14 4RN, UK. Periodicals postage paid (Permit no. 13095) at Brooklyn, NY 11256.

Airfreight and mailing in the USA by agent named World Container Inc., c/o BBT 150-15, 183rd Street, Jamaica, NY 11413, USA.

US Postmaster: Send address changes to Survival, World Container Inc., c/o BBT 150-15, 183rd Street, Jamaica, NY 11413, USA.

Subscription records are maintained at Taylor & Francis Group, 4 Park Square, Milton Park, Abingdon, OX14 4RN, UK.

Subscription information: For more information and subscription rates, please see tandfonline.com/pricing/journal/TSUR. Taylor & Francis journals are available in a range of different packages, designed to suit every library's needs and budget. This journal is available for institutional subscriptions with online-only or print & online options. This journal may also be available as part of our libraries, subject collections or archives. For more information on our sales packages, please visit librarianresources.taylorandfrancis.com.

For support with any institutional subscription, please visit help.tandfonline.com or email our dedicated team at subscriptions@tandf.co.uk.

Subscriptions purchased at the personal rate are strictly for personal, non-commercial use only. The reselling of personal subscriptions is prohibited. Personal subscriptions must be purchased with a personal cheque, credit card or BAC/wire transfer. Proof of personal status may be requested.

Back issues: Taylor & Francis Group retains a current and one-year back-issue stock of journals. Older volumes are held by our official stockists to whom all orders and enquiries should be addressed: Periodicals Service Company, 351 Fairview Avenue, Suite 300, Hudson, NY 12534, USA. Tel: +1 518 537 4700; email psc@periodicals.com.

Ordering information: To subscribe to the journal, please contact T&F Customer Services, Informa UK Ltd, Sheepen Place, Colchester, Essex, CO3 3LP, UK. Tel: +44 (0) 20 8052 2030; email subscriptions@tandf.co.uk.

Taylor & Francis journals are priced in USD, GBP and EUR (as well as AUD and CAD for a limited number of journals). All subscriptions are charged depending on where the end customer is based. If you are unsure which rate applies to you, please contact Customer Services. All subscriptions are payable in advance and all rates include postage. We are required to charge applicable VAT/GST on all print and online combination subscriptions, in addition to our online-only journals. Subscriptions are entered on an annual basis, i.e., January to December. Payment may be made by sterling cheque, dollar cheque, euro cheque, international money order, National Giro or credit cards (Amex, Visa and Mastercard).

Disclaimer: The International Institute for Strategic Studies (IISS) and our publisher Informa UK Limited, trading as Taylor & Francis Group ('T&F'), make every effort to ensure the accuracy of all the information (the 'Content') contained in our publications. However, IISS and our publisher T&F, our agents and our licensors make no representations or warranties whatsoever as to the accuracy, completeness or suitability for any purpose of the Content. Any opinions and views expressed in this publication are the opinions and views of the authors, and are not the views of or endorsed by IISS or our publisher T&F. The accuracy of the Content should not be relied upon and should be independently verified with primary sources of information, and any reliance on the Content is at your own risk. IISS and our publisher T&F make no representations, warranties or guarantees, whether express or implied, that the Content is accurate, complete or up to date. IISS and our publisher T&F shall not be liable for any losses, actions, claims, proceedings, demands, costs, expenses, damages and other liabilities whatsoever or howsoever caused arising directly or indirectly in connection with, in relation to or arising out of the use of the Content. Full Terms & Conditions of access and use can be found at http://www.tandfonline.com/page/terms-and-conditions.

Informa UK Limited, trading as Taylor & Francis Group, grants authorisation for individuals to photocopy copyright material for private research use, on the sole basis that requests for such use are referred directly to the requestor's local Reproduction Rights Organization (RRO). The copyright fee is exclusive of any charge or fee levied. In order to contact your local RRO, please contact International Federation of Reproduction Rights Organizations (IFRRO), rue du Prince Royal, 87, B-1050 Brussels, Belgium; email ifrro@skynet.be; Copyright Clearance Center Inc., 222 Rosewood Drive, Danvers, MA 01923, USA; email info@copyright.com; or Copyright Licensing Agency, 90 Tottenham Court Road, London, W1P 0LP, UK; email cla@cla.co.uk. This authorisation does not extend to any other kind of copying, by any means, in any form, for any purpose other than private research use.

Submission information: See https://www.tandfonline.com/journals/tsur20

Advertising: See https://taylorandfrancis.com/contact/advertising/

Permissions: See help.tandfonline.com/Librarian/s/article/Permissions

All Taylor & Francis Group journals are printed on paper from renewable sources by accredited partners.

December 2023–January 2024

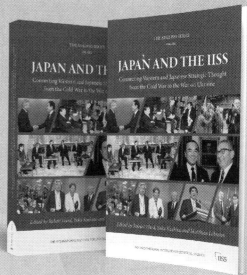

The Russo-Ukrainian War and the Durability of Deterrence

Lawrence Freedman

It has become commonplace to observe that the Russo-Ukrainian war has brought the world closer to nuclear war than at any time since the 1962 Cuban Missile Crisis without being clear how close. A state of anxiety has accompanied every stage of the war since Russia's full-scale invasion of 24 February 2022, intensifying as it struggled to overcome Ukrainian resistance. Could a nuclear power restrain itself from using its most powerful weapons against a non-nuclear and non-NATO power when it was losing? And to the extent that it saw its struggle as the result of the support given to Ukraine by the United States and its allies, might it draw them into the war, adding to the risk of nuclear escalation?

Thus far, the weapons have not been used and the speculation that they might soon be used has subsided, although it is unlikely to end until there is some sort of ceasefire in the war. Both the Russian Federation and the US and its allies have avoided taking actions carrying the greatest escalatory risk. NATO countries have not committed forces to the fighting and Russia has not attacked NATO states despite their active support for Ukraine in all other respects.

This restraint has bounded the conflict. Left uncertain is whether there are contingencies in which nuclear use might nonetheless be prompted. As

Lawrence Freedman is Emeritus Professor of War Studies at King's College London.

Survival | vol. 65 no. 6 | December 2023–January 2024 | pp. 7–36 https://doi.org/10.1080/00396338.2023.2285598

Russia is the only belligerent nuclear power, this would be a decision for Moscow, perhaps the result of Russian forces facing defeat in Ukraine, or Russian territory being struck with systems provided by Western countries. Moscow has therefore had the most to gain by emphasising the risk, and has done so regularly in the hope of deterring Western allies from transferring even more capable, long-range systems to Ukraine, or Ukrainian forces from attempting to take Crimea.

These threats have had some effect, at least in delaying some arms transfers, which has led to arguments that the US has allowed itself to be intimidated unnecessarily, thereby either prolonging the war because Ukraine lacks the wherewithal to liberate its territories, or allowing a dangerous situation to develop that could yield a Russian victory. Thus, Anne Applebaum has complained:

> Our self-imposed limitations may well have encouraged Putin to believe that American support for Ukraine is limited and will soon end. Our insistence that Ukraine not harm Russia or Russians in its own defense might explain why he keeps fighting. Perhaps our nuclear anxiety actually encourages him to carry out nonnuclear mass atrocities; he does so because he believes he will not face any consequences, because we will not escalate.[1]

Against this claim comes the warning that the risk of a nuclear catastrophe is real and that the US is bound to be cautious in these circumstances. Steve Cimbala and Lawrence Korb admonish:

> Concerns about the possibility of nuclear escalation are not to be dismissed, and they go beyond accepting any obviously tendentious Russian propaganda. In addition to high-end conventional military performance by Ukraine and NATO political unity, another requirement for success in defending Ukraine is escalation control.[2]

Much of the debate about the role of nuclear weapons in this war has, unavoidably, sought to identify the contingencies in which the fateful step might be taken. But the war has now been going on long enough for us to be able to ground the debate much more in what has been said and done during its course. There have been authoritative and consequential statements of policy from both Russian President Vladimir Putin and US President Joe Biden, and numerous comments from Russian sources, some quite inflammatory in their language, raising anxiety levels but with few tangible effects. There have also been interventions by other world figures, including Chinese President Xi Jinping, urging caution. We are no longer flying blind on this matter. There is a record to assess.

Crystal balls, taboos and red lines

The literature on nuclear deterrence is immense.[3] For the sake of simplicity we can identify the tension at its heart as one between the potential advantage of persuading a potential adversary that nuclear weapons might be used and the formidable reasons for not using them. These reasons come down to the proposition that any use would be both mad and bad: potentially suicidal for the instigator and widely condemned internationally because of the dire consequences for everyone else.

The 'mad' part is captured not just by the notorious acronym for 'mutual assured destruction' but also by the 'crystal-ball effect'.[4] When contemplating moves that could conceivably lead to nuclear exchanges, even if the risk is small, political leaders look into their crystal balls and see them full of mushroom clouds, leading to the end of civilisations and ecological disaster. Setting in motion the steps that could lead to such a terminal tragedy would go well beyond normal risk-taking. As the effects of multiple nuclear detonations, even only a few, would be horrific, and spread randomly and linger, setting a frightful precedent, the natural caution induced by the crystal ball is reinforced by strong normative constraints. These add up to the so-called 'nuclear taboo', ensuring that any state that broke it would be condemned as an international pariah. Over the years since 1945, a tradition of non-use has been established, reinforced by regular declarations that fighting a nuclear war would be irresponsible and unthinkable.[5]

Not completely unthinkable, of course, because substantial nuclear arsenals have been constructed and maintained. Governments on occasion may speak wistfully of a time when the arsenals might be dismantled, but for now they also believe in their strategic value, not least in reminding potential adversaries of the dangers of making war against them. So they continue to have a role as weapons of last resort.

But what constitutes the last resort? One obvious one would arise when a territory was being subjected to a nuclear attack. Then retaliation in kind would be both natural and justified, albeit in some ways pointless because the harm would already have been done. Nuclear powers, however, seek to do more than neutralise each other's arsenals. They wish to deter other types of threats to the existence of the state. This includes an enemy seizing sovereign territory, or using chemical or biological weapons (even though these are not in the same league in terms of their effects as nuclear weapons). Then there is the even more demanding task of deterring existential threats against allied states, thereby creating an immediate risk to one's own state that might not otherwise have been present.

Identifying the point of nuclear last resort is crucial for purposes of deterrence from the perspective of both the state doing the deterring and those to be deterred. This point is now often described as a 'red line', which if crossed must put the transgressor in danger. A red line will be the point at which a vital interest is irretrievably threatened, so it must in some ways be a point of no return. As such, it needs to be defined with specificity and clarity so that the transgression does not occur by accident. If one is transgressed without response, as for example when Barack Obama decided against punishing Syria for its use of chemical weapons in 2013, this may affect not only the immediate crisis but the wider credibility of the party setting the red line.[6]

If the red line is pulled back to a moment of truly last resort, the deterrent threat may be convincing, but fewer acts might then be deterred. It may ease the opponent's risk calculus as it contemplates what might still constitute significant aggression. Alternatively, setting the red line early – possibly well before all non-nuclear means of resistance have been exhausted – carries the risk that the deterrent effect will be ignored. This is why there can be a temptation to avoid clarity, to rely instead on uncertainty and fear of the unknown to encourage caution – what Thomas C. Schelling called the 'threat that leaves something to chance'.[7] Ambiguity leaves the potential adversary guessing about what comes next. Rather than attempt to clarify what they might do in extreme contingencies, better to assume that their opponents also have no idea.

Putin seeks to deter

It is Russian nuclear decision-making that requires the most attention because Russia, having embarked on a war which it expected to win easily before discovering it could not, faced the greatest strategic predicament. The most authoritative statements on Russian policy were Putin's.

For him, the Russian Federation's large and varied nuclear arsenal helps define the country. It is not only essential to its defence but also provides its international status and validates its mission as a vital counter to American power. It is 'the key guarantee of Russia's military security and global stability'.[8] At times he has shown a streak of apocalyptical thinking, remarking that a world that could do without the Russian state did not deserve to continue, and that, because Russians uphold the core values of civilisation, they could at least expect to get to paradise as martyrs in a nuclear cataclysm.[9]

The official line on nuclear use is set down in more prosaic terms in 'The Fundamentals of the State Policy of the Russian Federation in the Field of Nuclear Deterrence', published in June 2020. This states that the policy is 'defensive in nature'. The right to use nuclear weapons is reserved

> in response to the use of nuclear weapons and other types of weapons of mass destruction against it and (or) its allies, as well as in the event of aggression against the Russian Federation with the use of conventional weapons, when the very existence of the state is threatened.

The relevant conditions would be:

(a) receipt of reliable information about the launch of ballistic missiles attacking the territory of the Russian Federation and (or) its allies;

(b) the use of nuclear weapons or other types of weapons of mass destruction by the enemy on the territories of the Russian Federation and (or) its allies;

(c) the impact of the enemy on critical state or military facilities of the Russian Federation, the incapacitation of which will lead to the disruption of the response of nuclear forces;

(d) aggression against the Russian Federation with the use of conventional weapons, when the very existence of the state is threatened.[10]

Note that condition (a) points to a launch-on-warning policy. If Russia's early-warning system picked up signs of incoming weapons, this would trigger the launch against American targets of the threatened Russian intercontinental ballistic missiles and bombers. In December 2022, when meeting with soldiers' mothers, Putin responded to a suggestion that as a 'true gesture of goodwill' he should pledge not to use nuclear weapons first by observing 'if we are not the first to use them under any circumstances, then we won't be the second to use them either, because the possibilities of their use in case of a nuclear strike on our territory are very limited'.[11]

Condition (d), when the Russian state faces an existential threat from an adversary employing conventional weapons, is the most relevant. Until well into 2022, Ukraine itself was not seen as being close to posing such a threat. The specific focus of nuclear deterrence was therefore the possibility that NATO countries might enter the war as allies of Ukraine. The issue arose in August 2014, when Russian regular troops were overtly involved for the first time – having been covertly involved before – in seeking to push back Ukrainian forces who had acted against Russian-sponsored militias in the Donbas. Putin was then quoted as saying that other countries 'should understand it's best not to mess with us', with a reminder that 'Russia is one of the leading nuclear powers'.[12] He re-emphasised the point on 24 February 2022 when he announced the full-scale invasion:

> I would now like to say something very important for those who may be tempted to interfere in these developments from the outside. No matter who tries to stand in our way or all the more so create threats for our country and our people, they must know that Russia will respond immediately, and the consequences will be such as you have never seen in your entire history.[13]

Three days later, he publicly ordered his defence minister, Sergei Shoigu, and chief of the general staff, General Valery V. Gerasimov, 'to transfer the army's deterrence forces to a special mode of combat duty'.[14] This did not amount to much in practice: the point was to underline the deterrent threat. An annual nuclear drill that took place a few days before the invasion served a similar purpose.

Putin regularly came back to this position. When announcing the annexation of four provinces and full mobilisation on 21 September 2022, he blamed the West for threatening a nuclear catastrophe. It was in response to this supposed NATO threat that he said:

> I want to remind you that our country also has various means of destruction, and in some components more modern than the NATO countries. And if the territorial integrity of our country is threatened, we will certainly use all the means at our disposal to protect Russia and our people. It's not a bluff. The citizens of Russia can be sure that the territorial integrity of our Motherland, our independence and freedom will be ensured – I emphasize this again – with all the means at our disposal.[15]

At a press conference on 14 October 2022, after a period in which there had been intense speculation about Russia 'going nuclear', Putin was asked what appeared to be a planted question: given that NATO officials are saying explicitly that Ukraine's defeat would mean the Alliance's defeat, do you think NATO will send troops into Ukraine if the situation on the battlefield becomes disastrous for Kyiv? He replied that 'sending troops into direct engagement, a direct clash with the Russian Army is a very dangerous step that could lead to a global catastrophe. I hope those who talk about this will be smart enough not to undertake such dangerous steps.'[16]

Putin consistently blamed the West for the increased risk of nuclear war.[17] But his definition of the red lines was also consistent and, compared to that of other senior figures, relatively restricted. In October 2022, he denied that Russia was preparing to use nuclear weapons in the war in Ukraine: 'We have no need to do this. There's no sense for us, neither political nor military.'[18] His joint statement with Xi on 21 March 2023 referred back to the 'joint statement by the leaders of the five countries, which possess nuclear weapons, on the prevention of a nuclear war and an arms race', and restated 'that there can be no winners in a nuclear war and it must never be unleashed'.[19] In June 2023, he rejected the idea of using tactical nuclear weapons: 'First, we see no need to use [them]; and second, considering this, even as a possibility, factors into lowering the threshold for the use of such weapons.'[20]

This does not mean that Putin could not change his mind, or that planning has not taken place. US intelligence has reportedly picked up such discussion among Russian military commanders, although there were no indications of any movement of systems or other measures that would imply serious preparations.[21] Not long after the March meeting with Xi, Putin announced that tactical nuclear weapons were being sent to Belarus. He explained that this had been done 'precisely as an element of deterrence so that all those who are thinking about inflicting a strategic defeat on us are not oblivious to this circumstance'.[22] But all of this was consistent with established doctrine, which reserved the threat of nuclear use for an existential threat to the state. Continual denials of any interest in using tactical nuclear weapons might not be the whole truth, but they do signify the Kremlin's assessment that no potential strategic value can be extracted from the threats.

Wider Russian threats

The relative specificity of Putin's deterrent threats has been combined with an incessant series of more general warnings and demands for tough action, including with nuclear weapons, from Russian pundits and even officials with some notional influence. Hanna Notte has referred to a 'nuclear fever' afflicting Russian media, quoting a Russian dissident's observation that 'on Russian television over the past two weeks they have said two hundred times that ... it is possible ... and how they should use nuclear weapons. Two hundred times. For two weeks. This already looks like an advertisement for dog food.'[23]

For example, Andrey Gurulev – a lieutenant-general, member of the Duma and regular media commentator – claimed in August 2022 that Russia was fighting both the United Kingdom and the US in Ukraine:

> Let's make it super simple. Two ships, 50 launches of Zircon [missiles] –
> and there is not a single power station left in the UK. Fifty more Zircons
> – and the entire port infrastructure is gone. One more – and we forget
> about the British Isles. A Third World country, destroyed and fallen apart
> because Scotland and Wales would leave. This would be the end of the
> British Crown. And they are scared of it.[24]

A month later, after noting that Biden had warned Russia against using nuclear weapons in Ukraine, Gurulev observed that 'we may use them but not in Ukraine'. This time he made particular mention of strikes against decision-making centres in Berlin, threatening Germany with total chaos, along with his familiar theme of turning the British Isles into a 'Martian desert in 3 minutes flat'. He added, oddly, that this could be done with 'tactical nuclear weapons, not strategic ones' and, confidently, that the US would not respond. All this was linked to preventing NATO from getting directly involved. 'We shouldn't be shy about it or fear it … They should tuck their tails in and keep up yapping.'[25]

Russian TV presenter Olga Skabeyeva, who regularly describes the conflict as 'World War III', made specific threats with regard to the potential delivery of the long-range (300-kilometre) Army Tactical Missile System (ATACMS) missiles from the US to Ukraine: 'Russia has every right to defend itself. That's to say, to strike Poland or the US's Ramstein base in Germany, for example.'[26] Former space chief Dmitry Rogozin proposed having tactical nuclear weapons available, which 'we have the right to use', to avoid casualties during Ukraine's offensive. They would be a 'great equalizer for the moments when there is a clear discrepancy in the enemy's favor'.[27]

Not everyone was impressed. Yevgeny Prigozhin, then extant and still head of the Wagner Group, said talking about such disproportionate threats made the Russians 'look like clowns'.[28] There was a lot of nuclear advocacy, of varying degrees of fatuousness, but in general it was no more than background noise. The effect was, if anything, to deprive nuclear warnings of their drama because they were so routine.

Officials tended to stick close to Putin's line. His spokesman, Dmitry Peskov, for example, was reassuring in March 2022:

> Any outcome of the operation (in Ukraine) of course is not a reason for
> usage of a nuclear weapon. We have a security concept that very clearly
> states that only when there is a threat for existence of the state, in our
> country, we can use and we will actually use nuclear weapons to eliminate
> the threat for the existence of our country.[29]

After Chechen leader Ramzan Kadyrov spoke in favour of using 'low-yield' nuclear weapons, Peskov dismissed this as an emotional assessment and reasserted the 2020 policy.[30] His stress was on the risks of escalation posed by Western actions. Foreign Minister Sergei Lavrov took the same position. On 26 April 2022, for example, he warned the West not to underestimate the elevated risks of nuclear conflict over Ukraine and explained that NATO was 'in essence' engaged in a proxy war with Russia by supplying Kyiv with weaponry. He said Russia wanted to prevent nuclear war but the 'risks now are considerable'.[31] Later pronouncements reinforced the theme that NATO was a 'serious threat' to Russia and risked a 'direct clash between nuclear powers with catastrophic consequences'.[32]

The exception in official circles was Dmitry Medvedev, the former president and now deputy chairman of Russia's Security Council, a body chaired by Putin. Medvedev regularly raised the spectre of nuclear war, habitually referred to as the 'nuclear apocalypse'. Sometimes this was no more than warning that as Western powers become more involved terrible things might happen.[33] Occasionally he was more specific, and went well beyond official doctrine. On 17 July 2022, following an American observation that it would be legitimate for Ukraine to attack Russian targets in Crimea, Medvedev was reported as saying that if Crimea was attacked, 'Judgment Day will come very fast and hard. It will be very difficult to hide.'[34] On 23 March 2023, in response to the International Criminal Court (ICC) arrest warrant issued for Putin on account of war crimes, Medvedev raised the hypothetical scenario of Putin being arrested on German soil. 'What would that be? It would be a declaration of war on the Russian Federation. And in that case, all our assets – all our missiles et cetera – would fly to the Bundestag, to the Chancellor's office.'[35] He also threatened the ICC judges with missile strikes, noting that it was 'quite possible to imagine a surgical application of a hypersonic Onyx from a Russian ship in the North Sea on The Hague courthouse', adding 'so, judges, look carefully to the sky'. This would not trigger a wider war, he reassured his audience, because 'the court is only a miserable international organization, not the population of a NATO country'.[36]

Over the course of 2023, with each announcement of more advanced Western weaponry for Ukraine, Medvedev's language became more vivid. After the announcement that Ukraine would be receiving F-16 aircraft, he described a scenario of 'loss for everyone. A collapse. Apocalypse. Where you forget for centuries about your former life, until the rubble ceases to emit radiation.'[37] He had also said that 'all of Ukraine that remains under Kyiv's rule will burn'.[38] Referring to US deliveries of *Abrams* tanks and potentially of ATACMS, he saw direct conflict with NATO coming. The Alliance, in his view, had 'turned into an openly fascist bloc like Hitler's Axis, albeit larger. We are ready, although the result will be achieved at a much greater cost to humanity than in 1945.'[39] On a potential German decision to send *Taurus* missiles, he commented: 'Strikes on German factories where these missiles are made would also be in full compliance with international law. All in all, these idiots are actively pushing us towards World War III.'[40]

It is fair to say that the tone and regularity of Medvedev's comments, the lack of follow-through and frequent rumours about his sobriety meant that these statements were taken less seriously than he might have wished.

The Karaganov debate

If Russia had as an objective deterring Western arms transfers to Ukraine, it failed. Such transfers did not decline, but instead became more extensive and intensive. This led to a debate among prominent Russian commentators on the possibility of restoring deterrence by lowering the nuclear threshold – that is, the point at which the weapons might be used. It was opened in June 2023, in an article entitled 'A Difficult but Necessary Decision' by Sergei Karaganov, honorary chairman of Russia's Council on Foreign and Defense Policy and an established figure in the Russian security-policy community.[41]

Karaganov's singular world view has Russia as the most important military barrier to the West's promotion of a globalist and 'anti-human' ideology. The West's need to subvert this barrier had led it 'to incite and support the Kiev junta', thereby creating a 'slide towards World War III'. In 'a fit of desperate rage, the ruling circles of a group of countries have unleashed a full-scale war in the underbelly of a nuclear superpower'. Russia now could not properly win in Ukraine until the West's will was broken, for otherwise even successful military operations would leave it with an embittered rump state or else a country wholly occupied but ruined 'with a population that mostly hates us'. Only if the West forced the Kyiv government to surrender could Russia secure a friendly buffer state. One reason why it was struggling to do so was that it had both 'thoughtlessly set too high a threshold for the use of nuclear weapons' and also 'inaccurately assessed the situation in Ukraine'. After 75 years of relative peace, people, especially in the West, had 'forgotten the horrors of war and even stopped fearing nuclear weapons'. Karaganov then amplified the singularity of his argument by asserting that nuclear weapons were created by 'divine intervention', so that God could hand to humanity this 'weapon of Armageddon' to remind those 'who had lost the fear of hell that it existed'. This fear worked for three-quarters of a century but had gone, and unless it could be revived, humanity was 'doomed'.[42]

According to Karaganov, somehow the West had to be persuaded to retreat or even surrender. 'Roughly speaking, it must "buzz off" so that Russia and the world could move forward unhindered.' This required making nuclear deterrence work by lowering the nuclear threshold. This could be done 'by rapidly but prudently moving up the deterrence–escalation ladder', even getting to the 'point when we will have to urge our compatriots and all people of goodwill to leave their places of residence near facilities that may become targets for strikes in countries that provide direct support to the puppet regime in Kiev'. To avoid retaliation against Russian cities, Karaganov proposed at first striking European targets, relying on the Americans not retaliating on their behalf, aware that the next step would involve Russia returning fire against American cities. He had no illusions about the likely reactions of friends and sympathisers. China would condemn a nuclear strike, even while rejoicing at the 'powerful blow' to 'the reputation and position of the United States'. Other members of the 'global majority' would find the end of the nuclear taboo unacceptable. 'But in the end, the winners are not judged. And the saviours are thanked.'[43]

Another figure who supported lowering the nuclear threshold was Dmitry Trenin, once a well-known explainer of Russia to the West and now a hardliner on the war. He wrote about 'NATO's creeping escalation of the crisis and increasingly growing involvement in the hostilities in Ukraine'. The US had 'essentially set itself the unthinkable task of defeating another nuclear superpower in a region that is strategically important for the latter, without resorting to nuclear weapons, but by arming and controlling a third country'. Having continuously tested Russia's reactions, NATO now believed that the Russian leadership would not dare use nuclear weapons and so 'references to Russia's nuclear capabilities are nothing but a bluff'. It therefore sought to 'wear Russia out on the battlefield and destabilize it from the inside'. If this process was allowed to continue, the war would spread to the rest of Europe and inevitably go nuclear, most likely leading to an exchange of strikes

China would condemn a nuclear strike

between Russia and the United States. His proposal was to send 'our main adversary an unambiguous – not verbal anymore – signal that Moscow will not play by its rules'.[44]

While Karaganov expected little from partners and neutral states, Trenin wanted Moscow to explain 'the motives and goals of our actions'. By not 'hushing up' the possibility of nuclear use, escalation should be curbed and stopped, paving the way for 'a strategic equilibrium in Europe that suits us'. While he did not anticipate a US nuclear attack on Russia by way of retaliation, there would be a non-nuclear response that 'in all probability will be sensitive and painful for us', with the aim (as was Russia's in the other direction) of 'paralyzing the will of the Russian leadership to continue the war and creating panic in Russian society'. As this would not work, the escalation would continue, leading Russia eventually to target the US. Trenin's conclusion echoed Karaganov. Precisely to avoid a global catastrophe, 'fear must be brought back into politics and public consciousness'. The 'nuclear bullet' must be put into the 'revolver drum'. He asked: 'Why do we need nuclear weapons if we refuse to use them in the face of an existential threat?'[45]

Within Russia these arguments were challenged. The critics stayed close to the official Russian doctrine, blaming a malevolent Western information campaign for suggesting that it was being abandoned, and praising the leadership for their responsible attitude to escalation.[46] Nuclear use, they noted, would fail to solve the issues between Russia and the West, aggravate Russia's international position and create a risk of all-out nuclear exchanges. They warned against underestimating the West's readiness to climb the escalation ladder, overestimating the possibility of China and others tolerating a strike and caricaturing Western politicians as sharing a perverse social ideology and being unable to respond intelligently to new challenges. Ivan Timofeev summed up the dilemma graphically:

> Roughly speaking, they [the West] are trying to cook Russia on a slow fire. Nuclear escalation is a way to jump out of the boiler, abruptly bringing the temperature to the boiling point. The problem is that after jumping out of the boiler, you can get directly into the fire.[47]

He came up with a complex scenario of moves and counter-moves that showed the possibilities of escalating to a shared catastrophe. He agreed with Karaganov that Russia might be stuck with a 'bleeding wound' in the form of a hostile West and Ukraine, finding some consolation that Russia would also be one for the West.[48]

Alexey Arbatov, Konstantin Bogdanov and Dmitry Stefanovich – analysts at the Center for International Security at IMEMO RAS – could see no sense in a strategy that required Russia to 'quickly rise through all stages of escalation'. They considered the idea that nuclear use could 'stop the escalation and solve strategic problems that conventional forces have not been able to solve' to be 'highly questionable and most likely erroneous'. After describing the consequences of nuclear exchanges, their conclusion was harsh: they said a game of 'nuclear roulette' was likely to lead to 'radioactive ruins', adding that 'fans of sensational ideas and dangerous gambling should remember this'.[49]

What conclusions can we draw from this survey of Russian statements on the role of nuclear deterrence in the war? A clear red line was identified from the start in Russian official pronouncements: the direct intervention by NATO forces in the war. NATO acknowledged and respected it. However, Russian commentators and officials, some quite senior, have added threats and warnings seeking to persuade NATO not to pass other lines. Here the effect, from a Russian perspective, has been less satisfactory. Arguments from ultra-nationalist circles to raise the threat level further have support but are not left unchallenged. Putin has notably kept his distance from this conversation. While it might suit him to encourage the idea that continued Western support for Ukraine risks a wider nuclear war, he has not broadened his original threat. The red line has yet to move.

At the October 2023 Valdai conference, Karaganov put his thesis directly to Putin: 'Isn't it time for us to change the doctrine of the use of nuclear weapons in the direction of lowering the nuclear threshold and move, of course, firmly, but quickly enough along the ladder of escalation of deterrence, sobering up our partners?' Putin responded that he understood the sentiment, but then reaffirmed established doctrine. Nuclear weapons would be used for a retaliatory strike in the event of a first US strike, if possible from when an incoming attack was first detected, and also when 'something would threaten Russian statehood and the existence of the Russian state'.[50] He went on to muse about the possibility of abandoning the 1996 Comprehensive Nuclear-Test-Ban Treaty, which the US Congress has never ratified, to allow nuclear testing for new weapons. This soon led to a vote in the Duma taking the first step to revoking Russia's ratification. It will remain a signatory, and no commitment was made actually to restart testing.[51] This was another way to emphasise the priority given to Russia's nuclear arsenal, and the readiness to abandon restrictions on its future development, without threatening nuclear use.

The Russian nuclear debate has been about how to deter the US and NATO, not Ukraine. In early 2022, the issue was largely one of when and how Ukrainian resistance would be overwhelmed. So, from Russia's perspective, what needed to be deterred was active support for Ukraine from NATO, especially any direct intervention. By spring 2022, it was apparent that Ukraine was fighting back effectively and was intent on liberating all its territory, including Crimea. The 'existential threat', therefore, would come from Ukraine and not NATO. This revelation complicated Russian narratives, as Ukraine was habitually presented as an instrument of the West as much as an independent actor.

A further complication was that as Ukraine's military operations were ongoing, the threat would need to be to a degree compellent (persuading Ukraine to stop doing something) rather than deterrent (persuading Ukraine not to start). This merged into the issue of whether so-called 'tactical' nuclear weapons could be used not for coercive purposes but to turn the course of a land battle. There is little evidence that Russia seriously considered this course of action. Putin publicly ruled it out. The scenario nonetheless played a prominent part in the Western debate.

When Moscow began to be attacked by Ukrainian drones, Putin did not wish to make a big deal about it because he was unsure what to do. All he could say was that 'the air defences had worked satisfactorily'. Tatiana Stanovaya observed:

> Within a few months, it seemed that the Kremlin's red lines had either never existed or had become extremely mobile. The reaction of the authorities was more or less the same every time: downplay the significance of the event, present Russia as the victim, and depoliticize the problem – all without any public involvement from Putin.[52]

Putin dared not give the appearance of panic because that would suggest to his people that the 'special military operation' was not going as well as they had been led to believe. Russia could explain reverses by noting that Russia was now really facing NATO and not just Ukraine, without indicating how the world's most formidable alliance could be defeated.

US policy

Once it became evident that Ukraine would effectively resist the Russian invasion, the US and its allies began to send it weapons as a matter of urgency. As they did so they stressed that their aim was to strengthen Ukrainian defences while avoiding nuclear escalation. As Russian forces started attacking civilian targets, Biden turned down Ukrainian President

Volodymyr Zelenskyy's request for a no-fly zone, as this would involve direct combat between US and Russian forces.[53]

The most authoritative statement on the US position came from Biden when he announced that the US would be sending 'advanced rocket systems and munitions' to Ukraine:

> We do not seek a war between NATO and Russia. As much as I disagree with Mr. Putin, and find his actions an outrage, the United States will not try to bring about his ouster in Moscow. So long as the United States or our allies are not attacked, we will not be directly engaged in this conflict, either by sending American troops to fight in Ukraine or by attacking Russian forces. We are not encouraging or enabling Ukraine to strike beyond its borders. We do not want to prolong the war just to inflict pain on Russia.

At the same time:

> I know many people around the world are concerned about the use of nuclear weapons. We currently see no indication that Russia has intent to use nuclear weapons in Ukraine, though Russia's occasional rhetoric to rattle the nuclear saber is itself dangerous and extremely irresponsible. Let me be clear: Any use of nuclear weapons in this conflict on any scale would be completely unacceptable to us as well as the rest of the world and would entail severe consequences.[54]

The most controversial aspect of Biden's position was denying Ukraine long-range systems that might reach into Russian territory. In the event, although it took time, the US relented on a number of these systems, such as ATACMS.[55] When the US pledged or delivered them, the Ukrainians explicitly promised that they would not be used to attack Russian territory, as they did with respect to British *Storm Shadow* air-launched missiles.[56] Though this was probably more the result of inherent caution – seeing what was possible before taking the next step – than a deliberate strategy, the effect of incremental steps was that Russia found each one insufficient to be worth a massive response of any nature, although the cumulative effect was to

make a substantial difference to Ukraine's capabilities. This was sometimes described as 'boiling the frog'; my preferred metaphor was 'salami-slicing'.[57]
As Janice Gross Stein observed,

> The United States and its partners had experimented, paused, and moved again when they found there was no material reaction from Moscow, and Ukraine made sure to follow the rules in the ways it used the equipment. Officials then waited again to assess Moscow's reaction. A year after the invasion, U.S. policymakers and analysts were more confident that they understood better what kinds of support for Ukraine would prompt verbal outrage rather than risk 'something more dangerous'.[58]

Yet this calculation was not simple. Firstly, as noted, the Ukrainians developed their own means of attacking Russian territory independent of allied systems, and did so with increasing regularity. Secondly, whatever restraint the Ukrainians promised the US they would observe in using American systems, the Russians could point to their actual range and the potential threat they posed. Most importantly, as NATO countries had never recognised Crimea to be part of Russia, they could not, and did not, object to attacks on Russian military assets on the peninsula.[59] In effect, this meant that while the US was trying to identify Russian red lines and avoid crossing them, it was not necessarily drawing them in the same place as Russia did.

In an interview with CBS, Biden was asked what he would say to Putin 'if he is considering using chemical or tactical nuclear weapons'. Biden replied: 'Don't. Don't. Don't. You will change the face of war unlike anything since World War II.' When asked about consequences, Biden said:

> You think I would tell you if I knew exactly what it would be? Of course, I'm not gonna tell you. It'll be consequential. They'll become more of a pariah in the world than they ever have been. And depending on the extent of what they do will determine what response would occur.[60]

National Security Advisor Jake Sullivan reported in September 2022 that 'Russia understands very well what the United States would do in response to nuclear weapons use in Ukraine because we have spelled it out for them'. He added that care had been taken when it came to public talk 'because from our perspective we want to lay down the principle that there would be catastrophic consequences, but not engage in a game of rhetorical tit for tat'.[61]

Much would depend on exactly how weapons were used. Possibilities considered by the administration ranged from a demonstration shot to the direct targeting of Russian military assets. According to the *New York Times*, 'administration officials have said they could think of almost no circumstances in which a nuclear detonation by Russia would result in a nuclear response. Non-nuclear responses ranged from a conventional strike against a unit or base responsible to providing longer-range systems to Ukraine, to other "forceful" responses, as well as using Russia breaking the "taboo" to get more neutral countries to adopt sanctions.'[62]

The next month there was a curious incident when Shoigu, apparently on Putin's direction, called his counterparts in four NATO countries to alert them to a planned detonation by Ukraine of a 'dirty bomb' – that is, a conventional weapon spiked with radioactive material – on its own territory.[63] It was unclear why Ukraine would spread radioactivity in its own country to inculpate Russia in the attack, and when the International Atomic Energy Agency (IAEA), already concerned about the risks to the Ukrainian nuclear plant in Russian-occupied Zaporizhzhia, investigated it found no evidence to support the allegation.[64] France, the United Kingdom and the United States issued a statement denouncing the claim. This led to more conversations between Sullivan and his Russian opposite number, Nikolai Patrushev.[65] There were also calls between General Mark A. Milley, then chairman of the Joint Chiefs of Staff, and his counterpart, Gerasimov, that confirmed that they understood each other's nuclear doctrine, and a meeting of CIA Director William Burns with FSB director Sergei Naryshkin in Turkiye, where Burns warned of the dangers associated with any nuclear use.

By February 2023, the view in the Biden administration was more sanguine. There was at least some communication between the two capitals, the military situation was more stable, the IAEA was playing an increased role and, prompted by China, Putin may have appreciated that the nuclear taboo had not gone away, so that nuclear threats were backfiring.[66]

Pre-emptive panic

One of the difficulties in discussing contingencies was that much speculation surrounded one that Russia refused to admit – potential defeat in battle. As we have seen, Russian nuclear threats were directed against NATO countries rather than Ukraine, but it was Ukrainian acts that put Russia in trouble. Colin H. Kahl, as US under secretary of defense for policy, acknowledged that concerns about escalation were a factor in US reticence when it came to arms transfers: 'Ukraine's success on the battlefield could cause Russia to feel backed into a corner', he said, 'and that is something we must remain mindful of.'[67]

A familiar argument was that if it came to a choice between losing and using nuclear weapons, Putin would barely hesitate. As Graham Allison put it, 'forced to choose between humiliating defeat, on the one hand, and escalating the level of destruction ... there's every reason to believe he chooses the latter'.[68] While a loss would not be existential for Russia, it would be for Putin. Nina Tannenwald, asking whether the nuclear taboo was still effective, observed that 'the worry is that if the war continues going badly for Russia, Putin might reach for a tactical nuclear weapon – a low-yield bomb designed for use on the battlefield – out of frustration'. Making a common point among those with these concerns, she added that 'while Russia's aggression, protected by nuclear threats, must not pay, the United States has an obligation to avoid a wider war that could increase the risk of direct U.S.–Russian confrontation'.[69] According to Kevin Ryan, what would lead to such a confrontation would

> most likely ... be the inability of the Russian military to escalate the war by conventional means when Putin demands. For example, if a Ukrainian offensive threatens the loss of Crimea or the provinces that form the land bridge to it, Putin would demand an escalation of the fighting to prevent that loss.[70]

Masha Gessen argued that Putin would use nuclear weapons because he could, almost as a matter of retribution: 'The losses the Russian military is suffering now can only motivate Putin to create more terror, against more people.'[71] Others saw advantages for Putin in coercing Ukraine to surrender. Matthew Kroenig warned that a Russian nuclear strike 'could cause a humanitarian catastrophe, deal a crippling blow to the Ukrainian military, divide the Western alliance, and compel Kyiv to sue for peace'.[72] Jeremy Shapiro set out a wholly speculative scenario involving an inexorable process of escalation. It would only require 'one side to feel that it is losing and that a military defeat will have catastrophic consequences for their regime and the personal safety of its leadership, and to convince itself, under the pressure of looming military defeat, that nuclear use is the way out'.[73] If the war settled down to a long war of attrition, noted Shapiro, his concerns would probably not apply. This is what has happened and so reduces the risk, at least for now.

Much of this speculation depended on the psychology of one man and suggested that it would be an easier decision for him than for others. Yet in no sense would this be an easy decision. Could he be sure the red line had been passed? As already noted, escalation does not always move forward in dramatic leaps, but may instead proceed in lots of small steps, each not providing an obvious moment to claim that a fateful new stage in a conflict has been reached. Even apparently large steps can be ambiguous. For example, since the end of September 2022, when Russia claimed four Ukrainian *oblast*s (Donetsk, Luhansk, Kherson and Zaporizhzhia) as sovereign territory, Russia could arguably claim that any attack on them would constitute an 'existential threat'. But at the time, Russia did not comprehensively control any of the *oblast*s, and fighting was under way in all of them. In addition, any 'tactical' use of weapons against military formations in those regions would be on territory claimed by the Russian Federation. Similarly, with Crimea, while Russian units struggling to hold off an actual invasion would have posed significant risks of escalation, the actual circumstance of random targets being struck by drones and missiles did not. The attack on the Kerch Bridge, linking Crimea to mainland Russia, elicited a sharp reaction from Russia, but only to the effect that it was not short of non-nuclear options to hurt Ukraine if that is what it wanted to do.

Then there were the operational issues. If Putin was bound to use nuclear weapons in the event he was losing the war, then some explanation was needed as to how this might help him win. Would there be a warning first to encourage Ukraine to capitulate? Might Russia start with a demonstration, to show readiness to use without initially doing serious damage? If so, where? Could Moscow be sure that the delivery systems would not be intercepted, or that the warheads would explode as advertised? Could surprise attacks be organised without US intelligence picking up what was going on? What would be their targets – Ukrainian formations in the field or civilian facilities and areas? If the latter, would the aim be decapitation of the Ukrainian leadership? Supposing a strike were successful, what would be the consequences in terms of both political and radioactive fallout? And then what would Russia do with Ukraine? Would nuclear use make any subsequent occupation harder or easier? And given that no effort was made to prepare the Russian public for such a desperate step, how would Russian citizens react? Would they stay calm?

Moreover, although there were occasional references to possible tactical nuclear use in Russian-media commentary, as there were to launching strikes against London or Berlin, by and large the focus was on the US as the real enemy and Ukraine as a puppet. Putin stuck to deterring the West from fighting alongside Ukraine, disregarding those who wanted to punish the West for the support it was providing. There was therefore little alignment between the Russian debate, such as it was, and the Western debate, which featured expressions of anxiety grounded in speculation and inclined towards the view that it might be wise for Ukraine to cut a deal before matters really got nasty.

Lastly, those worried about the contingency of nuclear use while acknowledging that it would be an extraordinary and dangerous gamble could point to a recklessness in Putin's character that he had demonstrated by deciding to invade Ukraine in the first place. The suggestion here was that the act would be more of an emotional spasm than a bold stroke of strategy. This is one of those propositions that is inherently unprovable, but it gained credibility from the fact that Putin had taken one irrational decision. But it seemed equally plausible that precisely because his crystal ball had let him down, if anything he might look more closely for his next big decision. As shown in this article, the policy he articulated during the course of the war was consistent and explicit. There is a difference between being completely deranged, when every perception might be wrong and responses random, and making one stupid decision.

So far NATO has respected Putin's red line. Even those who worry that the fear of nuclear war has led to too much caution focus more on arms supplies than on the refusal to intervene directly in the fighting. So long as NATO continues to follow that policy, there is no reason why Putin should authorise nuclear use. Of course, once war begins factors of chance can play a part and situations might develop that get out of hand. Responsible statecraft requires paying close attention to all potential developments, but that does not dictate pre-emptive panic.

Notes

1   Anne Applebaum, 'Fear of Nuclear War Has Warped the West's Ukraine Strategy: Leaders Shouldn't Give in to Putin's Nuclear Rhetoric', *Atlantic*, 7 November 2022, https://www.theatlantic.com/ideas/archive/2022/11/russia-ukraine-nuclear-war-fear-us-policy/672020/.

2   Stephen Cimbala and Lawrence Korb, 'Putin's "Bluff": A Cautionary Note About Underestimating the Possibility of Nuclear Escalation in Ukraine', *Bulletin of the Atomic Scientists*, 2 October 2023, https://thebulletin.org/2023/10/putins-bluff-a-cautionary-note-about-underestimating-the-possibility-of-nuclear-escalation-in-ukraine/.

3   I cover it with Jeff Michaels in *The Evolution of Nuclear Strategy*, 4th ed. (London: Palgrave Macmillan, 2019).

4   Joseph S. Nye, Jr, Graham T. Allison and Albert Carnesale (eds), *Fateful Visions: Avoiding Nuclear Catastrophe* (New York: Harper & Row, 1988); and James Blight, *The Shattered Crystal Ball: Fear and Learning in the Cuban Missile Crisis* (New York: Rowman & Littlefield, 1990).

5   See Nina Tannenwald, *The Nuclear Taboo: The United States and the Non-use of Nuclear Weapons Since 1945* (Cambridge: Cambridge University Press, 2007); and T.V. Paul, *The Tradition of Non-use of Nuclear Weapons* (Stanford, CA: Stanford University Press, 2009).

6   See 'Reassessing Obama's Biggest Mistake: How Much Was His Red Line in Syria to Blame for America's Lost Credibility?', *The Economist*, 22 August 2023, https://www.economist.com/international/2023/08/22/reassessing-barack-obamas-red-line-in-syria.

7   Thomas C. Schelling, *The Strategy of Conflict* (Cambridge, MA: Harvard University Press, 1960), ch. 8. Janice Gross Stein uses this concept to frame her analysis of this topic, which covers some of the same ground to this piece, in 'Escalation Management

in Ukraine: "Learning by Doing" in Response to the "Threat that Leaves Something to Chance"', *Texas National Security Review*, vol. 6, no. 3, Summer 2023, pp. 29–50, https://tnsr.org/2023/06/escalation-management-in-ukraine-learning-by-doing-in-response-to-the-threat-that-leaves-something-to-chance/.

8   President of Russia, 'Meeting with Top Graduates of Higher Military Schools', 21 June 2023, http://en.kremlin.ru/events/president/news/71472.

9   '"We'll Go to Paradise as Martyrs, While They Will Just Die." What Putin Said at "Valdai"', RIA Novosti, 18 October 2018, https://ria.ru/20181018/1530999011.html?ysclid=lkwx69r8vb384344075.

10   President of Russia, 'Decree of the President of the Russian Federation No. 02 of 06.2020.355', 2 June 2020, http://www.kremlin.ru/acts/bank/45562.

11   President of Russia, 'Meeting of the Council for Civil Society and Human Rights', 7 December 2022, http://kremlin.ru/events/president/news/70046/videos.

12   Quoted in Colin Freeman, 'Vladimir Putin: Don't Mess with Nuclear-armed Russia', *Daily Telegraph*, 29 August 2014, https://www.telegraph.co.uk/news/world-news/vladimir-putin/11064209/Vladimir-Putin-Dont-mess-with-nuclear-armed-Russia.html.

13   Quoted in Max Fisher, 'Putin's Case for War, Annotated', *New York Times*, 24 February 2022, https://www.nytimes.com/2022/02/24/world/europe/putin-ukraine-speech.html.

14   Matthew Luxmore, 'Putin Puts Nuclear Forces in a "Special Mode of Combat Duty"', *Wall Street Journal*, 27 February 2022, https://www.wsj.com/livecoverage/russia-ukraine-latest-news-2022-02-26/card/putin-puts-nuclear-forces-in-a-special-mode-of-combat-duty--WKMRkTauWFNnWy26hZar.

15   President of Russia, 'Address by the President of the Russian Federation', 21 September 2022, http://en.kremlin.ru/events/president/news/69390.

16   President of Russia, 'Vladimir Putin Answered Media Questions', 14 October 2022, http://en.kremlin.ru/events/president/transcripts/69604.

17   See President of Russia, 'Meeting of the Council for Civil Society and Human Rights'.

18   Quoted in Anton Troianovski, 'Playing to Western Discord, Putin Says Russia Is Battling "Strange" Elites', *New York Times*, 27 October 2022, https://www.nytimes.com/2022/10/27/world/europe/ukraine-russia-war-putin.html.

19   'Russia, China Convinced that Nuclear War Must Never Be Unleashed – Joint Statement', TASS, 21 March 2023, https://tass.com/russia/1592589. The joint statement of the five nations had been issued at the start of 2022. See White House, 'Joint Statement of the Leaders of the Five Nuclear-weapon States on Preventing Nuclear War and Avoiding Arms Races', 3 January 2022, https://www.whitehouse.gov/briefing-room/statements-releases/2022/01/03/p5-statement-on-preventing-nuclear-war-and-avoiding-arms-races/. On 5 July 2023, the *Financial Times* reported that China took credit for 'convincing the Russian president to

back down from his veiled threats of using a nuclear weapon against Ukraine'. It quoted Josep Borrell, the EU's foreign-policy chief, that Xi's visit 'reduces the risk of nuclear war and they [the Chinese] have made it very, very clear'. Max Siddon et al., 'Xi Jinping Warned Vladimir Putin Against Nuclear Attack in Ukraine', *Financial Times*, 5 July 2023, https://www.ft.com/content/c5ce76df-9b1b-4dfc-a619-07da1d40cbd3.

20   President of Russia, 'Plenary Session of the St Petersburg International Economic Forum', 16 June 2023, http://en.kremlin.ru/events/president/news/71445. He described Russia's large nuclear arsenal as its 'comparative advantage'.

21   See Helene Cooper, Julian E. Barnes and Eric Schmitt, 'Russian Military Leaders Discussed Use of Nuclear Weapons, U.S. Officials Say', *New York Times*, 2 November 2022, https://www.nytimes.com/2022/11/02/us/politics/russia-ukraine-nuclear-weapons.html.

22   Quoted in Andrew Osborn, 'Putin Says Russia Put Nuclear Bombs in Belarus as Warning to West', Reuters, 17 June 2023, https://www.reuters.com/world/europe/putin-says-russia-positions-nuclear-bombs-belarus-warning-west-2023-06-16/.

23   Dmitry Muratov, 'There Will Be a Coup in Russia Without Overthrowing the Government', *Moscow Times*, 21 June 2023, https://www.moscowtimes.ru/2023/06/21/analiz-rosneft-predlagaet-monitorit-nefteeksport-v-ramkakh-opek-no-vryad-li-naydyot-otklik-a46687. See also Hanna Notte, 'The West Cannot

Cure Russia's Nuclear Fever', *War on the Rocks*, 18 July 2023, https://warontherocks.com/2023/07/the-west-cannot-cure-russias-nuclear-fever/.

24   Quoted in Zoe Strozewski, 'Putin's U.K. Missile Strike Would "End British Crown": Russian General', *Newsweek*, 30 August 2022, https://www.newsweek.com/putins-uk-missile-strike-would-end-british-crown-russian-general-1738120.

25   In presenting Gurulev's news spot on X, the *Daily Beast*'s Julia Davis said: 'Meanwhile in Russia, more of the usual: nuclear threats against Germany and Britain, cautioning NATO against going into Ukraine. This directly clashes with their lies, constantly spewed by state TV, that Russia is already at war with NATO & "uniformed NATO troops" are in Ukraine.' Julia David (@JuliaDavisNews), post to X, 19 September 2022, https://twitter.com/JuliaDavisNews/status/1571712271063072773.

26   Quoted in Francis Scarr (@francis_scarr), post to X, 19 September 2022, https://twitter.com/francis_scarr/status/1571821303253946368?lang=en.

27   'Putin Allies Split over Using Tactical Nuclear Weapons in Ukraine', *Moscow Times*, 4 May 2023, https://www.themoscowtimes.com/2023/05/04/putin-allies-split-on-using-tactical-nuclear-weapons-in-ukraine-a81038.

28   *Ibid.*

29   'Kremlin Spokesman: Russia Would Use Nuclear Weapons Only in Case of "Threat to Existence of State"', Reuters, 28 March 2022, https://www.reuters.com/world/kremlin-spokesman-russia-would-

use-nuclear-weapons-only-case-threat-existence-2022-03-28/.

30 See 'Kremlin Takes Distance from Kadyrov's Call to Use Nuclear Bomb in Ukraine', Euractiv, 3 October 2022, https://www.euractiv.com/section/global-europe/news/kremlin-takes-distance-from-kadyrovs-call-to-use-nuclear-bomb-in-ukraine/.

31 'Russia's Lavrov: Do Not Underestimate Threat of Nuclear War', Reuters, 25 April 2022, https://www.reuters.com/world/russia-says-western-weapons-ukraine-legitimate-targets-russian-military-2022-04-25/.

32 'Russia's Lavrov: NATO Policy Risks "Direct Clash" Between Nuclear Powers', Reuters, 5 December 2022, https://www.reuters.com/article/ukraine-crisis-nuclear-lavrov-idUSS-8N3oXoM5.

33 In early July, for example, Medvedev said: 'The idea of punishing a country that has one of the largest nuclear potentials is absurd. And potentially poses a threat to the existence of humanity.' Quoted in 'Russia's Medvedev Warns United States: Messing with a Nuclear Power Is Folly', Reuters, 6 July 2022, https://www.reuters.com/world/russias-medvedev-warns-united-states-messing-with-nuclear-power-is-folly-2022-07-06/. In late September, he stated: 'I have to remind you again – for those deaf ears who hear only themselves – Russia has the right to use nuclear weapons if necessary.' Quoted in Guy Faulconbridge and Caleb Davis, 'Medvedev Raises Spectre of Russian Nuclear Strike on Ukraine', Reuters, 27 September 2022, https://www.reuters.com/world/europe/

russias-medvedev-warns-west-that-nuclear-threat-is-not-bluff-2022-09-27/. In January 2023, he said: 'Nuclear powers have never lost major conflicts on which their fate depends.' Quoted in Guy Faulconbridge and Felix Light, 'Putin Ally Warns NATO of Nuclear War if Russia Is Defeated in Ukraine', Reuters, 19 January 2023, https://www.reuters.com/world/europe/putin-ally-medvedev-warns-nuclear-war-if-russia-defeated-ukraine-2023-01-19/.

34 Quoted in 'Russia's Medvedev: Attack on Crimea Will Ignite "Judgement Day" Response', Reuters, 17 July 2022, https://www.reuters.com/world/europe/medvedev-wests-refusal-recognise-crimea-russian-is-threat-2022-07-17/.

35 Quoted in Guy Faulconbridge, 'Any Attempt to Arrest Putin Would Be Declaration of War on Russia, Ally Says', Reuters, 23 March 2023, https://www.reuters.com/world/europe/russias-medvedev-says-west-wont-leave-russia-china-alone-tass-2023-03-23/.

36 Quoted in 'Russian Hawks Threaten Nuclear Strikes over Putin Hague Warrant', Moscow Times, 20 March 2023, https://www.themoscowtimes.com/2023/03/20/russian-hawks-threaten-nuclear-strikes-over-putin-hague-warrant-a80544. Margarita Simonyan, editor-in-chief of the Kremlin-funded broadcaster RT, also observed: 'I'd like to see a country that would arrest Putin under the ruling of The Hague. In about eight minutes, or whatever the [missile] flight time to its capital.'

37 Quoted in 'Russia's Medvedev Says Arms Supplies to Kyiv Threaten

Global Nuclear Catastrophe', Reuters, 27 February 2023, https://www.reuters.com/world/europe/russias-medvedev-says-arms-supplies-kyiv-threaten-global-nuclear-catastrophe-2023-02-27. See also 'Western Arms for Ukraine Make "Nuclear Apocalypse" More Likely: Russia's Medvedev', Reuters, 23 May 2023, https://www.reuters.com/world/europe/russias-medvedev-western-arms-ukraine-make-nuclear-apocalypse-more-likely-2023-05-23/. Lavrov warned in connection with the F-16s supplied to Ukraine that as these aircraft could carry nuclear weapons, 'we will regard the very fact that the Ukrainian armed forces have such systems as a threat from the West in the nuclear sphere'. They were creating risks of a direct armed clash with Russia, which he said was 'fraught with catastrophic consequences'. '"This Is Fraught with Catastrophic Consequences" – Sergey Lavrov on the Conflict with NATO and the Risks of Using Nuclear Weapons', Lenta.ru, 12 July 2023, https://lenta.ru/articles/2023/07/13/lavrov/.

38 Quoted in 'Russia's Medvedev Says More U.S. Weapons Supplies Mean "All of Ukraine Will Burn"', Reuters, 4 February 2023, https://www.reuters.com/world/europe/russias-medvedev-says-more-us-weapons-supplies-mean-all-ukraine-will-burn-2023-02-04/.

39 Translated and quoted in Anton Gerashchenko (@Gerashchenko_en), post to X, 26 September 2023, https://x.com/Gerashchenko_en/status/1706678776967430547?s=20.

40 Translated and quoted in Anton Gerashchenko (@Gerashchenko_en), post to X, 1 October 2023, https://x.com/Gerashchenko_en/status/1708430418901340205?s=20.

41 Sergei A. Karaganov, 'A Difficult but Necessary Decision', *Russia in Global Affairs*, 13 June 2023, https://eng.globalaffairs.ru/articles/a-difficult-but-necessary-decision/.

42 *Ibid.*

43 *Ibid.*

44 Dmitry V. Trenin, 'Conflict in Ukraine and Nuclear Weapons', *Russia in Global Affairs*, 22 June 2023, https://eng.globalaffairs.ru/articles/ukraine-and-nuclear-weapons/.

45 *Ibid.*

46 *Russia in Global Affairs*, the journal that published the two articles, carried a number of responses, including those from Ilya S. Fabrichnikov of the Council on Foreign and Defence Policy, Ivan N. Timofeev of MGIMO University and the Valdai Club, and Fyodor A. Lukyanov, the journal's editor-in-chief. See Ilya S. Fabrichnikov, 'Demonstrative Restraint as a Recipe Against Unnecessary Decisions', *Russia in Global Affairs*, 16 June 2023, https://eng.globalaffairs.ru/articles/demonstrative-restraint/; Ivan N. Timofeev, 'A Preemptive Nuclear Strike? No!', *Russia in Global Affairs*, 20 June 2023, https://eng.globalaffairs.ru/articles/a-preemptive-nuclear-strike-no/; and Fyodor A. Lukyanov, 'Why We Won't Be Able to "Sober Up the West" with a Nuclear Bomb', *Russia in Global Affairs*, 26 June 2023, https://eng.globalaffairs.ru/articles/sober-up-the-west/. On the debate, see Andrey Baklitskiy, 'What We Learned from Recent Calls for a Russian Nuclear Attack', Carnegie Politika, 20

July 2023, https://carnegieendowment.
org/politika/90232.

47 Timofeev, 'A Preemptive Nuclear
    Strike? No!'.

48 *Ibid*.

49 Alexey Arbatov, Konstantin Bogdanov
    and Dmitry Stefanovich, 'Nuclear
    War Is a Poor Solution to Problems',
    Kommersant, 21 June 2023, https://
    www.kommersant.ru/doc/6055340.

50 President of Russia, 'Valdai
    International Discussion Club
    Meeting', 5 October 2023, http://
    en.kremlin.ru/events/president/
    news/72444.

51 See Guy Faulconbridge and Filipp
    Lebedev, 'Russian Duma Takes First
    Step to Revoke Ratification of Nuclear
    Test Ban Treaty', Reuters, 17 October
    2023, https://www.reuters.com/world/
    europe/russia-is-revoking-ratification-
    nuclear-test-ban-treaty-parliament-
    speaker-2023-10-17/.

52 Tatiana Stanovaya, 'Why Is the
    Russian Regime Ignoring the Moscow
    Drone Attacks?', Carnegie Politika, 31
    May 2023, https://carnegieendowment.
    org/politika/89851.

53 See James Hohmann, 'Why Biden's
    Response to Zelensky's No-fly
    Zone Request Was So Wise',
    Washington Post, 16 March 2022,
    https://www.washingtonpost.
    com/opinions/2022/03/16/
    zelensky-biden-no-fly-zone/.

54 Joseph R. Biden, Jr, 'What America
    Will and Will Not Do in Ukraine', *New
    York Times*, 31 May 2022, https://www.
    nytimes.com/2022/05/31/opinion/
    biden-ukraine-strategy.html.

55 See Emma Graham-Harrison, 'US
    Agrees to Send Long-range Missiles
    to Ukraine in Military Boost for Kyiv',

Guardian, 23 September 2023, https://
www.theguardian.com/world/2023/
sep/23/us-agrees-to-send-long-
range-missiles-atacms-to-ukraine-in-
military-boost-for-kyiv.

56 A spokesman for the British prime
    minister stated that Britain had 'received
    reassurances from Ukraine that these
    missiles like all other military support
    we have provided will only be used
    to defend their sovereign territory in
    keeping with international law'. Quoted
    in Matthew Mpoke Bigg and Stephen
    Castle, 'Britain Says It Is Donating
    Long-range "Storm Shadow" Missiles to
    Ukraine', *New York Times*, 11 May 2023,
    https://www.nytimes.com/2023/05/11/
    world/europe/ukraine-storm-shadow-
    missiles-uk.html.

57 See Lawrence Freedman, 'Salami
    Slicing, Boiled Frogs, and Russian Red
    Lines', Comment Is Freed, Substack,
    4 June 2023, https://samf.substack.
    com/p/salami-slicing-boiled-frogs-
    and-russian.

58 Stein, 'Escalation Management
    in Ukraine'.

59 See Alexander Ward, 'U.S. Approves
    of Ukraine Striking Russian-occupied
    Crimea', *Politico*, 17 August 2022,
    https://www.politico.com/newsletters/
    national-security-daily/2022/08/17/u-s-
    approves-of-ukraine-striking-russian-
    occupied-crimea-00052364.

60 'President Biden Warns Vladimir
    Putin Not to Use Nuclear
    Weapons: "Don't. Don't. Don't."',
    CBS News, 16 September 2022,
    https://www.cbsnews.com/news/
    president-joe-biden-vladimir-putin-
    60-minutes-2022-09-16/.

61 Quoted in David E. Sanger and Jim
    Tankersley, 'U.S. Warns Russia of

"Catastrophic Consequences" if It Uses Nuclear Weapons', *New York Times*, 25 September 2022, https://www.nytimes.com/2022/09/25/us/politics/us-russia-nuclear.html.

62 *Ibid.*

63 'Kremlin Says It Will Keep Making "Vigorous" Case on Alleged Ukraine Dirty Bomb Threat', Reuters, 26 October 2022, https://www.reuters.com/world/kremlin-says-it-will-keep-making-case-alleged-ukraine-dirty-bomb-threat-2022-10-26/. Putin reportedly told a meeting of intelligence officials from ex-Soviet countries that the West was 'pumping' Ukraine with heavy weapons, and that 'there are also plans to use a so-called "dirty bomb" for provocations'.

64 See David E. Sanger, 'Russia's Occupation of Nuclear Plant Gives Moscow a New Way to Intimidate', *New York Times*, 30 August 2022, https://www.nytimes.com/2022/08/30/us/politics/russia-ukraine-nuclear-plant.html.

65 See Vivian Salama and Michael R. Gordon, 'Senior White House Official Involved in Undisclosed Talks with Top Putin Aides', *Wall Street Journal*, 7 November 2022, https://www.wsj.com/articles/senior-white-house-official-involved-in-undisclosed-talks-with-top-putin-aides-11667768988.

66 See Julian Barnes and David E. Sanger, 'Fears of Russia's Use of Nuclear Weapons Diminished, but Could Re-emerge', *New York Times*, 4 February 2023, https://www.nytimes.com/2023/02/03/us/politics/russia-nuclear-weapons.html.

67 Quoted in David E. Sanger et al., 'Ukraine Wants the U.S. to Send More Powerful Weapons. Biden Is Not So Sure', *New York Times*, 17 September 2022, https://www.nytimes.com/2022/09/17/us/politics/ukraine-biden-weapons.html.

68 Quoted in Vazha Tavberidze, 'Interview: Why Putin Might Prefer a Stalemate to Going Nuclear on Ukraine', Radio Free Europe/Radio Liberty, 22 October 2022, https://www.rferl.org/a/russia-ukrain-putin-nuclear-escalation-allison/32095783.html.

69 Nina Tannenwald, 'Is Using Nuclear Weapons Still Taboo?', *Foreign Policy*, Summer 2022, https://foreignpolicy.com/2022/07/01/nuclear-war-taboo-arms-control-russia-ukraine-deterrence.

70 Kevin Ryan, 'Why Putin Will Use Nuclear Weapons in Ukraine', Russia Matters, 17 May 2023, https://www.russiamatters.org/analysis/why-putin-will-use-nuclear-weapons-ukraine.

71 Masha Gessen, 'Why Vladimir Putin Would Use Nuclear Weapons in Ukraine', *New Yorker*, 1 November 2022, https://www.newyorker.com/news/our-columnists/why-vladimir-putin-would-use-nuclear-weapons-in-ukraine.

72 Matthew Kroenig, 'Memo to the President: How to Deter Russian Nuclear Use in Ukraine – and Respond if Deterrence Fails', Atlantic Council, September 2022, https://www.atlanticcouncil.org/wp-content/uploads/2022/09/Memo-Ukraine.pdf.

73 Jeremy Shapiro, 'We Are on a Path to Nuclear War', *War on the Rocks*, 12 October 2022, https://warontherocks.com/2022/10/the-end-of-the-world-is-nigh/.

The Gaza Horror and US Policy

Steven Simon and Jonathan Stevenson

On 7 October 2023, Hamas, the militant Islamist Palestinian group that controls Gaza and is dedicated to eradicating the Israeli state, led a coordinated, large-scale surprise attack across Israel's border with Gaza. Some 1,500 Hamas and Palestinian Islamic Jihad fighters breached about 30 points along the border barrier, killing over 1,200 Israelis, including more than 300 soldiers, and taking around 240 hostages.[1]

Officials and analysts have various theories about exactly why Hamas chose to stage a major attack at this moment, but most are mere speculation.[2] All anyone has to go on are a few scattered statements from Hamas officials, none of which clearly states the group's war aims. Accordingly, any assessment is highly inferential and tentative. *New York Times* reporting, based on interviews with Hamas leaders in Gaza, portrays the group as seeking to re-establish itself as a military force and the Palestinians' primary agent of violent confrontation, as opposed to Gaza's caretaker, and to decisively reinvigorate the armed struggle with Israel by creating a 'permanent' state of war.[3] Other theories include a move to pre-empt Israeli–Saudi normalisation, which was thought to marginalise Palestinians for good. By drawing Israel into an extremely violent response, Hamas might have calculated that

Steven Simon is visiting professor of practice in Middle East Studies at the University of Washington and author of *Grand Delusion: The Rise and Fall of American Ambition in the Middle East* (Penguin, 2023). He served as senior director for the Middle East and North Africa at the National Security Council (NSC) during the Obama administration, and senior director for transnational threats at the NSC during the Clinton administration. **Jonathan Stevenson** is an IISS senior fellow and managing editor of *Survival*, and served as director for political–military affairs, Middle East and North Africa, at the NSC during the Obama administration.

Survival | vol. 65 no. 6 | December 2023–January 2024 | pp. 37–56 https://doi.org/10.1080/00396338.2023.2285600

it would be harder for the Saudis to proceed. Planning for the 7 October attack, however, seems to have begun well before Israeli–Saudi normalisation had been formally broached, so it is hard to argue that 7 October was a reaction to it. Thus far, Israeli prisoner-of-war interrogators have had access only to low-level fighters who have shed no reliable light on the questions of why and why now. But that might change in the coming weeks.[4]

The scale and sadistic zeal of the Hamas attack were shocking. The incursion was the most lethal in Israel's history, more Jews having died in a single day than on any other since the Holocaust.[5] In proportion to Israel's population, it was the equivalent of about 15 9/11s.[6] Beyond that, Hamas heedlessly killed civilians – many of them women, children and the elderly, and most non-military – in close quarters, and apparently executed some captives.[7] The torture and mutilation of civilian victims were distressing features of the raid. The secular Palestinian Authority (PA), Hamas's sclerotic political nemesis with which Israel has had an uneasy security partnership, condemned the attack. Hamas, by its charter, is doctrinally jihadist, and sees Muslim and Jewish interests in a zero-sum framework. Its foundational eschatology calls for the extermination of Jews, even if some more recent documents made a nod towards religious tolerance. The stated determination to eradicate the Jews' nation-state is, in any event, unaltered.[8] But the group is also descended from the Muslim Brotherhood, which contemplates politically controlling traditional states. The Brotherhood had taken pains to separate itself from groups like al-Qaeda and the Islamic State. It has not relied on violence to press its objectives in a very long time. Moreover, Brotherhood offshoots in Egypt, Jordan and Syria differ programmatically depending on their local political contexts. Thus, the degree to which Hamas's Muslim Brotherhood origins are useful for understanding Hamas's current posture is debatable.

In any case, times change. Nearly a decade of gruesome Islamic State videos of beheadings and other atrocities, combined with that group's reputation for success in Iraq and Syria, have apparently recast the culture of jihadism.[9] Hamas, however, is not the Islamic State; among other things, it enjoys open state support, specifically embraces Palestinian nationalism and does not have a global agenda. But on 7 October, it behaved like the

Islamic State.[10] The nature of the Hamas assault, and the lengthy period of preparation that preceded it, signalled the organisation's abandonment of its long-standing transactional approach to managing its relationship with Israel. From Israel's standpoint, this shift will necessitate Hamas's complete removal from Gaza, and has therefore complicated Washington's attempts to regulate its actions. Many observers have noted correctly that Hamas represents an idea that resonates deeply in Gazan society and that such ideas cannot be erased, especially by violence.[11] This is true, but irrelevant since many Israelis assume that the idea of resistance is fundamentally ineradicable, which is why they do not place much stock in the idea of land for peace. Their objective is therefore to destroy not an indestructible, intangible phenomenon but rather the heavily armed, deeply entrenched and implacable organisation that attacked them on 7 October.

Hamas and Israel in Gaza

Israel captured Gaza a second time from Egypt (the first time was in 1956) in the 1967 War, in which it also took the West Bank from Jordan and the Golan Heights from Syria. In the years after the Palestinians' second intifada erupted in July 2000, following the Camp David Summit's failure to produce a final-status accord, Ariel Sharon, who was elected Israel's prime minister a year later, concluded that Israel's best option vis-à-vis the Palestinians was to sever Israel's ties to at least some part of the occupied territories, in much the same way as King Hussein of Jordan had done with the West Bank in July 1998. In August 2005, Sharon took an audacious step towards this objective by withdrawing Israel's presence from Gaza, dismantling settlements, redeploying Israeli forces and leaving Gaza to the PA. Pruning Gaza from Israel might have been a good thing had it been negotiated with the Palestinians. But it was not. The Israelis' attitude seemed to be that one doesn't negotiate the amputation of a gangrenous toe with one's foot. In any case, the initiative was controversial in Israel and had not been carefully thought through.

The George W. Bush administration cynically and carelessly pushed the PA to reclaim its local legitimacy by holding elections, which Hamas jarringly won in January 2006. The White House believed that the resulting mayhem would 'rip the ugly mask off Hamas', which it considered a more important objective than a durable, stable outcome for ordinary Palestinians.[12] The PA tried to negate the results, but Hamas killed or ejected its operatives and exerted a tight grip on Gazan society. Because Hamas refused to recognise Israel, renounce violence or abide by agreements already made between the PA and Israel, Washington and Jerusalem considered it ineligible to compete in subsequent elections.[13] Hamas had split the Palestinians and, owing to poor governance or simple indifference, did little to improve their lives. In Hamas's view, Israel is responsible for Gazans' welfare as an occupying power and, as a practical matter, the United Nations Relief and Works Agency for Palestine Refugees in the Near East exists to ensure it. Hamas also perversely served as Israeli Prime Minister Benjamin Netanyahu's 'objective partner', since both were opposed to a two-state solution. Satisfied with this state of affairs, Netanyahu was content to periodically 'mow the grass' of Palestinian militancy rather than seek a political solution. In a 2015 interview, Bezalel Smotrich, Israel's present finance minister and among its most extreme-right cabinet members, voiced Israel's theretofore tacit assumptions: 'The Palestinian Authority is a burden, and Hamas is an asset. It's a terrorist organization, no one will recognize it, no one will give it status at the [International Criminal Court], no one will let it put forth a resolution at the UN Security Council.'[14]

For the last 17 years, Israel's strategy has been to neuter Palestinian politics by using Hamas to weaken the credibility of the PA, which in turn helped to undermine it as a plausible partner for peace. Over that period, armed conflict in Gaza has flared up repeatedly. In June 2006, Hamas captured Israeli army conscript Gilad Shalit in a cross-border raid from Gaza, prompting Israeli air raids and incursions. In December 2008, Hamas rocket attacks on the southern Israeli town of Sderot prompted a 22-day Israeli military offensive in Gaza – officially dubbed *Operation Cast Lead* and known as the Gaza Massacre among Palestinians – in which about 1,400 Palestinians and 13 Israelis were killed. In November 2012, Israel killed Hamas military chief of staff Ahmad Jabari, following up with eight days of air raids. In summer 2014, Hamas's kidnapping and killing of three Israeli teenagers led to a seven-week war in which more than 2,100 Palestinians and 73 Israelis, including 67 soldiers, were killed. In response to Palestinian protests at Gaza's fenced border with Israel in March 2018, Israeli troops opened fire. More than 170 Palestinians were killed in several months of protests, prompting fighting between Hamas and Israeli forces. In May 2021, after weeks of tension during the Muslim holy month of Ramadan, Israeli security forces injured hundreds of Palestinians at the Al-Aqsa Mosque compound in Jerusalem. Hamas demanded that Israel withdraw security forces from the compound and fired rockets on Israel from Gaza, giving rise to Israeli air raids. In fighting that lasted 11 days, at least 260 people were killed in Gaza and 13 in Israel. More than 30 Palestinians, including women and children, died in Israeli airstrikes in August 2022. Palestinian Islamic Jihad, which lost commanders in the airstrikes, fired dozens of rockets into Israel. This ongoing carnage did not sway Israel from its instrumental approach to Hamas. The 7 October attack, however, indicated decisively that it had backfired.

The US response

The United States has two strategic interests related to the Gaza crisis: a geopolitical interest in preventing the conflict from widening; and a reputational interest in forestalling an even worse humanitarian catastrophe. The unsustainability of the status quo ante and Israel's willingness to inflict heavy civilian casualties there have shaped the United States' current crisis-management effort. In attempting to restrain the Israeli government, the US has had to account for Israel's predisposition towards punitive counter-terrorism, its horror over Hamas's jaw-dropping cruelty, and its need to rebuild its deterrent and re-establish the safety, security and confidence of its people after a massive intelligence and military failure.[15] Hamas's meticulous planning was a rude revelation. It used drones to take out key Israeli surveillance and communications towers, effectively blinding the Israeli military, and explosives and tractors to obliterate border barricades, paving the way for a first wave of 200 attackers and 1,800 more later that day. On motorcycles and in pickup trucks, with precise intelligence, they located and assaulted eight military bases and more than 15 villages and cities.[16] Also notable were Hamas's unexpectedly airtight operational security and innovative penetration tactics. These factors combined with Israel's confirmation bias, institutional complacency and diversion of forces from the south to the West Bank to deal with the repercussions of settler violence to produce major vulnerabilities.[17] Devastating retaliation was in the cards, as was the lure of pre-empting Hizbullah's intervention in the north.

Washington has exuded sympathy with Israel's declared intention to wipe out Hamas. But President Joe Biden's noted bear hug with Netanyahu – towards whom he has been cool for years – and his rousing words of friendship and support for Israel were not intended as expressions of blank-cheque acquiescence in all-out Israeli payback. Biden's very public trip to and presence in Israel appeared intended to serve as a kind of deterrent, giving all sides pause about initiating major hostilities and imperilling a US president while cooler heads prevailed on strategic issues.[18] Although the administration has not questioned whether Israel should act decisively, it has weighed in on how it should do so, counselling caution and deliberation to buy time for hostage negotiations and to shape operations that minimise civilian casualties while achieving Israeli objectives. It is likely that, in private, many American officials would concede that Netanyahu's callous policies – expanding West Bank settlements, shelving the two-state solution, embracing the religious ultra-right at home and the Arab Gulf monarchies – had set the conditions for a major Hamas operation, albeit not one of such utter perversity. The real aim of the speech, the hug, and US military and economic support was to ensure American influence and leverage over Israel's decisions at a time when its impulse towards vengeance was extraordinarily high.[19] Indeed, the key line in Biden's speech stressed that what separated the US and Israel from Hamas was their aversion to targeting civilians. In short, Biden approached Netanyahu on Israel's response the way he did Senator Joe Manchin on domestic economic legislation: as a potential obstacle to US policy objectives who needed to be placated.

Over the first three weeks of the crisis, this design appeared to work, to some extent capitalising on Netanyahu's reluctance to commit to an all-out invasion.[20] Israel did, of course, rain abundant indirect fires and airstrikes on Gaza – killing far more Palestinians than Hamas killed Israelis on 7 October[21] – as well as imposing a security crackdown on the West Bank and punishing

Hizbullah for anti-tank missile attacks in the north intended to harass Israel.[22] More strategically, it undertook a massive military mobilisation – among Israel's biggest ever, at nearly 500,000 soldiers including 360,000 reserves – in less than 36 hours, deploying forces around Gaza and in the north near Lebanon, and established a substantial naval deployment off the Gaza coast. And Israeli officials have issued numerous threats of annihilation. But US officials and analysts worried that the Israel Defense Forces (IDF), designed for state-on-state manoeuvre operations in open terrain, were unprepared for the bloody, close-in urban warfare that it would inevitably encounter in Gaza, and that a full-scale invasion would invite opportunistic piling on by Iran and Hizbullah.[23] Biden slowed down the Israeli ground campaign, got the humanitarian corridor to Gaza that he wanted and staved off Israel's pre-emption of Hizbullah by reinforcing his rumoured private warning not to proceed by augmenting Israeli air defences and deploying two US Navy carrier strike groups to the Mediterranean to bolster Israel's deterrent. In late October, however, the IDF finally entered Gaza in force.

Prospects

The IDF's commencement of its ground incursion into Gaza has generated more open friction with the United States.[24] Yet Israeli ground forces, at least initially, refrained from moving heavily into Gaza City and declined to call the operation an invasion. Israel's ambiguity about the nature of the operation – officials said merely that it was 'expanding ground activity' and Netanyahu blandly characterised it as the 'second stage' of the war[25] – suggested some deference to US admonitions of restraint, or at least the appearance thereof. Israel's posture also afforded it a measure of tactical unpredictability, aided by its disabling of Gaza internet and telecommunications networks. The IDF's envelopment of Gaza City initially deferred penetration of the city's interior by infantry, such that Israel's fight on the ground largely involved armoured manoeuvring to seal off the urban centre, with its network of underground tunnels and fortifications, without engaging in messy urban combat. Israeli caution bought it time to assess the effect that a full-blown Israeli invasion would have on dangerous allies of Hamas – in particular, Iran and Hizbullah – but did not really keep a lid on mounting international criticism of Israeli conduct and pressure for a ceasefire.

At the same time, Netanyahu rejected a ceasefire as tantamount to 'surrender to terrorism' and attributed civilians' deaths to Hamas's practice of using human shields.[26] The law of armed conflict prohibits the killing of civilians interposed in this way by combatants, depending on the proportionality between military necessity and the expected toll in civilian lives. But these factors are very much in the eye of the beholder and thus not a very compelling constraint for either side. As it is, Israeli airstrikes have already claimed more than 10,000 Palestinian lives, including thousands of children, since 7 October and set the stage for a public-health crisis that will endanger many more.[27] On 8 November, Israel agreed to four-hour daily humanitarian pauses in northern Gaza.[28] These were not insignificant: two humanitarian corridors were established, enabling thousands of Palestinians to reach safer ground, while 96 trucks carrying needed supplies entered Gaza territory on the first day and 106 on the next. US officials applauded these developments and were pushing for 150 trucks daily, but stressed that Israel was running the military operation in Gaza.[29] Neither Israel nor Hamas is likely to agree to a sustainable ceasefire in present circumstances insofar as it could jeopardise its tactical advantage – Israel's by allowing Hamas and allied militants to regroup, Hamas's by permitting the IDF to consolidate its positions in Gaza and rest its troops. For a cessation to be plausible, independent monitors would have to be in place and empowered to enforce compliance with the status quo, and no state would be inclined to volunteer its forces for this mission. Israel will remain resistant to any durable cessation until it has achieved its war objectives.[30]

In the near to medium term, the Israelis intend to chew through as much of Gaza as necessary to capture or kill Hamas leaders and fighters, destroy its subsurface infrastructure and dismantle its missile factories. As of mid-November, Israel had enveloped Gaza City and cut the strip in half crosswise, delinking northern and southern Gaza. Israel anticipates a long, bloody slog. To the extent possible, the IDF will try to shunt the casualty burden of urban combat onto its adversary, but this in turn will ramp up civilian casualties in a self-defeating way. On 6 November, Netanyahu declared that Israel would continue to police Gaza well after it had dispensed with Hamas.[31] On 21 November, Hamas and Israel agreed to a four-day truce to allow for Hamas's release of 50 hostages and Israel's release of 150 Palestinian prisoners.[32] This reflected the intense pressure on both parties to focus on the hostages, but it was unclear whether it also signified a more subtle change in either side's overall game plan.

The United States' strategic priority, however, remains avoiding a wider war that involves Iran and Hizbullah. Provided it continues to be able to impress the importance of restraint on Israeli leaders, it stands a good chance of succeeding insofar as neither Iran nor Hizbullah is likely to consider a major war to be in its current interest. Iran's leadership faces a restive domestic population that is divided about its support for Hamas, and cannot risk a direct military confrontation with the United States, having taken conspicuous pains to deny an Iranian role in the 7 October attack.[33] Hizbullah has equities to protect in Lebanon: if it is not already at risk for its participation in a multiparty regime that has cannibalised Lebanon and its population, it could be if it presides over a smouldering replica of Gaza. Iran and Hizbullah will continue to support Hamas politically and materially on principle and to retain regional clout. But their military restraint in the wake of the Hamas attack suggests that they prefer to hang back as long as Israeli military action stays below the threshold at which they would lose face absent robust military action. Easily thwarted missile and drone attacks on Israeli targets by the Houthi rebels, Iran's proxies in Yemen, would seem to confirm this reading.[34]

A regional war could still erupt if Israel crossed an as yet unspecified red line. The only one Iran or Hizbullah has articulated thus far has been the Israeli military's entry on the ground into Gaza, which has so far proceeded without drawing significant fire. In a speech on 3 November, Hassan Nasrallah, Hizbullah's leader, diverted the question of intervention thresholds and deadlines by insisting that Hizbullah had in fact been engaged in the fight against Israel in support of Hamas since 7 October, incurring nearly 60 fatalities, and was prepared to endure more.[35] Iran and Hizbullah

> *The US priority remains avoiding a wider war*

have suggested that Israel's imminent or actual destruction of Hamas might constitute another red line, as it is key to the credibility of their 'axis of resistance'.[36] It is not certain, of course, that this eventuality would trigger Iran's or Hizbullah's entry into the war; red lines can shift during critical moments, as they have on occasion for the United States. Biden's ongoing aim will be the same as his initial one: to temper Israel's impulse to retaliate to the maximum. Merely presenting the alternative of a grislier, open-ended status quo is unlikely to be persuasive. Moreover, the rococo horror of the 7 October attack makes the argument for restraint more difficult to make. To minimise chaos and maximise manageability, the US would ideally present to Israel, other regional actors and especially Palestinians a more agreeable future that, improbable as it sounds, recasts the crisis as cut-rate catharsis. Given the multiplicity of conflicting stances, this is a tall diplomatic order.

One concept that has gained traction, put forward by one of us as well as others, is that of re-establishing PA control in Gaza, which might require the deployment there of a peacekeeping force – mainly Arab and possibly United Nations-mandated, problematic though that would be for Israel – pending PA reform and possibly new elections in Gaza to re-establish its legitimacy.[37] While this would require the abject marginalisation of Hamas, it would not require Israel to hunt and kill every Gazan affiliated with it.[38] It would call for committed buy-in from key Arab countries that have peace or normalisation agreements with Israel – Egypt, Jordan, Bahrain, Morocco and the United Arab Emirates – as well as support from Saudi Arabia, which would presumably carry the labouring oar on Gaza reconstruction, and Qatar, a key Hamas patron. This will not work in the absence of a revived peace process, presumed dead for years, and a priori Israeli concessions to the PA. The war cabinet and public opinion in Israel will likely reject a plan along these lines, at least initially. It will not get much of a reception until the Israelis assess that Hamas at a minimum has its back to the wall and is incapable of sustained resistance. Indeed, Netanyahu has indicated that it would be unacceptable to Israel for a Western-backed PA to administer Gaza unless the PA condemned the 7 October attack and were thoroughgoingly reformed, and Gaza comprehensively demilitarised.[39]

Egypt and Jordan, which strongly condemned the Hamas attack, both have interests in containing spillover violence and insecurity as swiftly as possible, and would be receptive to a dispensation that ends the war while preserving the Palestinian cause.[40] The four Arab Abraham Accords signatories likewise favour an expeditious restoration of relative security and stability.[41] Saudi Arabia, which condemned the Hamas attack but has been diplomatically somnolent, similarly prioritises stability, retains some hope of normalisation with Israel and might ultimately welcome the regional disempowerment of Iran that corralling Hamas would imply.[42] Qatar has hosted Hamas's leadership and economically supported Gaza, and has long seen the Brotherhood as the wave of the future. But on this score, insofar as it also seeks full legitimacy as a regional player and is enabled as well as constrained by the substantial US military presence in-country at Al Udeid Air Base, it has flown close to the sun, and must now be having second thoughts about Hamas's viability. Qatar too may be convincible.[43]

Washington's quandaries

Although the extreme nature of Hamas's provocation no doubt diminished international sympathy with the group, an Israeli overreaction has boosted it – a factor Hamas may well have been counting on.[44] Probably on account of long-standing distaste for Israeli policies under Netanyahu, a creeping tendency has developed to minimise and thus to under-appreciate Israeli motivations and objectives that flow from it.[45] To the extent that this tendency has affected American officials, the Biden administration is compelled to hold it in check, as it seems to have done so far. Senior American and Israeli officials also need to maintain the close, minute-to-minute liaison that they appeared to establish in the first weeks of the crisis. This would of course strengthen perceptions of US complicity in what many regard as an inexcusably excessive Israeli response. Unfortunately, there is not much Washington can do to counter this. While the savvy and craftiness reminiscent of a Henry Kissinger would be useful and welcome, American officials today face an even more formidable task than he did in 1973 during and after the Yom Kippur War. Back then, Egyptian president Anwar Sadat and his

Israeli counterparts were already open to some kind of accommodation. Netanyahu and the Hamas leadership are not.

Adding to the Biden administration's burden, domestic political fallout in the United States is unavoidable. In a sharply divided Congress, and especially the incohesive and unruly House of Representatives, backing for White House policy is likely to be tethered to concessions in other areas.[46] Over the course of the next year, Biden and his team will be obliged to take the 2024 US presidential election into account in formulating and implementing policy on Gaza. His support for even calibrated Israeli retaliation has already incurred the wrath of Arab-American voters, critical in swing states, who have urged a ceasefire. According to an Arab American Institute poll taken after the Gaza crisis erupted, only 17% supported him, down from 59% in 2020 and 35% immediately before the crisis.[47] Support for the president among Democrats more broadly, especially those under 35, has also flagged, fracturing Democratic unity.[48] US government employees from some 40 federal agencies, many of them political appointees, have also opposed the Biden administration's support for Israeli policy – in particular, its refusal to demand a ceasefire – by way of a letter to Biden as well as several internal State Department 'dissent cables'.[49] Overall, however, a slight plurality of 47% of Americans still favours Biden's policy on Gaza.[50] If the administration tilted in a more neutral direction, moderates and traditional conservatives hardwired for strongly backing Israel would surely object.[51] Presumably, Israelis can read these survey results too, and, if they assess that Biden is merely a speed bump en route to a second Trump administration, might feel immune to American pressure.

> *Israel might feel immune to American pressure*

International perceptions are also significant factors in US calculations. American support for Israel against Hamas has increased scepticism and distrust of the United States among countries in the Global South, which consider the US to be hypocritical in light of what they see as an inconsistent stance in favour of Ukraine – like the Palestinians, an underdog – against Russia.[52] The fear is that in backing Israel, and to some appearing an accomplice in something akin to ethnic cleansing, Washington will increasingly lose credibility to the point where its influence on other strategic issues – including the Russia–Ukraine war – flags. With India firmly in Israel's court and most Global South states lacking a stake in the Gaza conflict, time will tell whether this concern is warranted. Nevertheless, questions will undoubtedly arise as to how the US can move Israel away from a maximally aggressive posture to preserve its bona fides with the rest of the world.

Critics of the Biden administration have focused mostly on a ceasefire, which the US endorses to the extent of brief, localised halts to the fighting to allow the delivery of humanitarian assistance, facilitate the evacuation of civilians and permit the return of hostages. As noted, in early November the Israelis provisionally agreed to such pauses. Mechanisms for compelling broader Israeli cooperation have not been addressed – perhaps because the same critics tacitly acknowledge that there are no promising ones. Notionally, the US could threaten to withhold ammunition shipments; to withdraw air defences, deployed troops and maritime assets; to disavow the 2016 Memorandum of Understanding on US security assistance for Israel; to vote in favour of anti-Israel UN Security Council or UN General Assembly resolutions; or to send American aid convoys into Gaza and dare the IDF to attack them.

Most of these measures would skewer other US interests without moving Israel's needle. Withholding certain munitions would merely push Israel into using less accurate ones producing more collateral damage. Removing air defences would open the door to Iranian, Hizbullah and Houthi missile attacks that would put thousands of Americans, as well as Israelis, in Israel at risk, and give the appearance of not merely chastising Israel but siding with its enemies. Withdrawing US troops, which are there mainly for hostage rescue and evacuation missions, would have the same effect. Redeploying carrier strike groups could encourage the wider war the US wants to avoid. Israel does not need foreign military financing, so cutting it would merely ignite a firestorm in Congress, potentially to Biden's domestic political detriment. US assertiveness at the UN would impress third countries – especially those in the Global South – while inflaming Israel and eroding whatever influence it now has on Israeli decisions. Finally, making US forces a tripwire in a combat zone would clearly be reckless. Given that Hamas itself is impeding the throughput of humanitarian assistance, pressures could mount for US forces to directly confront Hamas, conjuring memories of the US Marine barracks bombing in Lebanon in 1982 and 'Black Hawk down' in Somalia in 1993.

Even leaving aside the own-goal character of most of the foregoing measures, the general rub now would be as it has been in the past: if the US acts or threatens to act punitively, Israel will feel isolated but also free to do whatever it wants, thus depriving the US of the very leverage it seeks to apply. It could also damage its credibility with allies and partners by appearing to stiff one of them, emboldening its adversaries. If Washington bears with Israel, it might be able to marginally restrain its conduct, though Israel is likely still to act in ways that damage US interests. Pressure on Israel in such circumstances often works by offering Israeli leaders political cover for steps that they themselves have concluded are necessary but would raise questions about the wisdom of their policies. In reversing their positions, Israeli leaders could argue that Washington forced them to do so, which, as usual, would be cast as its having snatched Israeli defeat from the jaws of victory. Such whipsawing considerations, both domestic and international, suggest that the United States should continue a middle course, supporting Israel's suppression of Hamas while doggedly counselling restraint, and devising an affirmative multilateral plan for the day after, as remote as that day might appear at this time.

Notes

1 See Shira Rubin and Loveday Morris, 'How Hamas Broke Through Israel's Border Defenses During Oct. 7 Attack', *Washington Post*, 27 October 2023, https://www.washingtonpost.com/world/2023/10/27/hamas-attack-israel-october-7-hostages/; and 'Israel Lowers Oct. 7 Death Toll Estimate to 1,200', *New York Times*, 10 November 2023, https://www.nytimes.com/live/2023/11/10/world/israel-hamas-war-gaza-news.

2 See Graeme Wood, 'Hamas May Not Have a Step Two', *Atlantic*, 11 October 2023, https://www.theatlantic.com/ideas/archive/2023/10/hamas-strategy-israel-gaza-war/675618/.

3 See Ben Hubbard and Maria Abi-Habib, 'Behind Hamas's Bloody Gambit to Create a "Permanent" State

of War', *New York Times*, 8 November 2023 (updated 9 November 2023), https://www.nytimes.com/2023/11/08/world/middleeast/hamas-israel-gaza-war.html.

4 See, for instance, 'Why Hamas Attacked – and Why Israel Was Taken by Surprise: A Conversation with Martin Indyk', *Foreign Affairs*, 7 October 2023, https://www.foreignaffairs.com/middle-east/martin-indyk-why-hamas-attacked-and-why-israel-was-taken-surprise. Hamas might have felt the need to put the Israeli–Palestinian conflict back in the headlines, get Washington's attention and reassert its claim to be the avatar of resistance. This hypothesis also jibes with the smaller-bore view that Hamas had taken this huge gamble to wrongfoot its rival, the Palestinian Authority. But that would be like flying transatlantic because you like those little bowls of soggy almonds. Moreover, Hamas does not address itself to the US, but rather to regional audiences. Hamas also does not regard the US as its saviour, even in some imagined, long-range scenario in which Washington and Jerusalem become adversaries because the US no longer countenances Israel's collective punishment of Gazans and denial of Palestinians' demand for self-determination. A more likely but still hypothetical explanation is that Hamas might have hoped to trigger a regional conflict drawing in Iran and Hizbullah. If so, why then did Hamas not coordinate its plan with either notional ally? Perhaps Hamas simply saw the handwriting on the wall and aimed to go out in a blaze of glory.

5 'Hamas's Attack Was the Bloodiest in Israel's History', *The Economist*, 12 October 2023, https://www.economist.com/briefing/2023/10/12/hamass-attack-was-the-bloodiest-in-israels-history.

6 See David Martin, 'Gen. David Petraeus: Hamas' Attack on Israel Was "Far Worse Than 9/11"', CBS News, 15 October 2023, https://www.cbsnews.com/news/general-david-petraeus-hamas-attack-on-israel-was-far-worse-than-911/.

7 See, for example, David Clarke and Sophie Meyer, 'The Deadly Hamas Rampage Across Southern Israel', Reuters, 12 October 2023, https://www.reuters.com/graphics/ISRAEL-PALESTINIANS/MASSACRES/zgporzedjvd/; Sheera Frenkel and Steven Lee Meyers, 'Hamas Seeds Violent Videos on Sites with Little Moderation', *New York Times*, 10 October 2023, https://www.nytimes.com/2023/10/10/technology/hamas-violent-videos-online.html; and Meg Kelly and Sarah Cahlan, 'Video Shows Apparent Death of Israeli Hostages in Hamas Custody', *Washington Post*, 9 October 2023, https://www.washingtonpost.com/investigations/2023/10/09/israel-hamas-hostage-death/. Some of the fighters are believed to have taken the amphetamine Captagon before the operation, but that would hardly explain the scope or manner of the carnage. See James Jackson, 'Hamas Gunmen Were "High on Drugs" During Terrorist Attacks on Israel', *Telegraph*, 22 October 2023, https://www.telegraph.co.uk/world-news/2023/10/22/fighters-took-captagon-attacks-israel-hamas-war/.

8 See Hamas, 'A Document of General Principles & Policies', May 2017, https://irp.fas.org/world/para/docs/hamas-2017.pdf. See also Bruce Hoffman, 'Understanding Hamas's Genocidal Ideology', *Atlantic*, 10 October 2023, https://www.theatlantic.com/international/archive/2023/10/hamas-covenant-israel-attack-war-genocide/675602/.

9 See Anna Schecter, 'Videos of Hamas Attack Suggest a Chilling Evolution of Jihadist Tactics', NBC News, 28 October 2023, https://www.nbcnews.com/news/investigations/videos-hamas-attack-suggest-jihadism-evolved-chilling-new-ways-rcna122564.

10 See Monica Marks, 'What the World Gets Wrong About Hamas', *Time*, 30 October 2023, https://time.com/6329776/hamas-isis-gaza/; and Graeme Wood, 'Hamas Is Not ISIS', *Atlantic*, 27 October 2023, https://www.theatlantic.com/ideas/archive/2023/10/hamas-isis-war-in-gaza/675786/.

11 See Daniel Levy, 'The Road Back from Hell', *New York Times*, 8 November 2023, https://www.nytimes.com/2023/11/08/opinion/israel-hamas-cease-fire.html.

12 The quoted phrase is from a member of the Bush administration's National Security Council staff, in a conversation with one of the authors.

13 See David Rose, 'The Gaza Bombshell', *Vanity Fair*, April 2008, https://www.vanityfair.com/news/2008/04/gaza200804.

14 Quoted in, for example, Alice Speri, 'Before They Vowed to Annihilate Hamas, Israeli Officials Considered It an Asset', *Intercept*, 14 October 2023, https://theintercept.com/2023/10/14/hamas-israel-palestinian-authority/. See also Meron Rapoport, 'The End of the Netanyahu Doctrine', Responsible Statecraft, 11 October 2023, https://responsiblestatecraft.org/benjamin-netanyahu-israel/; and Tal Schneider, 'For Years, Netanyahu Propped Up Hamas. Now It's Blown Up in Our Faces', *Times of Israel*, 8 October 2023, https://www.timesofisrael.com/for-years-netanyahu-propped-up-hamas-now-its-blown-up-in-our-faces/.

15 It was especially galling and ominous that the Hamas operation came at the 50th anniversary of the momentous Arab surprise attack that initiated the near-catastrophic Yom Kippur War, which drew notice and comment before and after the fact. See Isabel Kershner, 'Hamas Attack Has Haunting Echoes of the 1973 Yom Kippur War', *New York Times*, 7 October 2023, https://www.nytimes.com/2023/10/07/world/middleeast/for-many-israelis-the-attacks-have-haunting-echoes-of-the-1973-yom-kippur-war.html; and Emily Rose and James Mackenzie, 'Fifty Years On, Divided Israel Remembers the War for Its Survival', Reuters, 6 October 2023, https://www.reuters.com/world/middle-east/fifty-years-divided-israel-remembers-war-its-survival-2023-10-06/.

16 See Patrick Kingsley and Ronen Bergman, 'The Secrets Hamas Knew About Israel's Military', *New York Times*, 13 October 2023, https://www.nytimes.com/2023/10/13/world/middleeast/hamas-israel-attack-gaza.html.

17 See Ronen Bergman, Mark Mazzetti and Maria Abi-Habib, 'How Years

of Israeli Failures on Hamas Led to a Devastating Attack', *New York Times*, 29 October 2023 (updated 1 November 2023), https://www.nytimes.com/2023/10/29/world/middleeast/israel-intelligence-hamas-attack.html.

18 See Peter Baker, 'How to Fly an American President into a Country at War', *New York Times*, 19 October 2023 (updated 23 October 2023), https://www.nytimes.com/2023/10/19/us/politics/biden-israel-trip.html.

19 See, for example, Franklin Foer, 'Inside Biden's "Hug Bibi" Strategy', *Atlantic*, 17 October 2023, https://www.theatlantic.com/ideas/archive/2023/10/biden-israel-tel-aviv-trip-netanyahu/675671/; and Susan B. Glasser, 'The Week When Biden Hugged Bibi', *New Yorker*, 20 October 2023, https://www.newyorker.com/news/letter-from-bidens-washington/the-week-when-biden-hugged-bibi.

20 See Patrick Kingsley and Ronen Bergman, 'Israel's Army Is Ready to Invade Gaza. Its Divided Government May Not Be', *New York Times*, 26 October 2023 (updated 30 October 2023), https://www.nytimes.com/2023/10/26/world/middleeast/israel-gaza-invasion-delay.html.

21 The Gaza Health Ministry put the number at more than 8,000 as of 29 October. See Wafaa Shurafa, Samy Magdy and Kareem Chehayeb, 'Gaza Receives Largest Aid Shipment So Far as Deaths Top 8,000 and Israel Widens Military Offensive', AP News, 29 October 2023, https://apnews.com/article/israel-hamas-war-news-10-29-2023-de1a7d660ba2f6d80b3d7aeaae5bb0f3.

22 Noga Tarnopolsky and Rick Noack, 'Hezbollah Steps Up Attacks, IDF Says, Fueling Fears of Wider Conflict', *Washington Post*, 22 October 2023, https://www.washingtonpost.com/world/2023/10/22/israel-gaza-war-hezbollah-iran/.

23 See Damien Cave, 'The "Devil's Playground" of Urban Combat that Israel Is Preparing to Enter', *New York Times*, 24 October 2023, https://www.nytimes.com/2023/10/24/world/middleeast/israel-hamas-invasion.html; and Helene Cooper, Adam Entous and Eric Schmitt, 'U.S. Raises Concerns About Israel's Plan of Action in Gaza, Officials Say', *New York Times*, 23 October 2023 (updated 31 October 2023), https://www.nytimes.com/2023/10/23/us/politics/israel-us-gaza-invasion.html.

24 See Michael D. Shear, David E. Sanger and Edward Wong, 'Biden's Support for Israel Now Comes with Words of Caution', *New York Times*, 30 October 2023, https://www.nytimes.com/2023/10/30/us/politics/biden-israel.html.

25 Patrick Kingsley and Ronen Bergman, 'Under Shroud of Secrecy, Israel Invasion of Gaza Has Begun', *New York Times*, 30 October 2023, https://www.nytimes.com/2023/10/30/world/middleeast/israel-gaza-invasion-secrecy.html.

26 *Ibid.*

27 See, for example, Nidal Al-Mughrabi, 'Gaza Death Toll Tops 10,000; UN Calls It a Children's Graveyard', Reuters, 6 November 2023, https://www.reuters.com/world/middle-east/pressure-israel-over-civilians-steps-up-ceasefire-calls-rebuffed-2023-11-06/.

28 See, for example, Aamer Madhani, Zeke Miller and Ellen Knickmeyer,

'Israel Agrees to 4-hour Daily Pauses in Gaza Fighting to Allow Civilians to Flee, White House Says', AP News, 10 November 2023, https://apnews.com/article/israel-gaza-humanitarian-pauses-b8fc613ffd8b9351c0dc37b90b6e10dd.

29 White House, 'Press Gaggle with NSC Coordinator for Strategic Communications John Kirby', 9 November 2023, https://www.whitehouse.gov/briefing-room/press-briefings/2023/11/09/press-gaggle-with-nsc-coordinator-for-strategic-communications-john-kirby/.

30 See Daniel Kurtzer, 'Why a Gaza Cease-fire Is Unrealistic', *Atlantic*, 8 November 2023, https://www.theatlantic.com/international/archive/2023/11/gaza-cease-fire-pause-israel-war/675933/.

31 See, for example, Isabel Kershner et al., 'Israel Plans to Control "Overall Security" of Gaza After War', *New York Times*, 7 November 2023, https://www.nytimes.com/2023/11/07/world/middleeast/israel-control-security-gaza-war.html.

32 See Nidal Al-Mughrabi and Rami Amichay, 'Israel, Hamas Agree on Four-day Truce, Hostage Release and Aid Into Gaza', Reuters, 21 November 2023, https://www.reuters.com/world/middle-east/israeli-government-debates-deal-release-gaza-hostages-truce-2023-11-21/.

33 See Scott Peterson, 'Gaza Crisis: After Strategic Gains, Iran Pivots to Prevent Losses', *Christian Science Monitor*, 25 October 2023, https://www.csmonitor.com/World/Middle-East/2023/1025/Gaza-crisis-After-strategic-gains-Iran-pivots-to-prevent-losses; and

Alex Vatanka, 'Iran's Calculations in the Israel–Hamas War', Middle East Institute, 19 October 2023, https://www.mei.edu/publications/irans-calculations-israel-hamas-war.

34 See Vivian Nereim and Saeed Al-Batati, 'Yemen's Houthi Militia Claims to Have Launched an Attack on Israel', *New York Times*, 31 October 2023, https://www.nytimes.com/2023/10/31/world/middleeast/yemen-houthi-militia-israel.html.

35 See, for instance, Ben Hubbard, 'In High-stakes Speech, Hezbollah's Leader Stops Short of Call to Expand Hamas War', *New York Times*, 3 November 2023, https://www.nytimes.com/2023/11/03/world/middleeast/hezbollah-leader-address-israel-hamas-war-gaza.html; and Hanin Ghaddar, 'What Did Nasrallah Really Say, and Why?', Policy Analysis, Washington Institute for Near East Policy, 3 November 2023, https://www.washingtoninstitute.org/policy-analysis/what-did-nasrallah-really-say-and-why.

36 See Michael Young, 'The Axis of Resistance Has Been Gathering Strength', *Atlantic*, 24 October 2023, https://www.theatlantic.com/international/archive/2023/10/-iran-axis-of-resistance-israel-gaza-conflict/675749/.

37 See Robert Satloff, Dennis Ross and David Makovsky, 'Israel's War Aims and the Principles of a Post-Hamas Administration in Gaza', PolicyWatch 3799, Washington Institute for Near East Policy, 17 October 2023, https://www.washingtoninstitute.org/pdf/view/18402/en; and Steven Simon, 'What Comes After Hamas?', *Foreign*

Affairs, 18 October 2023, https://www.
foreignaffairs.com/israel/what-comes-
after-hamas. See also Josh Marshall,
'Who Takes Over Gaza?', Talking
Points Memo, 31 October 2023, https://
talkingpointsmemo.com/edblog/who-
takes-over-gaza; and Bret Stephens,
'A Plan to Defeat Hamas and Avoid
a Bloodbath', *New York Times*, 27
October 2023, https://www.nytimes.
com/2023/10/27/opinion/israel-hamas-
strategy-bennett.html.

38 See Satloff, Ross and Makovsky,
'Israel's War Aims and the Principles of
a Post-Hamas Administration in Gaza'.

39 See Isabel Kershner, 'Netanyahu Pushes
Back on Idea of Palestinian Authority
Running Gaza', *New York Times*, 12
November 2023, https://www.nytimes.
com/2023/11/12/world/middleeast/
netanyahu-palestinian-authority.html.

40 See Samy Magdy, 'At Cairo Summit,
Even Arab Leaders at Peace with Israel
Expressed Growing Anger over the
Gaza War', AP News, 21 October 2023,
https://apnews.com/article/israel-gaza-
egypt-jordon-palestinians-hamas-
997fe6fd3dcbc08f97b2168744180af1.

41 See, for example, Vivian Nereim,
'Israel–Hamas War Threatens Wider
Unrest and Crushes Hopes for
Calmer Mideast', *New York Times*, 13
October 2023, https://www.nytimes.
com/2023/10/13/world/middleeast/
israel-hamas-war-mideast.html.

42 See Kate Kelly et al., 'Saudi Arabia
Warns U.S.: Israeli Invasion of Gaza
Could Be Catastrophic', *New York Times*,
27 October 2023, https://www.nytimes.
com/2023/10/27/world/middleeast/
saudi-arabia-israel-us-invasion.html.

43 See Hussein Ibish, 'The Reckoning
That Is Coming for Qatar', *Atlantic*, 20
October 2023, https://www.theatlantic.
com/international/archive/2023/10/
israel-gaza-conflict-qatar-hamas-
muslim-brotherhood/675702/.

44 See William McGurn, 'Hamas's
Second-stage Strategy', *Wall Street
Journal*, 30 October 2023, https://www.
wsj.com/articles/hamass-second-stage-
strategy-palestinians-gaza-civilian-
casualties-israel-hamas-a63b6abc.

45 See, for instance, David Ignatius, 'In
Fight Against Hamas, Israel Needs
to Be Certain of Its "Big Ideas"',
Washington Post, 24 October 2023,
https://www.washingtonpost.
com/opinions/2023/10/24/
hamas-israel-gaza-war-strategy/.

46 See, for example, Michael Birnbaum
et al., 'Biden's Aid Plan for Israel,
Ukraine Splits Republicans in
Congress', *Washington Post*, 31 October
2023, https://www.washingtonpost.
com/national-security/2023/10/31/
blinken-austin-senate-israel-ukraine/.

47 Andrea Shalal, 'Arab American
Support for Biden, Democrats
Plummets over Israel, Poll Shows',
Reuters, 31 October 2023, https://
www.reuters.com/world/us/arab-
american-support-biden-democrats-
plummets-over-israel-poll-2023-10-31/.

48 See Reid J. Epstein and Anjali Huynh,
'Democrats Splinter over Israel as the
Young, Diverse Left Rages at Biden',
New York Times, 27 October 2023
(updated 28 October 2023), https://www.
nytimes.com/2023/10/27/us/politics/
biden-democrats-israel-2024.html.

49 See Maria Abi-Habib, Michael
Crowley and Edward Wong, 'More
Than 500 U.S. Officials Sign Letter
Protesting Biden's Israel Policy', *New
York Times*, 14 November 2023, https://

www.nytimes.com/2023/11/14/us/
politics/israel-biden-letter-gaza-cease-
fire.html.

50 Harry Enten, 'Polls Show Americans
Agree with Biden on US Foreign
Policy on Israel', CNN, 19
October 2023, https://www.cnn.
com/2023/10/19/politics/polling-israel-
hamas-biden/index.html.

51 See, for instance, Caroline Downey,
'Prominent Democrats Turn on
Rashida Tlaib as She Escalates
Anti-Israel Vitriol', *National Review*,
6 November 2023, https://www.
nationalreview.com/news/prominent-
democrats-turn-on-rashida-tlaib-as-
she-escalates-anti-israel-vitriol/.

52 See Oliver Stuenkel, 'Why the
Global South Is Accusing America
of Hypocrisy', *Foreign Policy*, 2
November 2023, https://foreignpolicy.
com/2023/11/02/israel-palestine-
hamas-gaza-war-russia-ukraine-
occupation-west-hypocrisy/.

The Gaza War and the Region

Emile Hokayem

The Islamist Palestinian militant group Hamas's 7 October attack on southern Israel from Gaza, in which roughly 1,200 Israeli civilians and security personnel were killed, often gruesomely, and more than 200 hostages were taken, was a generation-defining event that has left Israel deeply traumatised, Palestine in even greater distress, and the region itself dangerously close to all-out war.[1] The assault was as much a Hamas military success as it was a comprehensive Israeli failure. In the past two decades, successive Israeli governments had believed that the Palestinian 'problem' could be boxed in, shrunk and ignored as they pursued territorial expansion in the West Bank and regional integration and normalisation with Arab states. Many Western and Arab states seemed satisfied, complacent or resigned. This mindset has badly backfired.

Hamas's nebulous agenda

Hamas's precise aims and motivations remain unclear, but the drivers of its action are evident. The organisation is less cohesive than it looks from the outside: its Gaza-based military wing, which has been ascendant in recent years, grew distrustful of a political leadership that is largely based abroad. The responsibility for governing Gaza felt like a trap insofar as it could have operated to weaken the group's ethos of resistance and further split the fates of Gaza and the West Bank. The intensification of Israeli occupation

Emile Hokayem is Director of Regional Security and Senior Fellow for Middle East Security at the IISS.

Survival | vol. 65 no. 6 | December 2023–January 2024 | pp. 57–66 https://doi.org/10.1080/00396338.2023.2285603

in the West Bank and East Jerusalem exposed the haplessness of the secular Palestinian Authority (PA) and did not deter several Arab states from normalising relations with Israel. Israeli–Saudi normalisation, which to many seemed imminent, would have been a symbolic humiliation and strategic setback.

The attack settled the debate about Hamas's identity: resistance prevailed over governance. It elevated the group's domestic and regional profile, as Hamas entered the premier league of non-state armed groups, joining the likes of Hizbullah, the Lebanese Shia militant group, among the stalwarts of the Iranian-backed *muqawama* front, or 'axis of resistance'. Hamas has also decisively overtaken the beleaguered PA in standing and credibility. It has achieved notable psychological and political effects, shattering Israeli perceptions of its own power, the competence of its security services and political leadership, and the manageability of its immediate neighbourhood.

Hamas's prospects will depend largely on how it emerges from the Israeli response. It has made extensive physical preparations (notably tunnels), acquired better capabilities and adapted its leadership structure. On 7 October, it fired nearly 3,000 rockets (as compared to a daily average of 124 by Hizbullah during the 2006 Lebanon War) and continues to strike deep into Israeli territory.[2] It will gear its hostage-release policy to its military and political goals. While Israel will focus on seizing territory and killing militants, Hamas will play for time and try to shape the narrative. Variables include how long its leadership will survive, what kind of tactical surprises it will achieve during the war, how long it can sustain rocket fire into Israel, how much additional harm Israel suffers, Israeli resolve and Israel's political stability.

As the Israeli air and ground campaign intensifies, the Israeli military is likely to achieve some operational success. The destruction of Hamas's advanced military capabilities and the decapitation of its Gaza-based command are realistic prospects. What is highly unlikely is the obliteration of Hamas as a social, political and ideological actor. Contrary to the Islamic State in Mosul or Raqqa, Hamas is entrenched in and extremely knowledgeable about the society that hosts it. Hamas will justify humanitarian suffering and high casualty levels among its fighters and civilians as the inevitable cost of future victory. To regenerate itself, it will find recruits among the many orphaned young men of Gaza and elsewhere. Many Palestinians beyond its immediate sympathisers accept its nationalist credentials, and, in the short term, many of its detractors are likely to overlook its Islamist agenda. A key factor is whether Palestinians in Gaza blame Hamas for the calamity as much as or possibly more than Israel. That may depend on the degree of human loss and displacement, the physical damage done to infrastructure and physical space, and the erosion of the social fabric. These, in turn, depend on the type of military campaign Israel conducts. Israel is likely to dismantle the United Nations infrastructure that has sustained Gaza since 1948. Hamas is just as likely to evolve into a determined insurgency.

Many outside parties have called for external forces to govern and police Gaza after the war, whether it is the PA, Arab forces, UN peacekeeping troops or a mixture of the three. But the obstacles to such arrangements are immense. Israel is inclined to insist on maintaining a large and active security presence within Gaza and to deny any ruling authority full control over border points, maritime access, movement of people and goods, or local governance. Israel is also likely to assume control of territory and unilaterally announce no-go zones on land and at sea. External forces would then be seen as mere enforcers of an Israeli occupation, and Arab forces fighting Hamas would be a political catastrophe for Arab governments. Furthermore, without a clear articulation and acceptance by the Israeli government of a political dispensation that spells out tangible steps towards Palestinian statehood, no external player is likely to be willing to take responsibility for Gaza's future. The most probable scenario is another Israeli ground occupation on territory fundamentally reshaped to suit Israeli security concerns and over a destitute population with dismal political or economic prospects.

A neighbourhood on the brink

The Israel–Hamas war is profoundly destabilising for the immediate neighbourhood, which was already reeling from successive Arab–Israeli wars and the Syrian conflict. A long and destructive war, followed by an insurgency, large-scale displacement and popular anger, has dangerous implications for Lebanon and Syria, the two Arab countries most opposed to Israel, as well as for Egypt and Jordan, the first two states to have signed peace agreements with Israel.

Egypt and Jordan have been concerned in recent years that other Arab states' focus on normalisation was diverting attention from worsening dynamics inside the Palestinian territories. From a political point of view, this alarm was awkward to express. Their main partners and financial backers, Saudi Arabia and the United Arab Emirates (UAE), have been positively inclined towards Israel. Neither is a front-line state, hosts refugees or needs to worry acutely about security and economic repercussions. Cairo and Amman also resented the fact that the normalisation push, energised by the Trump administration, was undermining their traditional roles as the lead Arab nations on Israel and Palestine. Jordan's King Abdullah II sees Israeli Prime Minister Benjamin Netanyahu as uniquely dangerous and unreliable. Jordan refused to take part in the Negev Forum, a small grouping endorsed by the United States that included Bahrain, Egypt, Israel, Morocco and the UAE, but excluded the PA.

Cairo and Amman's fear that ethnic cleansing will produce new waves of refugees – reinforced by statements by senior Israeli officials and a leaked Israeli intelligence memo – has motivated their frenetic diplomatic outreach pressing for an immediate ceasefire. While a ceasefire has not been forthcoming, the US and other Western countries are emphatically opposed to forced displacement.[3]

In the short term, Egypt is the most exposed. As desperate civilians congregate in southern Gaza and Israel shifts its operational focus from the north to the south, the humanitarian situation could deteriorate quickly. Cairo has publicly warned that it would not allow crossings into Sinai, but this position may become untenable if suffering increases significantly. Jordan has sought an immediate ceasefire so as to avoid such a scenario in the West Bank. This will be difficult to arrange. Israeli settlers and extremist politicians perceive a moment of opportunity to expand further into the West Bank. Settler violence has increased and is rarely stopped or contained by the Israeli military. While Hamas's presence in the West Bank is small, other militant groups, civil-society organisations and political parties may respond to calls for solidarity with Gaza. The PA, institutionally battered and regarded as illegitimate by many Palestinians, would struggle to contain such an outburst unless backed by regional powers and a Western push for statehood.[4]

Popular solidarity with the Palestinians has also produced large demonstrations that serve as platforms for broad criticism of the Egyptian and Jordanian governments. In turn, dislocations of the war further stoke discontent.[5] Egypt has faced energy cuts as Israeli gas production and transport has been suspended due to concerns about the security of the production facilities and underwater pipeline.

Dislodged regional prospects

In the days preceding the 7 October attack, regional discussion centred on the mesmerising possibility of US-facilitated Saudi–Israeli normalisation. Riyadh primarily sought US security, political and economic benefits. Jerusalem saw a deal with the Arab world's political, religious and economic powerhouse as the ultimate validation of its regional strategy. Washington focused on economically driven regional integration. The region-wide trend towards de-escalation made normalisation an understandable if overhyped prospect. Saudi Arabia and Iran had restored relations; Turkiye and the UAE had suspended their rivalry; Gulf reconciliation had ended Qatar's isolation; conflicts in Libya, Syria and Yemen were frozen; and the Abraham Accords had normalised relations between Israel and several Arab states. This fostered relief and enthusiasm in Western, Asian and many Arab capitals, but also complacency and wishful thinking.[6] The India–Middle East–Europe Economic Corridor, in which Israel played a central role, is a prime example. It was unveiled at the G20 meeting less than a month before the 7 October attack. In late September, when Netanyahu brandished a map entitled 'The New Middle East' showing Israel as including all the Palestinian territories and the Golan Heights during his speech at the UN General Assembly, there was at best tepid objection by a few member states.[7]

In reality, the Middle East's de-escalation has been thin, tactical, bilateral and unstructured. None of the core issues have been addressed, let alone resolved. Instead, grand plans for regional integration and cooperation ignored or understated the persistence of conflict, bleak economic and fiscal prospects, and the worsening of domestic political trends in many countries. It was not difficult for the Israel–Hamas war to overturn the apparent regional agenda, as indeed it has. The war has forced the Palestinian question back to the top of the Middle Eastern agenda after years of neglect. Arab states' relations with Israel will be constrained for years to come. In Arab forums, Palestine is likely to overshadow other conflicts. Palestinians' faraway supporters, such as Algeria, Iraq and Kuwait, will be comforted in their uncompromising positions. Even Israel's closest partners in the Arab world despair at their lack of leverage over Israeli decision-making. Crucially, the crisis will allow Arab states to resist Western policies and professed norms. Disingenuously or not, a wide segment of Arab society considers Western outrage over Saudi Arabia's conduct of its war in Yemen and Syrian President Bashar al-Assad's large-scale killing in Syria selective and hypocritical.

In private, however, there is considerable Arab anger at Hamas, especially insofar as the 7 October attack increases Iran's ability to upend regional dynamics. Many Arab states will decline to embrace Hamas's maximalist objective of a state comprising the totality of pre-1948 Palestine, to support a sustained war with Israel, or to deploy instruments of economic coercion such as an oil embargo. The ongoing war is unlikely to reverse de-escalation among major players. Signatories to the Abraham Accords are unlikely to pull out. While stalled at present, Saudi normalisation with Israel remains on the table, though the Saudi ask is likely to be considerably higher.

At the same time, the prospect of wider conflict, the relative futility of US diplomacy thus far and the contradictions of Western policy have energised regional diplomacy. In recent weeks, contacts among erstwhile enemies and rivals have multiplied. Saudi Crown Prince Muhammad bin Salman held his first meeting with Iranian President Ebrahim Raisi at the height of the crisis. Assad, Iran's foremost partner in the Arab world, attended an emergency session of the Arab League in Riyadh, as did Turkish President Recep Tayyip Erdoğan. The Qatari emir has met the Egyptian and Emirati presidents. Arab capitals' main effort is likely to be directed at the United States, which, however diminished, is seen as the only player able to restrain Israel, put a political process on track and provide guarantees.

Iran's calculations

Other than Israel, the state that will most shape the trajectory of the conflict is Iran. Exactly how informed and involved Iran was in the October Hamas attack remains a matter of debate. It empowers, guides and supports, but does not necessarily order or approve, its partners' actions. They are like junior brothers-in-arms. Hamas may have hoped for, but likely did not expect, direct and sustained Iranian help during a conflict. Early US intelligence has indicated that Iran did not play a direct role in the 7 October operation.[8]

Furthermore, Iran's relations with non-state groups vary according to political context, local conditions and risk appetite. Iran's relationship with Hamas soured during the Syrian civil war when Hamas sided with the Syrian rebels, with hundreds of its fighters operating from Palestinian refugee camps against Assad's forces and their Shia allies. Assad's victory in 2017, a change in Hamas leadership and then Hizbullah's mediation has since improved relations. Iran has consolidated its network of partners, opening a joint operations room in Beirut and encouraging operational and strategic cooperation. Hamas's ability to rebound after its costly conflict with Israel in 2014 owes much to Iranian support. But Iran's relationship with Hamas is still less organic and strategic than its ties with Hizbullah and Palestinian Islamic Jihad, Hamas's smaller rival in Gaza.[9]

On balance, Tehran has emerged a beneficiary of the 7 October attack. The crisis has terrified Israeli society, re-energised Iran's axis of resistance and shaken its regional rivals. Iran can credibly present itself as the righteous supporter of Palestine in contrast with Arab states whose support had receded, allowing it to brush aside the criticism of its actions in Iraq, Syria and Yemen.

In the short term, Iran does not appear to have an interest in expanding the war. Rather, the Gaza war is an affirmation of its forward-defence strategy. The more crucial question is whether Hizbullah should join the fight. The Lebanese group has become Iran's most effective instrument of punishment and deterrence against the US and Israel, and is the one best suited for an existential conflict as opposed to a contained and possibly inconclusive regional war. Much will depend on how the war unfolds and what lessons Israel derives from it. Under the two most likely scenarios, Iran faces risks. An easy defeat of Hamas could motivate Israel to pursue an aggressive approach in Syria and Lebanon, which are strategically vital from Iran's standpoint. A slow, grinding war would raise questions about Iran's credibility. As Gaza got pounded and Hamas weakened, Iran would be asked why its fiery rhetoric and professed solidarity had not translated into supportive action. But should Hamas resist more stiffly than expected, inflicting serious damage on the Israeli military, and Israel come under sustained international condemnation, Iran would be able to keep avoiding a direct military role.

In any case, Iran's ability to operate through partners in various arenas gives it options short of all-out war. Iran-backed Shia militias have hit US bases in Syria and Iraq with mortar rounds and rockets; Hizbullah and Syria-based militias have fired rockets on northern Israel; and the Houthi rebels have launched ballistic and cruise missiles, as well as uncrewed aerial vehicles, at Israel from Yemen. This activity can be interpreted as Iran using its partners for strategic signalling of support while resisting pressure for greater direct involvement.

*   *   *

The Israeli military response to the October attack is unprecedented in scope and brutality, with a stated if probably unattainable objective of destroying Hamas. It is unclear as yet how the war will unfold, whether it will spread, and what Israel will do if its military objectives are or are not met. The prospect of a consequential Israeli strategic failure cannot be discounted. At a minimum, the war's human and other costs are likely to exceed anything that Israelis and especially Palestinians have endured in the past.

Notes

[1] For a detailed account of how the attack unfolded, see Jason Burke, 'A Deadly Cascade: How Secret Hamas Attack Orders Were Passed Down at Last Minute', *Guardian*, 7 November 2023, https://www.theguardian.com/world/2023/nov/07/secret-hamas-attack-orders-israel-gaza-7-october.

2 See, for example, Emanuel Fabian, 'IDF: 9,500 Rockets Fired at Israel Since Oct. 7, Including 3,000 in 1st Hours of Onslaught', *Times of Israel*, 9 November 2023, https://www.timesofisrael.com/liveblog_entry/idf-9500-rockets-fired-at-israel-since-oct-7-including-3000-in-1st-hours-of-onslaught/.

3 See, for instance, Yasmeen Serhan, 'Why Palestinians Fear Permanent Displacement from Gaza', *Time*, 2 November 2023, https://time.com/6330904/palestinians-gaza-fear-permanent-expulsion/.

4 See Mairav Zonszein, 'Settler Violence Rises in the West Bank During the Gaza War', International Crisis Group, 6 November 2023, https://www.crisisgroup.org/middle-east-north-africa/east-mediterranean-mena/israelpalestine/settler-violence-rises-west-bank-gaza-war.

5 See 'Israel–Hamas War Fuels Anger and Protests Across the Middle East amid Fears of a Wider Conflict', CBS News, 18 October 2023, https://www.cbsnews.com/news/israel-hamas-war-protests-middle-east/.

6 See Jake Sullivan, 'The Sources of American Power', *Foreign Affairs*, vol. 102, no. 6, November/December 2023, pp. 8–29, esp. pp. 22–3.

7 See, for instance, Daniel Edelson, 'Germany, U.S. Slam Netanyahu's Middle East Map Presented at UN', ynetnews, 26 September 2023, https://www.ynetnews.com/article/b10ibyxgt.

8 Adam Entous, Julian E. Barnes and Jonathan Swan, 'Early Intelligence Shows Hamas Attack Surprised Iranian Leaders, U.S. Says', *New York Times*, 11 October 2023, https://www.nytimes.com/2023/10/11/us/politics/iran-israel-gaza-hamas-us-intelligence.html.

9 See Nadeen Ebrahim, 'Hamas and Iran Are Longtime Allies. Did Tehran Help with Its Attack on Israel?', CNN, 10 October 2023, https://www.cnn.com/2023/10/09/middleeast/hamas-iran-israel-attack-analysis-intl/index.html.

Israel and the Palestinians:
The Day After

Chuck Freilich

Predictions of Israeli politics are notoriously perilous, but a broad consensus anticipates a major political reckoning after the current war, precipitated by Hamas's historic 7 October attack, ends. Israeli Prime Minister Benjamin Netanyahu's ultra-right-wing government was already in trouble before the war began, having overplayed its hand with the so-called judicial overhaul and problematic stewardship of a number of major issues, including the economy and the critically important relationship with the United States. The war's horrific outset, and the widely shared public perception ever since that the government had failed to manage the home front and left it to civil-society organisations, have greatly undermined Netanyahu's claim to ongoing leadership on the basis of his reputation as Israel's 'Mr Security' and his presumptively unparalleled ability to chart its course through dangerous times.

The polls show a collapse in support for Netanyahu personally and his Likud party as a whole.[1] The public appears to be tired of Netanyahu's high-octane partisanship and the low performance and accountability of Likud governments in recent years, and desirous of more responsible, unifying and centrist governance. Most Israelis, left and right, are likely to feel the need to reassess some of their fundamental beliefs. Existing parties will

Chuck Freilich, a former Israeli deputy national security advisor, is a senior fellow at the Institute for National Security Studies in Tel Aviv and the MirYam Institute. He is the author of *Zion's Dilemmas: How Israel Makes National Security Policy* (Cornell, 2012), *Israeli National Security: A New Strategy for an Era of Change* (Oxford, 2018) and *Israel and the Cyber Threat: How the Startup Nation Became a Global Cyber Power* (Oxford, 2023).

Survival | vol. 65 no. 6 | December 2023–January 2024 | pp. 67–73 https://doi.org/10.1080/00396338.2023.2285602

probably split and new ones arise, leading to a range of new choices on both the left and right. An overall right-of-centre orientation is probable, but it will be pragmatic and security-minded right rather than ideological.

Limited options, daunting obstacles

US President Joe Biden has repeatedly stated that the war must end with the defeat of Hamas and a revival of the long-moribund two-state solution.[2] The administration has already begun working towards the latter, meeting with the leaders of Israel, the Palestinian Authority (PA), primary Arab states and international partners. International crises can provide an opportunity for unexpected and constructive diplomacy, and the administration is wise to try to provide it. It is, however, exceedingly hard to see why the two-state solution should not now be considered dead in the water.

There is room for blame on all sides. Israel's settlement policies under the right-wing governments in recent decades were intentionally designed to make a two-state solution practically unachievable. The Palestinians have repeatedly rejected peace proposals that would have given them a state on essentially 100% of West Bank and Gaza territory, with an unlimited return of refugees to the Palestinian state and a capital in east Jerusalem. Indeed, they have spurned every possible compromise ever since the British Peel Commission first recommended the division of Mandatory Palestine into Arab and Jewish states in 1937.

The genocidal character of Hamas's attack on Israel was the living embodiment of the latter's deepest national nightmare: that its enemies' true objective was the annihilation of Jews, as Jews, and ultimately the destruction of the state of Israel. In an unprecedentedly brutal fashion, Hamas effectively took a page out of Iran and Hizbullah's playbook, which calls for repeated limited conflicts against Israel designed to lead to its long-term weakening and eventual collapse.[3]

Israel's most basic demand in any peace negotiation has always been for essentially ironclad security arrangements. Following the catastrophic onset of the war, few in Israel will continue to believe in their viability. Peace may be the best ultimate guarantor of safety, but most Israelis will require a level of tangible military security that will be very hard to achieve.

A two-state solution must now be predicated on a number of eventualities that may not be feasible. The first, and a prerequisite for the others, is that Israel can successfully destroy Hamas as a coherent military force and topple it as the governing body in Gaza. If not, the most likely outcome is a restoration of the pre-war status quo and ever-bloodier rounds of violence in the future. Peace will be unachievable as long as Hamas remains a viable force.

Even assuming Israel can destroy Hamas – an increasingly questionable proposition given the rising death toll and international backlash – the next question is whether the PA can be reinstated in Gaza, after having been overthrown by Hamas in 2007. The PA has repeatedly failed to re-establish itself there and has consistently refused to hold elections since 2006 out of fear that Hamas would gain control over the West Bank as well.

Yet even if the PA were to regain control over Gaza, an international or Arab force would have to be deployed to Gaza for a lengthy period to ensure that PA leaders were not killed by remnants of Hamas and other rejectionist organisations, and that they did not topple the PA once again. To prop up the PA, this force would need to have effective interim control. This too is a highly dubious condition. International peacekeeping forces can work when the sides are sincerely interested in their success; they are of little value when they must actually fight. In this case, fighting would almost certainly be necessary. Furthermore, prospects that an international force could prevent the re-emergence of the internal and external violence endemic to an overpopulated and impoverished strip of land are prohibitively low. And few states, if any, would volunteer to send their forces directly into such a perilous situation.

If no acceptable party is likely to take control of Gaza, Israel will face a number of critical decisions. Netanyahu has already stated that Israel will have to maintain some sort of security control over Gaza after the war. One possibility, a highly undesirable one, is to remain deployed in Gaza indefinitely, in effect imposing a renewed occupation. Alternatively, Israel could withdraw, as it has done following all previous conflicts with Hamas, and leave the way open to the next cycle of violence. But this would contravene its entire rationale for fighting the war: the permanent suppression of Hamas.

Looming over the Gaza crisis is the uncertain future of the West Bank. If a two-state solution can no longer be achieved but Israel reverts to more centrist and moderate governance, how does it address the demographic ramifications of the ongoing occupation of the West Bank for its character as a predominantly Jewish and democratic state? This long-standing conundrum may produce renewed interest in the concept of civil (as opposed to military) withdrawal from the West Bank. Under this approach, Israel would gradually dismantle settlements in those parts of the West Bank that a centrist government would not wish to retain in a final peace agreement – probably over 90% of West Bank territory. The Israel Defense Forces (IDF), however, would remain fully and indefinitely deployed throughout the West Bank for security purposes. Palestinian statehood would be put off for the foreseeable future and beyond.

From the outset of the Oslo peace process in the 1990s, the Palestinians utterly failed to meet the fundamental criteria on which it was predicated: establishment of a responsible government, an end to terrorism and a demonstrated willingness to live in peace next to Israel. Instead, they established a corrupt dictatorship in the West Bank and a radical theocracy in Gaza, conducted unending terrorism and rejected all peace proposals, no matter how close they came to meeting their demands in full. The Palestinians are not solely to blame, of course. Israel's settlement policy has corroded Palestinian faith in the peace process. Settlements, however, can be dismantled, as Israel has demonstrated more than once.

Accordingly, the conclusive demise of Palestinians' hopes for an independent state is a likely consequence of Hamas's attack and the ensuing war. In an optimistic scenario, they may enjoy heightened autonomy and self-government in the West Bank and Gaza, but probably not independent statehood.

The role of the international community

Gaza, hardly in great shape before the war, will end it in a state of severe destruction. It is doubtful that Arab countries and the wider international community will actually fulfil pledges of aid to Gaza more fully this time than they have in the past. Given the ongoing war in Ukraine and other challenges around the world, the collective capacity for significant aid to Gaza will likely prove limited.

In any case, it is time for the international community to hold the Palestinians accountable for their actions and to stop treating them as helpless, childlike victims. Palestinians are among the highest per capita recipients of international aid.[4] Merely pouring more resources into Gazan recovery and development in the West Bank, well-intentioned as this may be, is not a sufficient answer. Palestinians should also be encouraged to fundamentally change their national narrative, truly disassociate themselves from the doctrines of murderous hatred on which generations have been educated, acknowledge that there will never be a return of refugees to Israel itself, and appreciate that Israel's national aspirations are no less legitimate than theirs and that all sides have to compromise. Only then will Israel be able to consider the painful concessions it too must make for peace, including a willingness to accept security guarantees.

The conflict, as pro-Palestinian voices are fond of noting, did not begin on 7 October, and all sides have made egregious errors over the decades. Nothing, however, justifies decades of terrorism culminating in the horrors of that day, and there is a price to be paid. While every Gazan casualty is to be regretted, the onus must be placed on Hamas, which incontrovertibly places its weapons among the civilian population, next to hospitals, schools, youth clubs and more, intentionally using ordinary Palestinians as human shields. Some Israeli attacks against military targets undoubtedly cause unintended civilian casualties, despite stringent targeting criteria. Critics of IDF actions should, however, go beyond empathy and suggest realistic alternatives. If Israel fails to win this war decisively, Hamas, Hizbullah and Iran may reprise what happened on 7 October, as they have repeatedly stated publicly.

One of Hamas's aims may have been to derail Israel's expanding relationships with the Sunni Arab states, especially its apparently imminent normalisation of ties with Saudi Arabia. For Iran too, the emerging US-led axis between Israel and the Sunni states constituted a severe strategic setback that would have negated years of progress in strengthening its overall strategic posture in the region. Normalisation between Saudi Arabia and Israel may still be salvageable, but will likely be put off for some time. The Saudis could both preserve the viability of that objective and promote an Israeli–Palestinian peace process by agreeing to play a significant role in resurrecting post-war Gaza – for example, by helping to reinstate the PA and participating in an international force, as well as providing reconstruction aid.

US–Israeli relations

Since the attack, US–Israeli relations have been marked by strategic cooperation of unprecedented depth and scope. Biden has forcefully emphasised Israel's right and even duty to defend its citizens, backing up rhetoric with proactive diplomacy and the deployment of two carrier strike groups to deter Hizbullah and Iran from broadening the war, while demanding that every effort be made to prevent civilian casualties. The president himself made a rare wartime visit to Israel, and US Secretary of State Antony Blinken has visited several times.

In the United States prior to the war, structural demographic changes unrelated to Israel but with significant ramifications for public opinion towards it, and the Democratic left's changing perceptions of Israel, appeared to be leading to an unprecedented crisis in US–Israeli relations.[5] But the war has demonstrated Israel's fragility and the accuracy of some of its claims regarding Arab intentions. Notwithstanding the highly corrosive impact that Israel's settlement policies have had on public opinion and the vociferous protests against Israel's military response to the Hamas attack, the crisis has revealed the depth and firmness of American public and congressional support for Israel, and led to an at least short- to medium-term strengthening of US–Israeli relations.

In the longer term, in the absence of a readily implementable peace process, sources of bilateral tension will likely re-emerge. Unless a new and more moderate government rapidly coalesces in Israel, diplomatic friction could become significant. The war has demonstrated Israel's heavy dependence on the US even in scenarios that are considered far less than existential, and thus the importance of adopting policies and measures that meet with American approval and counter percolating American discontent.

Notes

[1] See, for example, 'Only 27% of Israelis Believe Netanyahu Is Suitable to Head Government', Middle East Monitor, 4 November 2023, https://www.middleeastmonitor.com/20231104-only-27-of-israelis-believe-netanyahu-is-suitable-to-head-government/.

[2] See, for instance, 'Biden Pushes Mideast Leaders to Consider Two-state Solution After Israel–Hamas War Ends', PBS News Hour, 29 October 2023, https://www.pbs.org/newshour/world/biden-pushes-mideast-leaders-to-consider-two-state-solution-after-israel-hamas-war-ends.

[3] See Robert Satloff et al., 'The New Middle East: Hamas Attack, Israel at War, and U.S. Policy', PolicyWatch 3797, Washington Institute for Near East Policy, 13 October 2023, https://www.washingtoninstitute.org/policy-analysis/new-middle-east-hamas-attack-israel-war-and-us-policy.

[4] See Jeremy Wildeman and Alaa Tartir, 'Political Economy of Foreign Aid in the Occupied Palestinian Territories: A Conceptual Framing', in Alaa Tartir, Tariq Dana and Timothy Seidel (eds), *Political Economy of Palestine: Critical, Interdisciplinary, and Decolonial Perspectives* (Cham: Palgrave Macmillan, 2021).

[5] See, for example, Dana H. Allin and Steven N. Simon, *Our Separate Ways: The Struggle for the Future of the U.S.–Israel Alliance* (New York: PublicAffairs, 2016).

Noteworthy

Nightmare: Israel, Hamas and Gaza

'We have decided to put an end to all of the occupation's crimes. The time is over for them to act without accountability. Thus, we announce the *Al-Aqsa Flood* operation, and in the first strike within 20 minutes, more than 5,000 rockets were launched.

[…]

Today, whoever has a gun, let him bring it out; it is time. Everyone should come out with their trucks, cars, or tools. Today, history opens its most pure and honorable pages.'

Mohammed Deif, commander of the Al-Qassam Brigades, the military wing of Hamas, declares the start of the Al-Aqsa Flood *operation against Israel in a televised speech on 7 October 2023.*[1]

'My husband is holding the door of the bomb shelter. Now they're shooting sprays of bullets at the bomb shelter's window. Sprays. And my three children are here with me.'

An Israeli woman named Doreen tells Israel's Channel 12 about coming under attack by Hamas militants in her home in Nahal Oz on 7 October.[2]

'My Administration's support for Israel's security is rock solid and unwavering.'

US President Joe Biden releases a statement on 7 October.[3]

'You cannot support freedom fighters in Ukraine as they resist Russian occupation but not in Palestine against Israeli occupation, unless you have no conscience.'

Egyptian human-rights activist Hossam Bahgat posts to X on 7 October.[4]

'The IDF [Israel Defense Forces] will immediately use all its strength to destroy the capabilities of Hamas. We will cripple them to the point of destruction and we will take revenge with might for this black day they have brought upon the State of Israel and its citizens. As [Hayim Nahman] Bialik said: "Satan has not yet created revenge for the blood of a small child." All the places where Hamas is organized, of this city of evil, all the places where Hamas hides, operates from – we will turn them into cities of ruins. I say to the residents of Gaza: get out of there now, because we will act everywhere and with all our strength.'

Israeli Prime Minister Benjamin Netanyahu makes a statement on 9 October.[5]

'Only a negotiated peace that fulfills the legitimate national aspirations of Palestinians and Israelis, together with their security alike – the long-held vision of a two-State solution, in line with United Nations resolutions, international law and previous agreements – can bring long-term stability to the people of this land and the wider Middle East region.'

UN Secretary-General António Guterres releases a statement on 9 October.[6]

'The Zionist regime's own actions are to blame for this disaster … The occupying regime seeks to portray itself as a victim to escalate its crimes further … This is a misguided calculation … It will result in even greater disaster.'

Ayatollah Ali Khamenei, Iran's supreme leader, gives a televised speech on 10 October.[7]

Survival | vol. 65 no. 6 | December 2023–January 2024 | pp. 74–76 https://doi.org/10.1080/00396338.2023.2285604

'Humanitarian aid to Gaza? No electrical switch will be turned on, no water pump will be opened and no fuel truck will enter until the Israeli abductees are returned home. Humanitarianism for humanitarianism. And no one can preach morality to us.'

Israel Katz, Israel's energy minister, posts to X on 12 October after Gaza is almost completely deprived of electricity.[8]

'Israel's actions have gone beyond the scope of self-defence. It should listen earnestly to the calls of the international community and the U.N. secretary general, and cease its collective punishment of the people of Gaza.'

China's Foreign Minister Wang Yi speaks to his Saudi Arabian counterpart Prince Faisal bin Farhan during a call on 14 October.[9]

'Gaza is being strangled and it seems that the world right now has lost its humanity … Gaza is running out of water, and Gaza is running out of life … An unprecedented humanitarian catastrophe is unfolding under our eyes.'

Philippe Lazzarini, commissioner-general of the United Nations Relief and Works Agency for Palestine Refugees in the Near East (UNRWA), speaks at a press conference on 15 October.[10]

'We remain committed to a lasting and sustainable peace based on the two-state solution through reinvigorated efforts in the Middle East Peace Process.'

The European Council releases a statement on 15 October.[11]

'Hamas and [Russian President Vladimir] Putin represent different threats, but they share this in common: They both want to completely annihilate a neighboring democracy – completely annihilate it. Hamas's stated purpose for existing is the destruction of the State of Israel and the murder of Jewish people. Hamas does not represent the Palestinian people. Hamas uses Palestinian civilians as human shields, and innocent Palestinian families are suffering greatly because of them.

Meanwhile, Putin denies Ukraine has or ever had real statehood. He claims the Soviet Union created Ukraine. And just two weeks ago, he told the world that if the United States and our allies withdraw – and if the United States withdraw, our allies will as well – military support for Ukraine, it would have, quote, "a week left to live." But we're not withdrawing.

[…]

American leadership is what holds the world together. American alliances are what keep us, America, safe. American values are what make us a partner that other nations want to work with. To put all that at risk if we walk away from Ukraine, if we turn our backs on Israel, it's just not worth it.

[…]

I know we have our divisions at home. We have to get past them. We can't let petty, partisan, angry politics get in the way of our responsibilities as a great nation. We cannot and will not let terrorists like Hamas and tyrants like Putin win. I refuse to let that happen.'

Biden addresses the American people in a broadcast on 20 October.[12]

'It's not a war, it's a genocide that has killed nearly two thousand children who have nothing to do with this war, they are victims of this war. And frankly, I don't know how a human being is capable of war knowing that the result of that war is the death of innocent children.'

Brazilian President Luiz Inácio Lula da Silva comments on the situation in Gaza on 25 October.[13]

'No one in the world is moving their finger: the United Nations Security Council, Organisation of Islamic Cooperation, League of Arab States, European Union, not one of the international blocs or organisations. On the contrary, the Palestinian cause and all what is happening in Palestine were totally forgotten. The whole world turns a blind eye to them.

[…]

Then came that glorious day: the operation of October 7.

[…]

The whole West, claiming and preaching about democracy … It's nothing but hypocrisy … The United States is totally responsible for the war raging in Gaza … It is the United States that stands in the way of a ceasefire. It is the United States proving once again, as described by [Ayatollah Ruhollah] Khomeini, it is the greatest Satan, the great devil … The United States must be held liable and then penalised for what it has been perpetrating against our people and the peoples of the region.

[…]

Some claim that we are about to engage in the war. I am telling you: we have been engaged in this battle since October 8 … What's taken place on our front is very important and significant. Those who claim that Hizbullah should engage swiftly in an all-out war with the enemy might see what's taken place on the border as minimal. But if we look at what's taken place on our border objectively, we will find it sizeable, yet I assure you: this will not be the end. This will not be sufficient.'

Hizbullah leader Hassan Nasrallah gives a speech on 3 November.[14]

Sources

1 "'Today, the People Claim Their Revolution". This Is What Al-Qassam Commander Said in His Speech', *Palestine Chronicle*, 7 October 2023, https://www.palestinechronicle.com/today-the-people-claim-their-revolution-this-is-what-al-qassam-commander-said-in-his-speech/.

2 Isabel Kershner, 'Some Israelis Are Barricading Themselves in Their Homes, Pleading for Help', *New York Times*, 7 October 2023, https://www.nytimes.com/live/2023/10/07/world/israel-gaza-attack/some-israelis-are-barricading-themselves-in-their-homes-pleading-for-help?smid=url-share.

3 White House, 'Statement from President Joe Biden Condemning Terrorist Attacks in Israel', 7 October 2023, https://www.whitehouse.gov/briefing-room/statements-releases/2023/10/07/statement-from-president-joe-biden-condemning-terrorist-attacks-in-israel/.

4 Hossam Bahgat (@hossambahgat), post to X, 7 October 2023, https://twitter.com/hossambahgat/status/1710545950907789725.

5 'Netanyahu: "We Will Take Revenge for This Black Day", Israel National News, 9 October 2023, https://www.israelnationalnews.com/news/378173.

6 United Nations Secretary-General, 'Secretary-General's Remarks to the Press on the Situation in the Middle East', 9 October 2023, https://www.un.org/sg/en/content/sg/press-encounter/2023-10-09/secretary-generals-remarks-the-press-the-situation-the-middle-east.

7 'Iran's Khamenei Says Tehran Was Not Behind Hamas Attack on Israel', Reuters, 10 October 2023, https://www.reuters.com/world/middle-east/irans-khamenei-says-tehran-was-not-behind-hamas-attack-israel-2023-10-10/.

8 See 'Energy Minister: No Electricity or Water to Gaza Until Abductees Returned

Home', *Times of Israel*, 12 October 2023, https://www.timesofisrael.com/liveblog_entry/energy-minister-no-electricity-or-water-to-gaza-until-abductees-returned-home/.

9 'China Says Israel Acting "Beyond Scope of Self-defense"', *Japan Times*, 15 October 2023, https://www.japantimes.co.jp/news/2023/10/15/world/politics/china-wang-israel-beyond-self-defense/.

10 UN Relief and Works Agency for Palestine Refugees in the Near East, 'UNRWA Commissioner-General Philippe Lazzarini Remarks on the Situation in the Gaza Strip', 15 October 2023, https://www.unrwa.org/newsroom/official-statements/unrwa-commissioner-general-philippe-lazzarini%E2%80%AF-remarks%E2%80%AF-situation-gaza-strip.

11 European Council, 'Statement of the Members of the European Council on the Situation in the Middle East', 15 October 2023, https://www.consilium.europa.eu/en/press/press-releases/2023/10/15/statement-agreed-by-the-27-members-of-the-european-council-on-the-situation-in-the-middle-east/.

12 White House, 'Remarks by President Biden on the United States' Response to Hamas's Terrorist Attacks Against Israel and Russia's Ongoing Brutal War Against Ukraine', 20 October 2023, https://www.whitehouse.gov/briefing-room/speeches-remarks/2023/10/20/remarks-by-president-biden-on-the-unites-states-response-to-hamass-terrorist-attacks-against-israel-and-russias-ongoing-brutal-war-against-ukraine/.

13 Andreia Verdélio, 'President Lula Says War in the Middle East Is Genocide', Agência Brasil, 25 October 2023, https://agenciabrasil.ebc.com.br/en/politica/noticia/2023-10/president-lula-says-war-middle-east-genocide.

14 'Hezbollah Chief Hassan Nasrallah Gives Gaza Speech', Al-Jazeera, 3 November 2023, https://www.youtube.com/watch?v=SsvgLulaDgs.

Time Is Short: Ukraine, Taiwan and the Echoes of 1941

Charlie Laderman

Two authoritarian powers, one in Europe and the other in Asia, are determined to overturn the global order. Both are resentful towards the Western democracies and believe the international system is rigged against them. With war already raging in Europe, relations between Asia's most powerful state and the United States are increasingly precarious. The world stands on the brink of a global conflict between the world's largest economy and the revisionist powers. This was December 1941, when Germany and Japan wrestled with the decision whether to confront the global hegemons before, from their perspective, it was too late.

Today, the world is entering another period of profound geopolitical uncertainty. That is not to say that the world of today and that of autumn 1941 are directly analogous. As L.P. Hartley quipped, 'the past is a foreign country; they do things differently there'.[1] While there is growing competition between pre-eminent democratic states and the principal authoritarian ones, the world is by no means destined for another great-power war. But some of the uncertainties that democratic and undemocratic statesmen alike faced in 1941 are comparable and enduring. Revisiting that pivotal moment in the twentieth century would help politicians, officials and strategists better navigate the precarious global context that now prevails.

Charlie Laderman is a senior lecturer in international history in the Department of War Studies at King's College London and a Visiting Fellow at the Hoover Institution on War, Revolution and Peace at Stanford University. His most recent book, co-authored with Brendan Simms, is *Hitler's American Gamble: Pearl Harbor and Germany's March to Global War* (Basic Books, 2021).

Survival | vol. 65 no. 6 | December 2023–January 2024 | pp. 77–90 https://doi.org/10.1080/00396338.2023.2285605

American indecision

On 6 December 1941, the history of the world seemed open. Nobody in Washington, London or Moscow could be certain whether Japan would strike west against the Soviet Union or south and east against the British and the Americans, or how Adolf Hitler would react to its decision. Even German and Japanese leaders did not know each other's intentions. Yet both independently had decided some time earlier to 'jump' – as the Japanese prime minister, General Tojo Hideki, put it – into the unknown.[2]

Why did they take this decision? At first glance, it seems inexplicable. The dominant view among Japan's leaders in 1941 was that, with its campaign in China stalled, the country could not afford another war. Conflict with the world's greatest industrial power was considered particularly perilous. The government's own planning agency estimated America's industrial output to be 20 times that of Japan.[3] Yet when the Imperial Conference met to decide on war with the United States, Britain and the Netherlands, all Japan's senior officials united in support.

They acted as much out of desperation as ambition. Crippled by the American oil embargo, imposed as punishment for Japan's aggressive policies in East Asia, Tokyo felt if it did not act soon, it would have no choice but to accept Washington's demands to withdraw from China. Hubristic nationalism encouraged its leaders to believe that, though Japan lacked natural resources, its destiny was to dominate East Asia. While most hoped to achieve this goal through diplomacy, they ultimately became captives of their bellicose rhetoric. None were ultimately willing to stop the escalation to war for fear that they would be held responsible for Japan missing its moment for greatness.

Likewise, Hitler felt he was running out of time. In August 1941, British prime minister Winston Churchill and American president Franklin D. Roosevelt had announced by way of the Atlantic Charter that they looked forward to a world after the defeat of Nazism. This convinced Hitler that America was, in effect, already at war with Germany and that direct US intervention was only a matter of time. He also appreciated the extent of US industrial power, some of which was already deployed against Germany through shipments of wartime supplies to Britain and the Soviet Union under the Lend-Lease Act, passed in March 1941.[4]

In fact, however, Roosevelt found himself in a very awkward political position that Hitler and the Japanese leaders did not fully appreciate. His rhetorical campaign to convince the American people that Hitler's Germany was their main enemy had secured support for his policy of aiding Britain, but had not persuaded them that direct American entry into the war was necessary. In mid-November 1941, a national poll suggested roughly as many Americans opposed as supported sending a large US army to Europe, even if required to defeat Hitler.[5] Isolationism remained a powerful force.

At the same time, Roosevelt learned through US intelligence that Japan was moving to expand its military operations in the Pacific. Yet the president was in the dark as to where, when or against whom it would strike. If Japan avoided attacking the US directly, Roosevelt would likely struggle to convince Americans to come to Britain's aid.

In the absence of full-scale belligerence, the US economy was not on a war footing. Lend-Lease shipments were merely providing short-term boosts to help the British and the Soviets through emergencies rather than furnishing the supplies necessary for them to turn the tide. In December 1941, the Nazis were on the outskirts of Moscow and the Soviets were dependent on British *Valentine* tanks to hold back the onslaught.[6] Yet the Brits themselves were stretched, with tanks and aircraft at a premium, and their position in North Africa in the balance. A German drive to the Suez Canal could not be discounted.

In sum, the world was on the brink in December 1941. But despite popular mythology, even Japan's attack on Pearl Harbor on 7 December did not fully resolve uncertainty about the United States' stance. Pearl Harbor united Americans, to be sure, but against Japan, not Germany. It certainly did not, contrary to the claim of the once stridently anti-interventionist senator Arthur Vandenberg, 'end isolationism for any realist'.[7] Vandenberg himself wrote in his diary on 8 December that although he and his fellow non-interventionists were now ready to 'go along' with war against Japan, they remained wedded to their core beliefs.[8] They showed little sign of embracing a wider war. Indeed, the founders of the America First Committee sent a circular shortly after the Japanese attack to its members saying that 'the facts and arguments against intervention in Europe remain the same as they were before the Japanese issue arose'.[9]

Roosevelt was now vulnerable to the charge that he had given equipment needed in the Pacific to the United Kingdom and Russia. Indeed, some non-interventionists, like senator Burton Wheeler and Charles Lindbergh, argued that Roosevelt's meddling in Europe, particularly the defence aid that he had provided to the Allies, had left the US even more exposed in East Asia.[10] Worse still, the war with Japan meant that Roosevelt had urgently to review Lend-Lease. With the Japanese dominating the Pacific, the US Army and Navy were determined to get hold of as many aircraft, tanks and ships, and as much ammunition, as possible. Immediately after Pearl Harbor, Lend-Lease was suspended.[11]

For several days, as George Kennan, then assigned to the US Embassy in Berlin, recalled, 'we lived in excruciating uncertainty'.[12] It was Hitler who finally resolved the tension by declaring war on the United States on 11 December 1941. He was determined to keep the promise of military support he had made to Tokyo, not least because he could not afford to see his ally defeated, which would allow the United States to devote all of its energies to fighting Germany. His expectation, as he told his advisers, was that the United States would for the foreseeable future be distracted by Japan. This seemed to solve what Robert Sherwood, Roosevelt's speechwriter, called the president's 'sorest problems'.[13] The president had been determined to bring a united nation into the war and, as a result, had been unwilling to pre-empt Hitler with his own declaration of war. Even if formal US–German hostilities were liable to ensue at some point after Pearl Harbor, the timing of Hitler's intervention was critical. Had the uncertainty persisted for weeks, the US aid embargo might have been extended, with serious consequences for Britain in North Africa and the Soviet defence of Moscow. Hitler's gamble turned two largely separate conflicts into the Second World War, whose outcome was as predictable – given the imbalance in resources – as it was murderous.

1941 and 2023

Today, the world again stares into an abyss, with striking similarities to 1941. The Russian invasion of Ukraine was a clear act of territorial aggression with deep roots in Moscow's imperialist attitude towards its near abroad, but in the mind of Russian President Vladimir Putin the conflict is also increasingly a proxy war with the wider West. He and his aides have repeatedly said that their country is effectively already at war with the West.[14] The framing of US military assistance as 'Lend-Lease' aid, recalling the 1941 act, has reinforced this view.[15]

In East Asia, the People's Republic of China is voicing more bellicose rhetoric about Taiwan and the South China Sea. If Japan was short of oil in 1941, China today lacks semiconductors. Liu He, then China's vice premier, told his nation's leading scientists in May 2021 that securing this technology is 'a matter of survival' for China.[16] Even more galling for Beijing, the world's predominant producer of semiconductors is a place that it regards as a recalcitrant province: Taiwan.

Partly as a response to the Australia–United Kingdom–United States (AUKUS) submarine agreement, Chinese President Xi Jinping has announced a massive increase in China's military budget. Rumours continue to circulate that he is preparing to supply Russia with weapons, thus acting as a kind of arsenal of tyranny. Ukrainians are already reportedly finding Chinese components in Russian weapons.[17] Nevertheless, British military analysts have suggested that for the moment, Russia is still overwhelmingly obliged to source the bulk of the equipment and ammunition it needs to fight its war with Ukraine from storage.[18] This puts huge pressure on its ability to continue fighting beyond 2024 unless it receives support from China on a large scale.

Both Moscow and Beijing refer bitterly to their exclusion by the 'Anglo-Americans' in terms remarkably similar to those used by the German–Japanese Axis during the Second World War. Putin blamed the 'Anglo-Saxons' for blowing up the Nord Stream 2 pipeline.[19] China's ambassador to Australia condemned AUKUS as an 'Anglo-Saxon bloc'.[20]

The outcome of these strategic confrontations remains unclear. So far, Putin has not sought open conflict with the West despite his rhetoric, and there are no signs of an imminent Chinese attack across the Taiwan Strait. We simply do not know what Xi's intentions are, and what effect any Chinese action might have on the war in Ukraine. What is clear is that the two spheres are linked, then as now. Like Roosevelt, US President Joe

Biden must take into account strong Republican sentiment that is not so much isolationist as fixated on Asia. If conflict were to break out in East Asia tomorrow, it would not only cast doubt over the continued military assistance to Ukraine, but also likely provoke accusations that the White House had become so obsessed with Ukraine that it had failed to deter China.[21]

As in 1941, time is of the essence. The fear, of course, is that China might be preparing to move on Taiwan while the regional military balance is in its favour. A recent war game organised and executed by the Center for Strategic and International Studies suggested that, in the event of an amphibious assault on Taiwan, the US would exhaust its long-range anti-ship cruise missiles in a week.[22] At the same time, Kyiv fears that critical American materiel may come too late to drive Russia from its territory and could even be diverted to East Asia in the event of a crisis there.

The limits of historical analogies

Historical analogies are invariably imperfect tools for understanding contemporary affairs. As Ernest May and Richard Neustadt made clear in their classic work, *Thinking in Time*, when looking to apply history to current statecraft, it is critical to keep in mind differences as well as similarities.[23]

Japan had been at war for much of the 47 years prior to 1941, and occupied much of Asia. Neither is the case with China today. Furthermore, the US is militarily much more powerful now than it was then, and has a much larger forward presence. Present US allies and partners in the region are also far more capable of defending themselves, and any coalition Washington might muster would present a far more formidable opponent than the one Japan faced in 1941.[24] Indeed, the US, Japan and Taiwan, with aid from South Korea and Australia – not to mention the potential support that they might receive from India and the European Union – would command productive capacities almost double those of China. Furthermore, most of its constituent militaries, unlike that of Beijing, have had real experience in conducting complex operations in modern warfare.[25]

In Europe, Russia's performance in the Russia–Ukraine war thus far should extinguish any sense that Putin's Russia is a great power on the scale of Hitler's Germany.[26] Indeed, if there is any similarity between contemporary Russia and any of the Axis combatants, it is with Benito Mussolini's Italy. In both cases, a country with a languid economy, a corrupt dictatorship and underdeveloped technological prowess holds a much stronger nation close – in Italy's case Germany, in Russia's case China – in a quixotic attempt to pursue great-power status. And Russia, like China, now faces a regional security environment that is inhospitable to its aggressive encroachments, having itself induced NATO to become a larger, stronger and more cohesive body today than it was at the start of the Russia–Ukraine war in February 2022. And, of course, in both current geopolitical spheres, unlike those of 1941, nuclear weapons affect the calculus of any nation that seeks to disturb the global order.

That said, military superiority and industrial potential alone do not necessarily translate into effective deterrence. As Germany and Japan showed in 1941, revisionist regimes are liable to choose war even when the odds are against them rather than reconciling themselves to a subordinate position in the international order.

Tentative lessons

Rather than offering neatly packaged lessons, history presents an array of enduring predicaments of which current decision-makers should be sharply conscious.

The first and foremost is that it takes only one side to decide that war is inevitable for that assessment to become a self-fulfilling prophecy. Axis powers' presumptions along these lines afforded America's allies an advantage in 1941. If Japan had attacked Britain but not the United States – Churchill's nightmare scenario and one that Hitler had promoted in 1940 and early 1941 – it would likely have been an even bigger disaster than British planners had expected. There is a strong chance that Roosevelt would have struggled to persuade the US public to join the war. British resources would have been stretched to the breaking point, critically diminishing its capacity to fight Hitler. Tokyo considered but rejected this option on the view that the United States would intervene on Britain's behalf in any case.[27] Likewise, Hitler's belief that war was unavoidable led him to ignore suggestions from his diplomats in Washington that there remained a distinction in the American mind between war with Japan and Germany, and he lost an opportunity to impose an acute strategic quandary on Roosevelt.

Secondly, the Axis powers considered economic warfare essentially equivalent to military confrontation and concluded that since the United States had already commenced the former, it would readily move to the latter. Economic sanctions had wreaked havoc on Japan, which was utterly reliant on international trade, inflicting damage on its industrial base that was potentially devastating to its fighting ability. As a result, distinctions between economic and military warfare that were salient in American domestic politics were ignored in Tokyo. Hitler, for his part, saw Lend-Lease aid to Germany's enemies as tantamount to a declaration of war and considered Roosevelt's careful presentation to his domestic audience – that he was employing 'all measures short of war' – as a distinction without a difference.

> *Hitler saw Lend-Lease as tantamount to war*

The larger point is that attempts to distinguish economic aid from direct military intervention might not be seen the same way for those on the receiving end. But the potential discrepancy need not diminish a state's options. It could also enable it to act with greater freedom, avoiding self-imposed constraints once it has crossed the Rubicon into economic warfare.

Thirdly, there is a danger that underlying, but as yet unrealised, military primacy might encourage rather than deter war by making time a critical factor. For Japanese and German leaders in 1941, the possibility for even qualified success would have disappeared once the colossal industrial and demographic weight of the United States was transformed into military reality. As they felt the strategic balance was turning irreversibly against them, they gambled on hastening war to exploit a narrow window of opportunity. Thus, the need to incorporate time into strategic calculations is essential. In 1941, Edward Stettinius, the Lend-Lease administrator, emblazoned a poster in his office with the words 'Time Is Short' to plant the idea that sufficient hardware needed to be produced and transferred quickly to those on the front line against authoritarian aggression.[28] Yet strategic empathy is also required to recognise that those against whom such kit is deployed will also be aware that 'time is short' for them to act before the tide has turned decisively against them.

The fourth problem is how to make deterrence credible. That, of course, depends on the perceptions of the party deterred, not the one trying to do the deterring. In 1941, leading figures in the Roosevelt administration believed that the preponderance of its industrial power would deter Tokyo. For domestic reasons, however, they avoided clearly threatening war and were unable to put the economy on a war footing to close the gap between potential and actual power. Deterrence thus failed.

To render deterrence credible, there must be sufficient munitions and materiel to go around. In 1941, prior to US entry into the war, Churchill was concerned that Lend-Lease provisions might be insufficient to feed the 'hungry table' of Allies.[29] Today, it is important to ensure that neither Taiwan nor Ukraine is deprived of what it needs. But if the table is to be sufficiently stocked, America's allies in Asia and Europe have to step up and share more of the burden. On that score, the recent NATO summit offered positive news in the form of large-scale support initiatives, including France's long-range missiles and Norway's financial packages. The Ukrainian defence minister suggested that there were even more munitions in the pipeline that needed to be kept quiet.[30] All the same, since 2015, France and Germany have only added a battalion's worth of forces, and Britain, albeit from a stronger position, has lost five. More is needed, particularly as the Russia–Ukraine war has demonstrated the brutally expensive nature of modern war, with Kyiv losing 10,000 drones per month and, during its spring offensive, having expended as many shells in ten days as the US produces in a month.[31]

The fifth challenge for the leader of a democratic state when contemplating a foreign war is to gauge accurately how far he or she can get ahead of domestic public opinion. Much was made of Pew Research Center polls in May 2023 that suggested that twice as many Americans, including 44% of Republicans, believed the US is doing too much on Ukraine as those who thought it was not doing enough.[32] Yet a Reuters poll the following month indicated that around three-quarters of the US public supported continuing military aid for Ukraine.[33] This significant uptick appeared to be due to the growing belief among Americans that aid to Ukraine would produce victory

– even if it was not clear precisely what that meant – and advance broader US interests. According to a Reagan Institute poll, when respondents were told that aid amounting to just 3% of the Pentagon's annual budget had helped Ukraine 'significantly degrade' the Russian military, while enabling Ukraine to retain control over 83% of its territory, there was a double-digit jump in support from both Republicans and Democrats.[34]

This is similar to the situation in 1941, when support for Lend-Lease reflected new confidence that the measure could win the war. Roosevelt had been hesitant about providing military aid in the weeks after the fall of France in summer 1940 for fear that Britain was doomed and would fall into Nazi hands. Even if he was privately sceptical that aid short of intervention was sufficient, Churchill's upbeat message to Americans to 'give us the tools and we will finish the job' was crucial in galvanising American public support behind congressional passage of Lend-Lease in March 1941.

A majority of Americans may eventually believe that Ukrainian victory is no longer viable or that the cost of supporting Kyiv is too high. Yet, particularly after aid to Ukraine was excluded from the funding measure to keep the federal government functioning, late-2023 polls suggested that bipartisan public support for aiding Ukraine, while slightly diminished, remained robust.[35] One poll, by a Ukrainian advocacy group, did sound a note of caution. There was broad bipartisan support for ending military support for Ukraine only when 'the region becomes stable and Russia leaves all Ukrainian territory', but this dropped off markedly if Americans would 'have to pay higher gas and food prices as a consequence'.[36] One corollary would be that the Biden administration's mantra that it will support Ukraine for 'as long as it takes' could need to be reframed to provide a clear plan for what ultimate victory will look like. Time, again, is of the essence.

*　　　*　　　*

Even if the relative strength of America's industrial economy is not comparable to its wholesale advantage over others in 1941, it has much stronger allies in East Asia and Europe now than it did then. They act as a critical force multiplier. While this edge may reassure the US and its allies that deterrence is sufficient across Eurasia, it should not lead to complacency.

In December 1940, a member of the German high command offered his view to the American journalist William Shirer that the Roosevelt administration thought time was on its side and that it could choose the most appropriate moment to intervene on behalf of Britain. 'Did you ever stop to think', this German officer continued, 'that Hitler, a master of timing, may choose the moment for war with America – a moment which he thinks would give him the advantage?'[37] In the event, of course, Hitler proved far from a 'master of timing', in December 1941 arriving at one of the most catastrophic military miscalculations in history. Yet he did so in spite of America's massive military potential, something that both he and his Japanese allies were fully aware of when they chose to launch their global war.

Today, a war among great powers is far from inevitable. By continuing to communicate this very fact, while also fielding credible deterrents, policymakers may be able to prevent it. But they should also apprehend 1941 as a sober reminder of how fluid geopolitics can be, how quickly apparently manageable situations can be brought to the brink of war, and how belligerent a nation can turn if it perceives that a historic window of opportunity is closing.

Notes

1 L.P. Hartley, *The Go-between* (London: Penguin, 1958), p. 1.

2 Quoted in Eri Hotta, *Japan 1941: Countdown to Infamy* (New York: Alfred A. Knopf, 2013), p. 201.

3 *Ibid.*, p. 167.

4 For an overview of Hitler's perspective on the looming war with the United States in the lead-up to Pearl Harbor, see Brendan Simms and Charlie Laderman, *Hitler's American Gamble: Pearl Harbor and Germany's March to Global War* (New York: Basic Books, 2021), pp. 1–87.

5 See Robert Dallek, *Franklin D. Roosevelt and American Foreign Policy, 1932–1945* (New York: Oxford University Press, 1979), p. 381.

6 See Alexander Hill, 'British Lend-Lease Tanks and the Battle of Moscow, November–December 1941 – Revisited', *Journal of Slavic Military Studies*, vol. 22, no. 4, November 2009, pp. 574–87.

7 Arthur H. Vandenberg, Jr (ed.), *The Private Papers of Senator Vandenberg* (Boston, MA: Houghton Mifflin, 1953), p. 1.

8 See *ibid.*, p. 16.

9 Quoted in Justus D. Doenecke (ed.), *In Danger Undaunted: The Anti-Interventionist Movement of 1940–41 as Revealed in the Papers of the America First Committee* (Stanford, CA: Stanford University Press, 1990), p. 461.

10 See James P. Duffy, *Lindbergh vs. Roosevelt: The Rivalry that Divided America* (Washington DC: Regnery, 2010), pp. 203–4; 'Japs Didn't Ask US to "Pink Tea", Wheeler Warns', *Chicago Tribune*, 10 December 1941, p. 10; and 'Wheeler Backs a War on Japan', *New York Times*, 8 December 1941, p. 6.

11 See Simms and Laderman, *Hitler's American Gamble*, pp. 184–5.

12 George F. Kennan, *Memoirs, 1925–1950* (Boston, MA: Little, Brown & Co., 1967), pp. 134–6.

13 Robert R. Sherwood, *Roosevelt and Hopkins: An Intimate History* (New York: Harper & Bros., 1950), p. 442.

14 See, for example, Guy Faulconbridge, 'Russia Is Now Fighting NATO in Ukraine, Top Putin Ally Says', Reuters, 10 January 2023, https://www.reuters.com/world/europe/putin-ally-patrushev-says-russia-is-now-fighting-nato-ukraine-2023-01-10/; President of Russia, 'Victory Parade on Red Square', 9 May 2023, http://en.kremlin.ru/events/president/news/71104; and 'Ukraine War: Russia Says It Is "Engaged in War" with NATO and Tells the West to Stop Supplying Weapons to Ukraine', Sky News, 26 April 2022, https://news.sky.com/story/ukraine-russia-says-it-is-engaged-in-war-with-nato-and-tells-the-west-to-stop-supplying-weapons-to-ukraine-12599126.

15 See, for example, Peter Baker, 'Biden Signs Bill to Allow Lending Arms to Ukraine, Which Will Speed Up Shipments', *New York Times*, 9 May 2022, https://www.nytimes.com/2022/05/09/world/europe/biden-lend-lease-act-ukraine.html.

16 Quoted in 'Xi Jinping Picks Top Lieutenant to Lead China's Chip Battle Against U.S.', Bloomberg, 17 June 2021, https://www.bloomberg.com/news/articles/2021-06-17/xi-taps-top-lieutenant-to-lead-china-s-chip-battle-against-u-s.

17 See Matthias Williams and John O'Donnell, 'Ukraine Says It Is Finding More Chinese Components in Russian Weapons', Reuters, 17 April 2023, https://www.reuters.com/world/europe/ukraine-says-it-is-finding-more-chinese-components-russian-weapons-2023-04-14/.

18 See House of Commons Defence Committee, 'Oral Evidence: Work of the Chief of the Defence Staff, HC 1689', 4 July 2023, https://committees.parliament.uk/oralevidence/13436/html/.

19 'Putin Says "Anglo-Saxon" Powers Blew Up Nord Stream Pipelines', Reuters, 30 September 2022, https://www.reuters.com/article/ukraine-crisis-putin-nordstream-idAFS8N2Z80FZ.

20 Matthew Knott and David Crowe, 'China Takes Aim at AUKUS as "Anglo-Saxon" Bloc', *Sydney Morning Herald*, 14 October 2022, https://www.smh.com.au/politics/federal/china-takes-aim-at-aukus-as-anglo-saxon-bloc-20221013-p5bpjm.html. On the potential rewards and pitfalls of AUKUS, see Nick Childs, 'The AUKUS Anvil: Promise and Peril',

Survival, vol. 65, no. 5, October–November 2023, pp. 7–24.

21 See, for example, Elbridge A. Colby and Alex Velez-Green, 'To Avert War with China, the U.S. Must Prioritize Taiwan over Ukraine', *Washington Post*, 18 May 2023, https://www.washingtonpost.com/opinions/2023/05/18/taiwan-ukraine-support-russia-china/.

22 See Gordon Lubold, 'U.S. Weapons Industry Unprepared for a China Conflict, Report Says', *Wall Street Journal*, 23 January 2023, https://www.wsj.com/articles/u-s-weapons-industry-unprepared-for-a-china-conflict-report-says-11674479916. Given the immense challenges of an amphibious landing, a campaign of destabilising interference is perhaps more likely, meaning deterrence will have to focus on preventing China from blockading or overtaking offshore islands. See Alessio Patalano, 'Taiwan Needs More than Weapons to Thwart China's Ambitions', *Telegraph*, 11 April 2023, https://www.telegraph.co.uk/opinion/2023/04/11/taiwan-needs-more-than-weapons-to-thwart-chinas-ambitions/.

23 See Richard Neustadt and Ernest May, *Thinking in Time: The Uses of History for Decision Makers* (New York: Free Press, 2011), p. 7.

24 See Abraham M. Denmark, 'The Promise and Perils of Historical Analogy: What the Pacific War Can, and Cannot, Tell Us About Asia Today', Wilson Center, August 2020, https://www.wilsoncenter.org/sites/default/files/media/uploads/documents/AP_2020-08%20Legacy%20of%20the%20Pacific%20War%20-%20Abraham%20Denmark.pdf.

25 See Phillips P. O'Brien, 'There's No Such Thing as a Great Power', *Foreign Affairs*, 29 June 2023, https://www.foreignaffairs.com/ukraine/theres-no-such-thing-great-power.

26 See, for instance, Robert Dalsjö, Michael Jonsson and Johan Norberg, 'A Brutal Examination: Russian Military Capability in Light of the Ukraine War', *Survival*, vol. 64, no. 3, June–July 2023, pp. 7–28.

27 For an incisive piece that stresses lessons from the Japanese case, see Jeffrey Record, *Japan's Decision for War in 1941: Some Enduring Lessons* (Carlisle, PA: US Army War College Press, 2009), https://press.armywarcollege.edu/monographs/633.

28 See Simms and Laderman, *Hitler's American Gamble*, p. 46.

29 Quoted in Martin Gilbert, *Churchill and America* (New York: Free Press, 2005), p. 233.

30 See Phillips P. O'Brien, 'Weekend Update #37', Phillips's Newsletter, Substack, 16 July 2023, https://phillipspobrien.substack.com/p/weekend-update37.

31 'NATO Is Drafting New Plans to Defend Europe', *The Economist*, 2 July 2023, https://www.economist.com/international/2023/07/02/nato-is-drafting-new-plans-to-defend-europe.

32 Jacob Poushter et al., 'Americans Hold Positive Feelings Toward NATO and Ukraine, See Russia as an Enemy', Pew Research Center, 10 May 2023, https://www.pewresearch.org/global/2023/05/10/americans-hold-positive-feelings-toward-nato-and-ukraine-see-russia-as-an-enemy/.

33 Jonathan Landay, 'Most Americans Support US Arming Ukraine, Reuters/

Ipsos Poll Shows', Reuters, 28 June 2023, https://www.reuters.com/world/most-americans-support-us-arming-ukraine-reutersipsos-2023-06-28/.

34 'Americans Know Victory in Ukraine Matters', *Wall Street Journal*, 25 June 2023, https://www.wsj.com/articles/ukraine-poll-reagan-institute-russia-americans-3c0c6f14.

35 See Dina Smeltz and Lama El Baz, 'American Public Support for Assistance to Ukraine Has Waned, but Still Considerable', Chicago Council on Global Affairs, October 2023, https://globalaffairs.org/sites/default/files/2023-10/CCS%202023%20Ukraine%20Brief.pdf.

36 Andrew D'Anieri, 'Are Americans More Supportive of Ukraine than Congress Is?', New Atlanticist, 4 October 2023, https://www.atlanticcouncil.org/blogs/new-atlanticist/are-americans-more-supportive-of-ukraine-than-congress/.

37 William L. Shirer, *Berlin Diary: The Journal of a Foreign Correspondent, 1934–1941* (London: Hamish Hamilton, 1942), pp. 463–4. This book was first published in September 1941, before Pearl Harbor.

NATO at 75: The Perils of Empty Promises

Sara Bjerg Moller

Almost two years out, NATO's performance in responding to Russia's invasion of Ukraine has been decidedly mixed. In the political sphere, the Alliance has performed remarkably well. Long-standing fears that the North Atlantic Council, the Alliance's highest political decision-making body, would be slow to respond in a crisis proved unfounded. Indeed, the council was convened within a few hours of the invasion on 24 February 2022 after eight allies invoked Article 4 of the founding treaty and requested the body hold crisis consultations.[1] Equally impressive, the council took swift and decisive action by granting immediate authorisation to NATO's military commander, the Supreme Allied Commander Europe (SACEUR), to activate the Alliance's defence plans and rapid-reaction forces. The very next day, NATO leaders gathered virtually to voice their determination to remain steadfast in the face of Russian aggression, a message that was repeated countless times in the ensuing months. At the 2022 Madrid Summit, NATO leaders unveiled a new Strategic Concept, the Alliance's main strategic document and its first since 2010, laying out its vision for navigating a more challenging strategic environment. After Turkiye lifted its block, the Alliance completed accession talks with Finland and Sweden in a record-setting five days.[2] Finland was successfully welcomed into NATO last year

Sara Bjerg Moller is an Associate Teaching Professor in the School of Foreign Service at Georgetown University and a Non-resident Senior Fellow at the Atlantic Council.

Survival | vol. 65 no. 6 | December 2023–January 2024 | pp. 91–118 https://doi.org/10.1080/00396338.2023.2285606

and the Alliance remains ready to do the same for Sweden when its turn eventually comes.

In the military sphere, however, the picture is more complicated. While NATO has made steady progress in updating its regional-defence plans and announcing an ambitious New Force Model to ensure deterrence and the defence of the entire Euro-Atlantic area, the non-US allies have not yet committed the resources necessary for the successful implementation of these and other urgently needed post-Ukraine adaptation measures. As a result, NATO missed several important political deadlines in 2023 to make progress on measures designed to help the Alliance refocus on collective defence after more than two decades spent on expeditionary and out-of-area operations. The possibility that these measures may fall behind schedule currently represents the best-case scenario. If the European and Canadian allies fail to follow through on the national-force contributions and other capability targets required by the new force structure before next summer's summit in Washington DC, NATO's ambitious post-Ukraine military reforms could end up permanently weakened. Russia's invasion presented NATO with a rare opportunity to modernise its military plans and structures. The risk is that, as time passes, the momentum and unity of purpose triggered by the shock of Moscow's aggression will dissipate, stalling implementation.

NATO's *force majeure* moment

Following Moscow's annexation of Crimea in 2014, NATO military planners began a multiyear adaptation process to update the Alliance's defence plans and force posture.[3] But outside the eastern-flank countries, many Western European allies did not adjust their national-defence plans. Some saw no need to do so, since the most substantive change to the NATO force structure after Crimea – the creation of a trip-wire defence in the east comprising four Enhanced Forward Presence (eFP) battlegroups totalling approximately 4,500 soldiers – required only minimal force contributions from them at the time. Russia's ongoing war against Ukraine and the ambitious plans set in motion by NATO last year mean this is no longer the case.

Initially, Russia's invasion appeared to serve as a wake-up call. On the morning of the invasion, Lieutenant-General Alfons Mais, the chief of the

Bundeswehr, took to LinkedIn to bemoan his country's neglect of its armed forces, warning that the German army was 'more or less empty-handed. The options we can offer the government in support of the alliance are extremely limited.'[4] While Mais's remarks were notable for their strong language and public nature, other allied military chiefs subsequently offered similar assessments to their governments. Among the more alarming shortages highlighted by the heads of Italy's armed forces to that country's parliament was the Italian Navy's inability to provide 'one full crew for any of our FREMMs [Fregata Europea Multi-Missione, or European multipurpose frigates]'.[5] Nevertheless, once the initial shock of the invasion wore off, many allies reacted quickly to bolster defence in the east through a series of measures initially termed Enhanced Vigilance Activities. Along with reinforcing the four original battalion-size battlegroups in the east, the Alliance conducted increased aerial and maritime activities throughout the north, east and southeast in the weeks following the invasion.[6] Nearly two years on, these multidomain vigilance activities – which allow NATO allies to demonstrate unity and practise readiness – have become the Alliance's 'new normal'.

Another early decision was to double the number of multinational battle-groups in the east from four to eight. Announced mere days after the invasion began, the new battlegroups (Bulgaria, Hungary, Romania and Slovakia) were fully operational by year's end. Additional changes to the NATO posture were announced at the Alliance's annual summit at Madrid in June 2022. The summit's main deliverable was initially intended to be the long-awaited new Strategic Concept laying out a road map for the Alliance until 2030. Commissioned in 2021, the strategy was largely completed prior to the war's outbreak and had to be hastily updated following Russia's invasion. Given the new reality, it was clear to all that the Alliance would need to deliver something more substantial than a revised Strategic Concept. Accordingly, the Madrid Summit communiqué announced a series of immediate and longer-term adaptation measures designed to enhance the Alliance's deterrence and defence capabilities.

Because NATO is constantly adapting and engaging in contingency planning, some of the deterrence and defence measures it adopted after February

2022 actually predated the war's onset. The idea for the Bulgarian and Romanian battlegroups, for example, was originally broached by SACEUR Tod Wolters in December 2021 in response to concerns over Russia's mobilisation.[7] Several of the longer-term adaptations can be traced to, or are an outgrowth of, the Alliance's newest military strategy (MC 400/4), which was adopted by the allies in 2019 following almost five years of work.[8] Unlike the previous military strategy (MC 400/3), which was last revised in 2012 but still largely rooted in the Cold War flexible-response strategy of deterrence by punishment, the 2019 strategy incorporated an element of deterrence by denial – which seeks to discourage the enemy from making an incursion by reducing the likelihood of it succeeding – in the form of increased emphasis on high-readiness forces. This modest adjustment was deemed necessary at the time because of Russia's annexation of Crimea, but was not emulated within the NATO force structure, which remained unchanged. Consequently, the eastern battlegroups, which were originally established in 2016, continued to operate heel-to-toe (using a continuous rotation of troops as opposed to permanently stationed troops), and the Alliance's force posture remained centred around the NATO Response Force, a rapid-reaction force numbering approximately 40,000 troops. The Alliance's decision to adopt a forward presence rather than a forward defence posture post-Crimea was driven by a combination of factors, including limitations in national capabilities and apprehensions about Russia's response. The resulting mismatch between NATO strategy and force posture unsettled the Baltic nations which, despite publicly expressing confidence that the allies would come to their assistance in the event of a Russian incursion, privately harboured doubts about whether 'NATO will get here in time'.[9]

The 2019 strategy incorporated deterrence by denial

The increased emphasis on deterrence by denial in the Alliance's 2019 military strategy became more pronounced with the adoption of NATO's Concept for Deterrence and Defence of the Euro-Atlantic Area (DDA) the following year. Described as a 'strategic redesign' of the Alliance's post-Cold War deterrence and defence strategy, which rested on threats arising from instability, the DDA military concept emphasises preventing the transition to conflict in peacetime rather than waiting to do so until crises emerge.[10] The DDA's heightened focus on deterrence in peacetime marked another modest step toward a deterrence-by-denial strategy. One of the guiding principles of the DDA is that every inch of Alliance territory will be defended. However, prior to Russia's February 2022 invasion, neither NATO's force posture nor its defence plans adequately mirrored the new strategy's elevated level of ambition. Similar to the force-posture debate, the defence plans established after 2014 emerged from a compromise between two camps within the Alliance: those wishing to return to Cold War-era defence planning against Russia and those favouring the continuation of contingency planning characteristic of the post-Cold War era.[11] Approved in 2015, the Alliance's post-Crimea defence plans, known as the Graduated Response Plans, consisted of a phased build-up of troops and were divided into five parts. Following the outbreak of the 2022 war, the revision of these plans, which was already under way as part of the 2020 DDA, was accelerated.[12]

The first opportunity allied national leaders had to gain clarity about the state of post-2014 military affairs within the Alliance, and to offer political direction to NATO military authorities in the wake of Russia's February 2022 invasion, arose at the Madrid Summit, four months into the conflict. Along with announcing an ambitious new baseline for its deterrence and defence posture in the form of the New Force Model and plans to scale up the existing battlegroups to brigade-size units, the allies agreed to initiate enhanced collective-defence exercises designed to strengthen the Alliance's ability to deny the enemy's objectives. NATO military authorities were charged with completing four tasks before the next summit in 2023: generating regional-defence plans; sourcing the requirements for the New Force Model; developing a new military alert system; and adjusting command and control.[13] Despite all the talk in the run-up to the Vilnius Summit about the necessity of providing Kyiv with a clear signal of its path to membership, the Alliance's foremost priority for 2023 was in fact advancing these significant military reforms.[14] Yet in the months leading up to Vilnius there were signs that some governments still weren't acting with the necessary urgency.

A new era in collective defence?

NATO has often fallen short in meeting the ambitious targets it has set itself, such as the much-hyped but soon forgotten 2012 'Smart Defence' attempt to pool military capabilities or the 2018 'Four Thirties Initiative' designed to strengthen European reinforcement against Russia.[15] Unfortunately, the latest efforts in European defence are shaping up to be no different. Privately, those with knowledge of the new adaptation plans say the Alliance is between two and ten years behind where it needs to be in implementing them.[16]

Although political leaders moved quickly in tasking NATO military authorities with updating the Alliance's defence plans and force structure, member states have not yet committed the resources required for their implementation. The plans were supposed to be the main summit input for Vilnius, and as such were originally slated to be approved at the June 2023 defence ministerial in Brussels. However, Turkiye initially blocked them, so they were not approved until the summit itself. This was not the first time that Turkiye had held up NATO defence plans: it did so in 2019 as well.[17] Still, for all the criticism surrounding Turkish President Recep Tayyip Erdoğan's obstruction of Sweden's membership and the regional-defence plans, the implementation of NATO's post-2022 defence transformation is being held up in many other capitals too.

The three recently approved defence plans – one for the High North and Atlantic; one for the Central Region covering the Baltics to the Alps; and one for the southeast covering the Mediterranean and the Black Sea – depart from the 2015 Graduated Response Plans in several significant ways. Unlike the post-Crimea plans – which were self-contained plans for five specific areas along the flanks of the Alliance's territory and were based on the existing NATO force structure – the regional plans are coordinated for theatre-wide scenarios and will draw units from the New Force Model.[18] Equally important, the regional plans are intended to be integrated with the national-defence plans of the countries in each region so that the allies know precisely what is expected of them in the event of their activation. Other reported changes include adjustments to the NATO activation warning system so that SACEUR will have access to units of higher readiness more quickly.

The planned modifications to NATO's conventional force structure are equally significant. During the Cold War, the Alliance's defence posture in Europe was centred around two Army Groups divided into eight corps sectors in Western Germany. In the event of an attack by Warsaw Pact forces, these in-place forces would be reinforced by follow-on forces from North America. The end of the Cold War prompted most European allies to decrease their national forces by more than 25%, causing NATO to switch to a leaner, more streamlined force structure with fewer assigned forces and headquarters.[19] Following 9/11, the realisation that many European countries lacked the kinds of high-mobility assets and forces required for new missions outside of Europe led planners to begin adapting the Alliance's force posture to enhance its flexibility. In 2006, the Alliance introduced the NATO Response Force, a multinational expeditionary force made up of ground, air and naval units designed to allow it to undertake a range of crisis-response missions. As part of the comprehensive package of assurance and adaptation measures (known as the Readiness Action Plan) adopted by the Alliance following Crimea's annexation, its members decided to expand the NATO Response Force from 25,000 to 40,000, and to establish a 'spearhead force' able to deploy at very short notice within it, called the Very High Readiness Joint Task Force (VJTF).[20] Elements of these high-readiness forces were deployed to Romania four days into the 2022 war, marking the Alliance's inaugural deployment of the VJTF in a deterrence and defence role.[21] At the Madrid Summit, rather than augment the NATO Response Force as it did following Crimea, NATO leaders opted for a comprehensive transformation of the Alliance's entire force structure.

Under the New Force Model, the size and preparedness levels of the Alliance's wider force pool will be enhanced considerably. To reflect the magnitude of the proposed changes, planners have embraced new terminology to refer to the different types of forces available to the Alliance. During the Cold War, NATO organised its forces into four categories: Immediate Reaction Forces, Reaction Forces, Main Defence Forces and Augmentation Forces.[22] In recent years, however, the Alliance has relied on a three-category structure consisting of the VJTF, which can be deployed almost immediately; the Initial Follow-on Forces Group comprising units with a longer

Figure 1: **NATO's New Force Model**

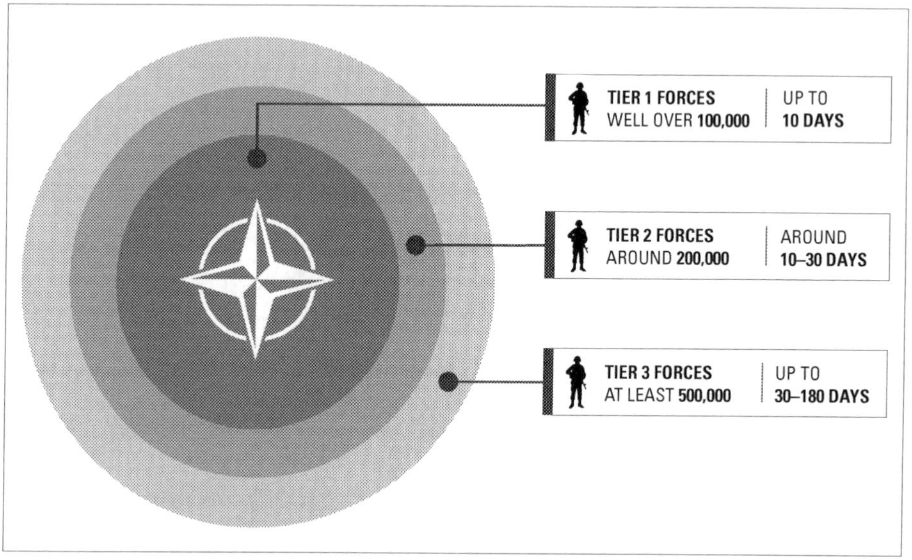

TIER 1 FORCES WELL OVER **100,000**	UP TO **10 DAYS**	
TIER 2 FORCES AROUND **200,000**	AROUND **10–30 DAYS**	
TIER 3 FORCES AT LEAST **500,000**	UP TO **30–180 DAYS**	

Source: NATO, 2022

response time, which can reinforce the VJTF; and the Follow-on Forces Group, which are national forces only assigned to NATO at the direction of the North Atlantic Council in a crisis.[23] The new framework maintains the tripartite structure but establishes new readiness statuses and force targets for each tier (see Figure 1). Under the new force structure, high-readiness Tier 1 forces (around 100,000) are expected to be ready within 7–10 days, while Tier 2 forces (around 200,000) are expected to be available in 10–30 days. Tier 3 forces (at least 500,000) are follow-on forces that will be made available up to 180 days after authorisation by the North Atlantic Council.[24]

The proposed changes to the NATO Command Structure, the entity responsible for deciding how the forces assigned to the Alliance are employed in crisis or wartime, are still in the early stages of development, but are equally consequential. Since 2004, the Alliance's Command Structure has consisted of two European operational-level commands: Joint Forces Command Brunssum, located in the Netherlands; and Joint Forces Command Naples in Italy. In 2018, the Alliance decided to establish a third operational-level command based at Norfolk, Virginia, which is home to NATO's North American strategic command, Allied Command

Transformation.[25] Shortly thereafter, in a departure from post-Cold War practices, military authorities decided to assign each operational command a specific geographic focus.[26] Until recently, the mission of Joint Forces Command Norfolk was to protect the Euro-Atlantic sea lanes and facilitate the reinforcement of Europe.[27] However, in the wake of the war in Ukraine and the subsequent accession of Finland (and eventually Sweden), some allies began lobbying for reassignment from the Brunssum command (whose current area of responsibility spans Western Europe through Scandinavia into Poland and the Baltics, and also includes Hungary) to Norfolk, which is under US command.[28] Citing the heightened importance of the High North for allied reinforcement from North America, Norway successfully secured its inclusion in Norfolk's area of responsibility in early 2023.[29] Finland, which was assigned to Brunssum upon its entry to the Alliance last year, has made no secret of its wish to follow suit. In a show of regional unity, all five Nordic defence chiefs (Denmark, Finland, Iceland, Norway and Sweden) stated last year that they wish to be housed within the same NATO command. While no official decision had been taken as of October 2023, SACEUR has reportedly indicated he supports moving responsibility for the defence of the Nordic nations from the Brunssum command once Sweden joins and the Norfolk command is ready.[30] Because of the additional personnel demands this move will place on many smaller nations, it could have far-reaching implications not just for the NATO Command Structure but also for its force posture. In addition to raising questions about where the new boundary between the defence of the High North and the eastern parts of the Alliance will be drawn, the inclusion of Nordic nations under Norfolk's area of responsibility will require filling several hundred additional staff billets at the Virginia command.[31] Requests for more personnel for the new Command Structure are unlikely to end there. In recent months, Norway's defence chief has begun lobbying for the creation of a forward-deployed headquarters element at Bodø to facilitate the coordination of Nordic defence.[32] Thus, one consequence of the Alliance's shift along the deterrence spectrum and heightened emphasis on defending every inch of territory is that some nations are now requesting more NATO resources for their defence.

Of course, Finland's accession has boosted Alliance personnel, and Finnish forces are likely to feature prominently in future plans for the north. Nevertheless, Helsinki could find itself juggling multiple appeals for troop contributions from elsewhere in the Alliance, including the Baltics, where several eFP lead nations are already eyeing Finnish troop contributions to the battlegroups as a way to help offset their own capability deficiencies.[33] Moreover, as a reserve-based force, the Finnish Army is organised around home defence, and only has one expeditionary battalion it can deploy. All this means NATO will likely have to look elsewhere for help offsetting the increased personnel requirements stemming from the Alliance's post-Ukraine reforms.

No man's land

Under NATO's updated defence plans, many national militaries are now, for the first time since the end of the Cold War, having to plan seriously for territorial defence, and are finding themselves caught short. After decades of downsizing their national forces, Canada and most of the European allies currently lack the ability to field the combat forces and associated combat-support elements required by the regional-defence plans and new force posture. Nowhere is this more apparent than in the land domain, from which the majority of the Alliance's high-readiness forces are expected to come.

In the almost 18 months since the reforms were first put in motion at Madrid, only a handful of capitals have shown any willingness to find the forces necessary to meet the challenge they set for NATO military authorities in 2022.[34] As late as June 2023, some capitals had still not finalised their offers for the New Force Model. (At the time, only one country, Germany, had publicly announced its contribution.) While precise details are hard to come by given the sensitivity of the subject, Admiral Rob Bauer, chair of NATO's Military Committee, admitted in July that the 2023 force-sourcing conference, the annual gathering at which allies pledge their force contributions, fell short of its goals.[35] The continued development of the regional plans depends on national military contributions and cannot advance until countries finalise these.[36] Coming up short at a force-generation conference is hardly a new experience for the Alliance, but the sheer scale of what is envisioned under the new plans makes the task of assembling the national force offers that much more difficult.

Moreover, by announcing the target numbers for the New Force Model (100,000 high-readiness troops ready at 10 days, with an additional 200,000 troops available at 30 days) at the 2022 Madrid Summit, before the NATO defence ministers approved the political guidance in February 2023 and the national militaries had prepared their 2024 force offers, the Alliance may have scored an own goal.[37] Given the war in Ukraine and allied leaders' desire to signal NATO's intention to rise to the challenge, the decision to preview the numbers in 2022 is perhaps understandable. But assurance measures and deterrence require credibility. By releasing the total force numbers early, before the national force packages were ready, Alliance officials may have hoped to tie the hands of allied governments. The only flaw in this plan, if there was such a plan, is that any scrutiny of the number of European and Canadian combat-capable units currently available quickly undermines the headline figures. Neither Canada nor the Europeans have the high-readiness personnel and associated assets required to sustain the ambitious new NATO force structure.

While NATO allies responded in record time last year to reinforce the eFP battlegroups, sustaining these alongside a return to Article 5-based defence planning will likely prove challenging for most non-US allies. On paper, the combined land forces of NATO's European allies number more than one million. However, along with apportioning forces to each of the three main Alliance responsibilities – national defence (Article 3); collective defence (Article 5); and ongoing NATO missions and operations (such as Baltic and Icelandic air policing, the Kosovo Force and NATO Mission Iraq) – Europe's militaries also have to maintain other international obligations and field personnel for non-NATO (United Nations, European Union) deployments. On paper, the Europeans have more than 150 brigades, but not all of them are employable, and most European armies have just two or three brigades each.[38] Because NATO's post-Cold War military plans rested on the assumption of allied forces being deployed for expeditionary operations and not continental defence, many smaller allies stripped their armies of the necessary combat-support elements (transport, intelligence, air defence) required for such operations. Instead of fielding these assets themselves, nations assumed that the United States and other larger nations would contribute them, and that the various units would simply 'plug and play' together once they were in theatre. While the same assumption applies to a certain extent for forward deployments such as the eastern battlegroups, their expansion from battalion to brigade size will require much more of the allies. NATO military officials openly admit that most allies can only field one full-strength brigade.[39] Barring reductions in contributions to non-NATO missions and operations by the Europeans and Canadians, it is hard to see how they will be able to maintain the Euro-Atlantic's new operational tempo without growing their armed forces (see Table 1).

Further complicating matters for many allied militaries is the New Force Model's requirement that troops be pre-assigned to particular countries. Under this change, nations will now be required to assign forces to each of the three core security tasks in advance. Maintaining rotational or persistently deployed forces for the latter requires operating according to the 'rule of three': for every unit deployed, another is preparing for deployment and a third is recovering from deployment. In the past, some allies could get away with double counting the same units for national and NATO planning purposes because of the reduced threat environment, but Russia's war in Ukraine has made this impossible.[40]

As Sven Biscop has shown, some European militaries were already finding it hard to reconcile their Alliance commitments even before the war in Ukraine.[41] Under pressure from the United States, the Europeans agreed at the 2018 NATO Summit to adopt the Four Thirties Initiative, which called for them to have 30 ships, 30 aircraft squadrons and 30 battalions ready at 30 days' notice by 2020.[42] At the time, many US and European defence experts openly questioned whether the Europeans would be able to uphold the pledge. Five years after the initiative was first introduced, neither NATO nor the Pentagon has provided an update on its status. From the limited information that is publicly available, it seems the Four Thirties goals went unmet.[43]

There are already signs that some European allies are struggling to meet the new NATO force requirements. At the time of the 2022 Madrid Summit, eFP forces numbered around 9,600, approximately twice the pre-war total.[44]

Table 1: **Personnel deployments in 2023 by non-US NATO allies**

Country	NATO missions and operations	Other missions and operations
Albania	463	73
Belgium	32	114
Bulgaria	32	114
Canada	931	175
Croatia	221	17
Czech Republic	687	126
Denmark	1,327	142
Estonia	50	16
Finland	100	227
France	1,478	16,958*
Germany	2,138	1,195
Greece	145	1,366
Hungary	685	247
Iceland	0	0
Italy	3,809	2,523
Latvia	138	7
Lithuania	35	65
Luxembourg	7	23
Montenegro	12	2
Netherlands	1,138	120
North Macedonia	78	5
Norway	402	62
Poland	824	241
Portugal	70	344
Romania	265	274
Slovakia	157	361
Slovenia	243	29
Spain	1,304	1,516
Sweden (pending)	6	259
Turkiye	761	39,325
United Kingdom	2,052	10,178
Total	19,590	76,104

*Figure includes the approximately 2,000 troops assigned to the joint Franco-German Eurocorps Brigade garrisoned in Germany
Source: IISS, *The Military Balance 2023*

Because the battlegroup deployments are typically six months long, most eFP contributor nations have already cycled through their larger 'enhanced vigilance' (that is, post-February 2022) rotations three times. Because every deployment overseas (regardless of location) places stress on troops and their families, smaller nations are already starting to worry about how the increased operational tempo will affect their personnel and unit preparedness over time, as well as how to sustain these contributions alongside other NATO and non-NATO force requirements.[45] Since units preparing to deploy or just returned from the battlegroups cannot be immediately assigned to other contingencies, national-defence planners are bound to face an added burden when trying to fill the ambitious new NATO targets. Lack of available troops is also likely one of the reasons (the other is host infrastructure) why plans for scaling up the Latvian and Lithuanian battlegroups from battalion size to brigades are not slated for completion until 2026. Difficulties sustaining the larger troop rotations could also be behind the United Kingdom's 2023 decision to keep the 'balance of a brigade' at high readiness at home, ready to deploy if needed, rather than replace the additional battlegroup forces it deployed to Estonia in 2022.[46]

Many allies lack not just troops, but equipment too. Last year, Canada – which, as an eFP lead nation, commands the Latvian battlegroup – was humiliated when the Danes showed up with better weapons and other gear, some of which was Canadian-made.[47] Meanwhile, it took the procurement office of Germany's Bundeswehr ten years to supply helmets to its high-readiness Rapid Forces Division.[48] Instances like these have generated plenty of discussion about equipment shortages, but while there has been some improvement in ammunition and other forms of defence production, many allied governments have not yet begun to have the difficult conversations with their populations that will determine the success of the NATO reforms. Above all, the allies face the need to increase their armed forces. Many national-defence establishments are all too aware of their personnel problems and have repeatedly stressed the importance of recruitment and retention, but elected officials have seemed unwilling to accord the issue the urgency it deserves.[49]

The 2% mirage

One reason for this lack of urgency is a fixation among the media and some defence analysts with the 2% defence-spending benchmark. The allies first committed to spending 2% of GDP on defence in 2006, and this commitment was repackaged as a Defence Investment Pledge at the 2014 Wales Summit following Russia's annexation of Crimea.[50] The Trump administration's strong emphasis on this benchmark encouraged European officials to find creative ways to game the books. Several European allies, including Germany, currently count their military aid to Ukraine toward the 2% figure.[51] After discovering that some allies include the cost of medical care for troops in their calculations, one Scandinavian country tried to add a portion of its national healthcare expenditure to its calculations in order to create the appearance of progress toward reaching the target. In some European defence circles it has become common to refer to the 2% target as 'phony money'.[52] Yet even with creative accounting tricks like these, only 11 countries managed to reach the 2% target in 2023.[53]

When it comes to burden-sharing in NATO, old habits die hard. Instead of working toward the investment target, some allies, such as Canada, instead spent 2022–23 lobbying to broaden the definition of what counts as defence spending. Canadian Prime Minister Justin Trudeau has reportedly acknowledged to NATO officials what many other allied governments will also privately admit: the 2% defence-spending target is beyond reach.[54] Denmark has stated publicly it won't be able to meet the NATO target until 2030; Spain's timetable for reaching the target is 2029; and Italy's is 2028.[55] Germany, a favourite target of American criticism for its lacklustre defence spending, may currently be basking in the fading glow of Olaf Scholz's *Zeitenwende* (political turning point), but it has only committed to reach 2% once (in 2024) before relying on an accounting sleight of hand and resorting to averages over a multiyear period. Even that may not end up being realistic given the difficult choices facing Scholz's coalition government after Germany's economy slipped into recession in 2023.[56] Although the government has stated that its projected €31 billion budget shortfall won't affect next year's defence budget, this could still change, especially if the anticipated cuts to social programmes become too costly politically. German public-policy experts are already sounding the alarm that the next federal government will have an even harder time closing the defence-spending gap.[57]

To help offset their dismal spending records, some European allies pledged special, one-time defence-investment packages to help boost their military capabilities in the wake of the Russian invasion. Denmark announced plans to spend DKK143bn (€19.2bn) on defence over the next ten years, but postponed making any final decisions about how the funds would be allocated until late 2023.[58] One year on, many questions remain about how Berlin will use the one-off €100bn 'special fund' for upgrading the long-neglected Bundeswehr. There is a real risk that the arcane bureaucracy of the Bundeswehr's procurement office will stifle the disbursement of funds while German parliamentary politics chokes off future spending increases.[59]

For all these reasons, the 2% target remains a bad metric for capturing Alliance burden-sharing or actual military capability. The real measure of whether the allies are serious about defence lies not simply in how much they spend, but what they choose to spend it on. To help ensure that European and Canadian governments were spending wisely, and not just on 'military pensions and fine barracks', Washington insisted on adding a second element to the 2014 Wales Defence Investment Pledge: a commitment to allocate at least 20% of defence spending to major-equipment expenditures.[60] The allies met the NATO target this year, but it is not clear whether they can continue to do so.[61] The 2022 German defence budget earmarked €10bn for new equipment, but the 2024 budget allocates less than €3bn for equipment, with many planned investments shifted to the one-time special fund. Given the dire straits the Bundeswehr finds itself in after decades of underinvestment, it will take much more than this to turn things around.[62] Following repeated complaints from current and former German military officials, Defence Minister Boris Pistorius admitted that Germany will not be able to bridge existing gaps in funding and equipment anytime soon. 'We all know that the existing gaps cannot be completely closed by 2030 … It will take years.'[63] Meanwhile, Ingo Gädechens, the Christian Democratic Union's representative on the defence-budget committee, told *Die Welt*: 'In truth, unfortunately, it's a two-percent fairy tale, because the goal can only be achieved with a lot of tricks and re-bookings.'[64] Germany's disappointing performance matters not only because it has the largest European economy and other European allies look to Berlin as a bellwether for determining their own investment levels, but also because US expectations for the defence of Europe and, increasingly, NATO defence plans themselves depend on Germany's ability to strengthen its military capabilities. Germany is one of only a handful of European countries that can sustain land forces at the division level.[65]

Falling short

National capability targets are prepared for each allied country as part of the NATO Defence Planning Process. The targets – which are the only element of Alliance business that does not operate according to the consensus rule (operating instead according to a 'consensus minus one' rule) – are prepared on four-year cycles and are evaluated every other year. While most NATO Defence Planning Capability Reviews are usually classified by the nations themselves to avoid public recriminations, a few countries have chosen to release them, affording researchers fascinating insight into NATO burden-sharing. Among other things, the previous two four-year planning cycles tasked several of the smaller Western European countries with developing a heavy infantry brigade. One of the recurring red flags from the 2019–20 and 2021–22 NATO reviews for these countries (admittedly an incomplete snapshot) are the ongoing qualitative and quantitative shortfalls identi-fied.[66] A recent report assessing Belgium's contribution to collective defence aptly captured the problem many smaller NATO allies now face, warning of ongoing 'challenges pertaining to recruitment, retention and attrition of personnel', which constrain 'the necessary growth of combat and combat support capabilities'.[67]

Meeting the force targets for NATO's new collective-defence posture will be made more difficult by the ongoing retention crises facing several of the larger non-US NATO countries, including Canada, France, Germany and the UK.[68] The warnings are coming from the allies themselves. Reports have been growing since last year that the British Army is unable to deploy larger formations to the Alliance's eastern flank in the event they are needed. Almost one-third of British high-readiness forces are reservists who are unable to mobilise within NATO timelines. On the eve of last year's Vilnius Summit, then-Deputy SACEUR Tim Radford, a British general, warned that, with fewer than 75,000 regular soldiers, the British Army is too small and must grow.[69] But whether London or other allied capitals are able to heed these warnings remains to be seen.

Work on the next four-year planning cycle (2026–30) is already under way. After spending 2023 determining which capabilities are needed, NATO military planners will begin apportioning requirements and setting national targets in 2024. Because the new Minimum Capability Requirements slated to be approved at the February 2024 defence ministerial are 'substantially larger' than the last review in 2020, the Canadians and Europeans will almost certainly see their apportioned force targets increased.[70] Yet judging by the discussions in allied capitals, many governments seem not to have grasped that they must grow their armed forces.[71] Apart from Poland, which has announced plans to establish two more divisions (bringing the total to six), few countries appear serious about meeting national personnel short-falls.[72] While it may be true that Europe does not require anywhere near the same number of combat-ready units it did during the Cold War, it still needs considerably more than it has today. Unlike munitions or other military hardware, some of which can be replenished quickly once production capacity kicks in, it typically takes much longer to train, prepare and field combat personnel. Although the Europeans and Canadians failed to address past shortfalls, they still have time to demonstrate their seriousness before the new targets are finalised next year, should they prove willing. Doing so will require that these governments initiate difficult discussions about national service and, for some countries, possibly even mandatory military service.

Europe needs considerably more combat-ready units

As part of the more than two decades of defence planning for 'eternal peace' in Europe, many Western European governments reduced the number of armoured infantry battalions in their armed forces in the 2000s.[73] Although some nations updated their postures following 2014, most European defence ministries have continued to pass over land forces in their defence reviews. While France, Germany, Norway and Poland have each added around one to two new battalions to their armies since Russia's annexation of Crimea, most NATO European militaries have either kept the number of combat-ready battalions the same or, in at least one case (the UK), actually shed units since 2014.[74] Other nations have retained the same number of units but shed forces, resulting in understrength units.

After ending conscription for all males aged 18–27 in 2011, the German Bundeswehr has shrunk almost 10% to 180,000.[75] In the wake of Russia's full-scale invasion, Berlin announced a new personnel target for the Bundeswehr, aiming to reach 203,000 by 2031. However, the number of recruits dropped 7% in the first half of 2023 from 2022 levels, leading the country's parliamentary commissioner for the armed forces to admit this goal is 'unattainable'.[76] Despite the war, the German bureaucracy is proceeding at its usual slow pace in addressing the Bundeswehr's recruitment challenges. In August 2023, Pistorius acknowledged the reforms were 'still pending'.[77] The lack of urgency is especially puzzling given the high approval numbers for military service among the public. A March 2023 poll found that 61% of Germans favour reintroducing compulsory military service.[78] Absent strong leadership and support from Chancellor Scholz, however, Germany could miss this once-in-a-generation opportunity to rebuild its armed forces. If the war itself isn't sufficient motivation for Berlin, Germany's demographic crisis – the country is ageing at one of the fastest rates globally – should be. By 2050, the country will have 12% fewer people in the 15–24 age cohort.[79] However, despite reviving discussions from 2018–20 about a mandatory national-service 'year for Germany', the German government continues to act far too cautiously in rehabilitating the armed forces.[80] In addition to reinstituting compulsory national service, the government should also open up national service to women. Ultimately, rebuilding the Bundeswehr will require more than just the backing of the defence minister; it will require marshalling the entire German government. As chancellor, Scholz has the ability to shape the national debate and propel reforms. Additional measures Scholz could take include urging those regions where the Bundeswehr is currently prohibited from advertising in schools to reconsider.[81] Absent leadership like this, Bundeswehr reforms will languish.

While the extent of the challenges varies by country, a version of this problem is playing out in capitals across Europe, where national leaders are failing to advocate for the reforms required to implement their 2022 commitments. Discrepancies between countries' pledges and what they can actually contribute are already starting to strain Alliance relations. This summer, tensions between Britain and Estonia spilled into the open after the Estonian officer earmarked to command the planned Estonian division (which will incorporate a British Army brigade) raised questions about the British Army's ability to implement what was previously agreed.[82] Similar frustrations have been voiced by officials in Lithuania, where officials have spent much of the last year seeking clarity from Berlin regarding the timing of the latter's proposed deployment of a permanent brigade to its territory.[83] In the coming years, such tensions will only increase as more and more European nations find themselves struggling to sustain NATO's enhanced posture in the east. Meanwhile, the demand for a more robust force presence on other parts of Alliance territory is likely to grow. There are calls, for example, to boost contributions to the Alliance's northern flank in the aftermath of Finland's (and eventually Sweden's) membership.[84]

*   *   *

For decades, in the belief that ground war in Europe was relegated to history, America's NATO allies have done the bare minimum to prepare their militaries for territorial collective defence. While the Europeans have taken some early positive steps to boost defence-industrial production and are now looking to acquire some of the armour and short-range air-defence systems their militaries shed during the post-Cold War years, they have yet to fully grapple with the long-term implications of NATO's new defence posture, especially in the land domain. Without a commitment by many of the non-US allies to grow the size of their armed forces, it is hard to see how NATO will be able to sustain its new posture.

Many of NATO's force-structure reforms since 2014 have involved division- or corps-level headquarters.[85] What NATO needs today is not more headquarters, but more troops assigned to them. The war in Ukraine has afforded European politicians a once-in-a-generation opportunity to restore the continent's ailing military power, but many capitals are squandering this opportunity. In the medium term, maintaining support for increased defence spending among European governments will likely depend on what happens in Ukraine. If the war grinds on and allies continue to draw down their own ammunition and weapons stockpiles to supply Ukraine, the gap between what the Europeans and Canadians are prepared to spend and what is required will only grow, not only because countries will want to refurbish national stockpiles, but also because some nations may view a Ukrainian stalemate as an excuse to kick the can down the road. Similarly, a cessation of hostilities could lead allies to conclude the present danger has passed and cause national leaders to slow-walk long-overdue reforms to their armed forces.

Vilnius was always intended to be a bridge to the forthcoming summit in Washington, at which the Alliance will celebrate its 75th anniversary.[86] To avoid casting a black cloud over the celebrations, allied governments should take concrete steps now to deliver on national targets and show how they plan to sustain the increased troop commitment to the eastern battlegroups while simultaneously supporting the New Force Model and defence plans. Without meaningful steps by the Canadian and European governments, the familiar accusations of uneven burden-sharing will resurface next summer, around the same time the 2024 US presidential campaign will kick into high gear. After an impressive initial response in February 2022, it remains to be seen if the Europeans and Canadians have it within them to deliver real change. Vilnius supplied a partial answer, but this was not the answer many NATO supporters hoped for.[87] What the Alliance needs now are deeds to match its members' promises.

Acknowledgements

The author would like to thank Max Margulies for helpful comments on an earlier draft.

Notes

1   NATO, 'The Consultation Process and Article 4', last updated 18 July 2023, https://www.nato.int/cps/en/natohq/topics_49187.htm.

2   NATO Parliamentary Assembly, 'Ratification of Finland and Sweden's Accession to NATO', https://www.nato-pa.int/content/finland-sweden-accession.

3   See Sara Bjerg Moller, 'Building the Airplane While Flying: Adapting NATO's Force Structure in an Era of Uncertainty', NDC Policy Brief 11-19, NATO Defense College, May 2019.

4   See 'German Army Chief "Fed Up" with Neglect of Country's Military', Reuters, 24 February 2022, https://www.reuters.com/world/europe/german-army-chief-fed-up-with-neglect-countrys-military-2022-02-24/; and Marco Seliger, 'Bedingt abwehrbereit:

Deutschlands Armee braucht mehr als nur neue Waffen', *Neue Zürcher Zeitung*, 30 July 2023, https://www.nzz.ch/deutschland/der-fall-deutschland/die-bundeswehr-braucht-juengere-soldaten-schlankere-strukturen-und-munition-ld.1747167.

5   See Tom Kingston, 'Meloni Vows Defense Hike as Generals Announce Shopping Lists', *Defense News*, 23 March 2023, https://www.defensenews.com/global/europe/2023/03/23/meloni-vows-defense-hike-as-generals-announce-shopping-lists/.

6   See Ministry of Defence, Republic of North Macedonia, 'NATO's Enhanced Forward Presence and Enhanced Vigilance Activities', https://mod.gov.mk/natos-enhanced-forward-presence/.

7   See John Vandiver, 'US General Seeks to Add NATO Battlegroups in Romania, Bulgaria, Media Report Says', *Stars and Stripes*, 30 December 2021, https://www.stripes.com/theaters/europe/2021-12-30/eucom-chief-wants-new-battlegroups-in-romania-bulgaria-over-Russia-concerns-4126998.html.

8   See Sten Rynning, 'Deterrence Rediscovered: NATO and Russia', in Frans Osinga and Tim Sweijs (eds), *NL ARMS Netherlands Annual Review of Military Studies 2020* (The Hague: T.M.C. Asser Press, 2020), pp. 29–45, https://doi.org/10.1007/978-94-6265-419-8_3.

9   Author interview with Lithuanian military staff member assigned to NATO Force Integration Unit, Vilnius, Lithuania, 22 May 2017. See also Jörg Noll, Osman Bojang and

Sebastiaan Rietjens, 'Deterrence by Punishment or Denial? The eFP Case', in Osinga and Sweijs (eds), *NL ARMS Netherlands Annual Review of Military Studies 2020*, pp. 109–28.

10   See Stephen Covington, 'NATO's Concept for Deterrence and Defence of the Euro-Atlantic Area (DDA)', Belfer Center for Science and International Affairs, Harvard Kennedy School, 2 August 2023.

11   See Rynning, 'Deterrence Rediscovered', p. 40.

12   See Jan Willem van Dijk, 'STRIKFORNATO's rol als Maritime Battle Staff Plannen en beleid binnen de NAVO', *Marineblad*, vol. 132, no. 3, May 2022, pp. 21–5.

13   See comments delivered by Major-General Matthew Van Wagenen in 'Session Two: NATO's New Force Posture', RUSI Land Warfare Conference 2023, 26 June 2023, available at https://www.rusi.org/events/research-event-recordings/recording-rusi-land-warfare-conference-2023.

14   See Alexander Ward and Paul Mcleary, 'Biden "Open" to Plan that Eases Ukraine's Path to NATO Membership', *Politico*, 15 June 2023, https://www.politico.com/news/2023/06/15/biden-ukraine-nato-membership-00102331.

15   See NATO, 'Smart Defence: What Does It Mean?', *NATO Review*, 1 April 2012, https://www.nato.int/docu/review/articles/2012/04/01/smart-defence-what-does-it-mean/index.html; and Ben Werner, 'SECDEF Mattis' New "Four Thirties" Initiative Designed to Reinforce NATO Against Russia', *USNI News*, 30 August 2018,

https://news.usni.org/2018/08/30/
mattis-says-natos-four-thirties-force-
structure-shows-political-strength.

16 Author interview with Nordic
defence official, 19 June 2023. See also
Christian Mölling et al., 'Sea Change
for Europe's Security Order: Three
Future Scenarios', DGAP Policy
Brief, no. 12, 27 April 2022, https://
dgap.org/en/research/publications/
sea-change-europes-security-order.

17 See Sabine Siebold and Andrew Gray,
'NATO Meeting Fails to Approve First
Defense Plans Since Cold War', Reuters,
16 June 2023, https://www.reuters.
com/world/europe/nato-meeting-fails-
approve-first-defence-plans-since-
cold-war-sources-2023-06-16/; and
'Some Still Oppose NATO's Regional
Defence Plans – Lithuanian Minister',
LRT, 16 June 2023, https://www.lrt.
lt/en/news-in-english/19/2015082/
some-still-oppose-nato-s-regional-
defence-plans-lithuanian-minister.

18 NATO, 'Joint Press Conference by
the Chair of the NATO Military
Committee, Admiral Rob Bauer
with Supreme Allied Commander
Europe, General Christopher Cavoli
and Supreme Allied Commander
Transformation, General Philippe
Lavigne', 10 May 2023, https://
www.nato.int/cps/en/natohq/
opinions_214382.htm?.

19 See Sara Bjerg Moller, 'Assessing the
Consequences of Enlargement for the
NATO Military Alliance', in James
Goldgeier and Joshua R. Itzkowitz
Shifrinson (eds), *Evaluating NATO
Enlargement: From Cold War Victory to
the Russia–Ukraine War* (London and
New York: Palgrave Macmillan, 2023),
pp. 459–93.

20 See Richard Kugler, 'The NATO
Response Force 2002–2006: Innovation
by the Atlantic Alliance', Case Studies
in National Security Transformation
Number 1, Center for Technology and
National Security Policy, December
2006, https://www.files.ethz.ch/
isn/136775/Case%201%20NATO%20
Response%20Force.pdf; NATO,
'Readiness Action Plan', last updated 1
September 2022, https://www.nato.int/
cps/en/natohq/119353.htm; and NATO,
'NATO Response Force', last updated
27 July 2023, https://www.nato.int/cps/
en/natolive/topics_49755.htm.

21 NATO, 'NATO Response Force
Land Elements Deploy to Romania',
1 March 2022, https://mncne.
nato.int/newsroom/news/2022/
the-nato-response-force-land-
elements-arrive-in-romania.

22 See Kugler, 'The NATO Response
Force 2002–2006'.

23 Netherlands Ministry of Defence,
'Rapid Reaction Force: Units
and Response Times', https://
english.defensie.nl/topics/
international-cooperation/
rapid-reaction-force.

24 See van Dijk, 'STRIKFORNATO's
rol als Maritime Battle Staff Plannen
en beleid binnen de NAVO', p. 23;
and NATO, 'New NATO Force
Model', https://www.nato.int/
nato_static_fl2014/assets/pdf/2022/6/
pdf/220629-infographic-new-nato-
force-model.pdf.

25 See 'The Role and Mission of NATO
Joint Force Command Norfolk: A
Conversation with Vice Admiral
Lewis', Chatham House, 18 November
2020, https://www.chathamhouse.
org/events/all/research-event/

role-and-mission-nato-joint-force-command-norfolk-conversation-vice.

26 Until recently, NATO's operational-level commands were not assigned regional areas of responsibility. Although NATO had regionally focused commands during the Cold War, the assignment of specific regional areas of operation to the Joint Forces Commands, which began after Crimea, was only finalised in 2022–23. Author interviews with Nordic defence officials, June 2023.

27 NATO, 'JFC Norfolk Commander Briefs Military Committee on Security Trends in the North Atlantic and Arctic Regions', 5 May 2022, https://www.nato.int/cps/en/natohq/news_195074.htm?.

28 See Allied Joint Force Command Brunssum, 'Mission', https://jfcbs.nato.int/page5815856; and Alf Bjarne Johnsen, 'Forsvaret av norge kan blir styrt fra usa: norge blir enda viktigere', Verdens Gang, 2 November 2022, https://www.vg.no/nyheter/innenriks/i/kEE5ma/forsvaret-av-norge-kan-bli-styrt-fra-usa-norge-blir-enda-viktigere.

29 Author interviews with Nordic defence officials, June 2023.

30 Ibid. See also 'Finland Joins NATO's Brunssum HQ in the Netherlands', YLE News, 24 May 2023, https://yle.fi/a/74-20033236.

31 One of the reasons for delay is Norfolk's capacity, which will need to expand by close to 50% to have the necessary staff to plan the defence of the entire Nordic region. See Ellen Ice, 'NATO Commander Discusses Recent Summit; Plans to Add Personnel in Hampton Roads', WTKR, 18 July 2023, https://www.wtkr.com/news/nato-commander-discusses-recent-summit-plans-to-add-personnel-in-hampton-roads.

32 Author interviews with Nordic Ministry of Defence official, June 2023; and Nordic defence attaché, Washington DC, 20 July 2023. See also Hilde-Gunn Bye, 'Chief of Norwegian Air Force Initiates Arctic Air Operations Center', High North News, 17 August 2023, https://www.highnorthnews.com/en/chief-norwegian-air-force-initiates-arctic-air-operations-center.

33 Author interviews with Nordic defence officials, June 2023.

34 See A. Wess Mitchell, 'Western Europe Is Still Falling Short in NATO's East', Foreign Affairs, 5 July 2023.

35 NATO, 'Media Briefing with Chair of the NATO Military Committee, Admiral Rob Bauer and SHAPE Deputy Chief of Staff Operations, Major General Matthew Van Wagenen', 3 July 2023, https://www.nato.int/cps/en/natohq/opinions_216728.htm.

36 See John Vandiver, 'Detailed Defense Plans for US and Allied Troops Remind Senior Army Leaders of Cold War', Stars and Stripes, 23 June 2023, https://www.stripes.com/branches/army/2023-06-23/army-nato-europe-ukraine-10527461.html.

37 See NATO, 'NATO Defence Planning Process', https://www.act.nato.int/our-work/network-community/nato-defence-planning-process/.

38 See International Institute for Strategic Studies (IISS), The Military Balance 2023 (Abingdon: Routledge for the IISS, 2023).

39 See RUSI Land Warfare Conference 2023, 26 June 2023, available at https://www.rusi.org/events/research-event-recordings/recording-rusi-land-warfare-conference-2023.

40 Previous defence plans targeted the same available units. See van Dijk, 'STRIKFORNATO's rol als Maritime Battle Staff Plannen en beleid binnen de NAVO', p. 22.

41 See Sven Biscop, 'Battalions to Brigades: The Future of European Defence', *Survival*, vol. 62, no. 5, October–November 2020, pp. 105–18.

42 See Jim Garamone, 'NATO Defense Chiefs Build 360-degree Defense on Maturing Framework, Dunford Says', DoD News, https://www.jcs.mil/Media/News/News-Display/Article/1651366/nato-defense-chiefs-build-360-degree-defense-on-maturing-framework-dunford-says/; and NATO, 'NATO Readiness Initiative', June 2018, https://www.nato.int/nato_static_fl2014/assets/pdf/pdf_2018_06/20180608_1806-NATO-Readiness-Initiative_en.pdf.

43 Author interviews with Nordic defence officials, June 2023. See also Hans Binnendijk and Timo S. Koster, 'Now for the Hard Part: A Guide to Implementing NATO's New Strategic Concept', *New Atlanticist*, 22 July 2022, https://www.atlanticcouncil.org/blogs/new-atlanticist/now-for-the-hard-part-a-guide-to-implementing-natos-new-strategic-concept/.

44 IISS, *The Military Balance 2023*, p. 53.

45 Author interviews with Nordic defence officials, June and July 2023.

46 See Louisa Brooke-Holland, 'UK Forces in Estonia', House of Commons Research Briefing, 21 November 2022, https://researchbriefings.files.parliament.uk/documents/CBP-9639/CBP-9639.pdf.

47 See Murray Brewster, 'An "Embarrassing" Gear Shortage Has Canadian Troops in Latvia Buying Their Own Helmets', CBC News, 5 June 2023.

48 Ralf Bosen, 'German Military: Strangled by Bureaucracy', *Deutsche Welle*, 6 July 2022.

49 See Dylan Dyson, 'Canadian Armed Forces Facing Member Shortage "Crisis"', CTV News, 5 April 2023; and Norwegian Defence Commission, 'Norwegian Defence Commission Proposes New Level of Ambition', 4 May 2023, https://forsvarskommisjonen.no/2023/05/04/norwegian-defence-commission-proposes-new-level-of-ambition/.

50 NATO, 'Funding NATO', last updated 19 July 2023, https://www.nato.int/cps/en/natohq/topics_67655.htm.

51 Author interviews with Nordic defence officials, June 2023. See also Alex Luck (@AlexLuck9), post to X, 7 July 2023, https://twitter.com/AlexLuck9/status/1677352650789261312.

52 Author interviews with Nordic defence officials, June 2023.

53 NATO, 'Defense Expenditures of NATO Countries (2014–2023)', press release, 7 July 2023, https://www.nato.int/nato_static_fl2014/assets/pdf/2023/7/pdf/230707-def-exp-2023-en.pdf.

54 See Murray Brewster, 'As NATO Firms Up Military Spending Target, Canada Is Trying to Broaden What Counts: Sources', CBC News, 10 July 2023; and Amanda Coletta, 'Trudeau Told

NATO that Canada Will Never Meet Spending Goal, Discord Leak Shows', *Washington Post*, 19 April 2023.

55 See Jacob Gronholt-Pedersen and Johannes Birkebaek, 'Denmark Plans Defence Spend of $21 Billion over Next Decade', Reuters, 30 May 2023, https://www.reuters.com/world/europe/denmark-plans-defence-investment-21-bln-over-next-decade-2023-05-30/; Joseph Wilson, 'Spain Boosts Military Spending to Close Gap with NATO', Associated Press, 5 July 2022, https://apnews.com/article/nato-russia-ukraine-spain-eastern-europe-madrid-61f2e9644404358defb517dcd37a2170; and Crispian Balmer and Angelo Amante, 'Italy Defers NATO Defence Spending Goal to 2028 in Coalition Compromise', Reuters, 31 March 2022, https://www.reuters.com/world/europe/italy-defers-nato-defence-spending-goal-2028-coalition-compromise-2022-03-31/.

56 See Ulrike Franke, 'Reading Between the Lines of Germany's New National Security Strategy', *Defense News*, 2 June 2023, https://www.defensenews.com/opinion/commentary/2023/06/22/reading-between-the-lines-of-germanys-new-national-security-strategy/; and Johanna Treeck, 'Germany's Slipped into Recession and Everyone Should Be Worried', *Politico*, 26 May 2023, https://www.politico.eu/article/germany-olaf-scholz-europe-eurozone-slipped-into-recession-and-everyone-should-be-worried/.

57 See Hubertus Bardt et al., 'Haushaltspolitik im Zeichen der "Zeitenwende" auf was müssen wir zugunsten der Verteidigung verzichten?', *Ifo Schnelldienst*, vol. 76, no. 7, 2023, https://www.ifo.de/publikationen/2023/aufsatz-zeitschrift/fiskalische-zeitenwende-deutschland.

58 Danish Ministry of Defence, 'A Milestone for Danish Defence and Security', 30 June 2023, https://www.fmn.dk/en/news/2023/a-milestone-for-danish-defence-and-security/.

59 See 'Germany Commits €100 Billion to Defense Spending', *Deutsche Welle*, 27 February 2022; Bosen, 'German Military: Strangled by Bureaucracy'; and Thorsten Benner, 'Germany Must Abandon Its Debt Brake to Make Up for the Lost Merkel Years', *New Statesmen*, 9 August 2022, available at https://gppi.net/2022/08/09/germany-must-abandon-its-debt-brake-to-make-up-for-the-lost-merkel-years.

60 See Signe Marie Frost and Emma Klinker Stephensen, 'Danmark indtager sidstepladsen på NATO-liste', TV2, 7 July 2023, https://nyheder.tv2.dk/2023-07-07-danmark-indtager-sidstepladsen-paa-nato-liste.

61 NATO, 'Defence Expenditures of NATO Countries (2014–2023)'.

62 See Michael Peck, 'Germany Is Finally Focusing on Defending NATO, but Its Military "Lacks Almost Everything" It Needs to Do It, a Former German General Says', *Business Insider*, 7 May 2023, https://www.businessinsider.com/germany-lacks-almost-everything-needed-to-rearm-former-general-says-2023-5; and Ifo Institute, 'Sondervermögen Bundeswehr nur zur Hälfte nutzbar – Zwei-Prozent-Ziel auf Dauer gefährdet', press release, 10 July 2023, https://www.ifo.de/pressemitteilung/2023-07-10/

sondervermoegen-bundeswehr-nur-zur-haelfte-nutzbar.

63 'Ausrüstungslücken bei Bundeswehr nicht bis 2030 geschlossen', *Welt am Sonntag*, 4 April 2023, https://www.welt.de/newsticker/dpa_nt/infoline_nt/Politik__Inland_/article244610358/Ausruestungsluecken-bei-Bundeswehr-nicht-bis-2030-geschlossen.html?.

64 Thorsten Junholt and Stefanie Bolts, 'Der deutsche Bluff beim NATO-Gipfel', *Die Welt*, 10 July 2023, https://www.welt.de/politik/deutschland/plus246298754/Nato-Gipfel-in-Vilnius-Der-Bluff-der-Bundesregierung.html.

65 See Ben Barry et al., 'The Future of NATO's European Land Forces: Plans, Challenges, Prospects', IISS research paper, 27 June 2023, p. 31.

66 See North Atlantic Council, 'NATO Defence Planning Capability Review 2019/2020 – The Netherlands', 14 October 2020; North Atlantic Council, 'NATO Defence Planning Capability Review 2019/2020 – Denmark', 14 October 2020; and North Atlantic Council, 'NATO Defence Planning Capability Review 2021/2022 – The Netherlands', 7 October 2022.

67 Alexander Mattelaer, 'Upgrading the Belgian Contribution to NATO's Collective Defence', Egmont Policy Brief 312, July 2023, p. 5.

68 See Elise Vincent, 'Les armées françaises confrontées à une évaporation croissante de leurs troupes', *Le Monde*, 10 May 2023, https://www.lemonde.fr/politique/article/2023/05/09/les-armees-confrontees-a-une-evaporation-croissante-de-leurs-troupes_6172570_823448.html; Dyson, 'Canadian Armed Forces Facing

Member Shortage "Crisis"'; and 'German Military Facing Recruitment Gap, Says Commissioner', *Deutsche Welle*, 4 February 2023.

69 See Dominic Nicholls, 'Britain "Just Holding On" to Nato Influence Because Army Is Now Too Small, Deputy Commander Warns', *Telegraph*, 20 June 2023.

70 See Alan Campbell, 'Analytic Implications of the NATO Defence Planning Process', SAS-081 Specialist Team Summary Report, NATO C3 Agency, https://www.sto.nato.int/publications/STO%20Meeting%20Proceedings/RTO-MP-SAS-081/MP-SAS-081-09.pdf; and Center for Strategic and International Studies, 'Transatlantic Defense in an Era of Strategic Competition', remarks by Jessica Cox on 'Panel 1: NATO and Geostrategic Competition', 27 October 2023, https://www.csis.org/events/transatlantic-defense-era-strategic-competition.

71 See Jan Walter, 'Europe: Is Compulsory Military Service Coming Back?', *Deutsche Welle*, 11 June 2023.

72 See IISS, *The Military Balance 2023*, p. 65.

73 Interview with Peter Viggo Jakobsen, Copenhagen, Denmark, 14 June 2023.

74 Barry et al., 'The Future of NATO's European Land Forces', p. 25.

75 Rudolf Schlaffer and Marina Sandig, *Die Bundeswehr 1955–2015: Sicherheitspolitik unde Streitkräfte in der Demokratie* (Freiburg im Breisgau: Rombach Verlag KG, 2015), pp. 215–16.

76 See 'Germany's Army Struggles to Recruit New Troops, Despite Official Push', EuroNews, 2 August 2023, https://www.euronews.com/2023/08/02/

germanys-army-struggles-to-recruit-new-troops-despite-official-push.

77 See 'Boris Pistorius plant "große Reform im Personalwesen" der Bundeswehr', *Zeit Online*, 4 August 2023, https://www.zeit.de/politik/deutschland/2023-08/boris-pistorius-bundeswehr-personal-ruecklaeufige-bewerberzahlen; and Julia Dahm, 'Military Recruiting Shortage Gums Up Germany's "Zeitenwende" Plans', Euractiv, 2 August 2023, https://www.euractiv.com/section/global-europe/news/military-recruiting-shortage-gums-up-germanys-zeitenwende-plans/.

78 IPSOS, 'Deutliche Mehrheit für Wiedereinführung der Wehrpflict', 9 March 2023, https://www.ipsos.com/de-de/deutliche-mehrheit-fur-wiederinfuhrung-der-wehrpflicht.

79 See 'Germany's Army Struggles to Recruit New Troops, Despite Official Push'.

80 See Jana Šafaříková, 'Bundeswehr lidi neláká, proto Berlín oprašuje brannou povinnost. Pro všechny', iDNES.cz, 25 July 2023, https://www.idnes.cz/zpravy/zahranicni/nemecko-bundeswehr-armada-branna-povinnost-nabor.A230725_085733_zahranicni_safaj?zdroj=top.

81 See Dahm, 'Military Recruiting Shortage Gums Up Germany's "Zeitenwende" Plans'.

82 See Meinhard Puik, 'Kannatused ja sõimuvalangud: brittide liitmine Eesti diviisi külge viib stressitaseme lakke', Postimees, 21 July 2023, https://www.postimees.ee/7818617/kannatused-ja-soimuvalangud-brittide-liitmine-eesti-diviisi-kulge-viib-stressitaseme-lakke; and 'Newspaper: The Addition of Brits to the Estonian Division Has Caused Tensions', *Estonian World*, 25 July 2023, https://estonianworld.com/security/newspaper-the-addition-of-brits-to-the-estonian-division-has-caused-tensions/.

83 See 'With Eyes on Russia, Germany Ready to Station Troops Permanently in Lithuania', Reuters, 26 July 2023, https://www.reuters.com/world/europe/germany-ready-permanent-brigade-presence-nato-member-lithuania-2023-06-26/.

84 See Alexander Gray, 'NATO's Northern Flank Has Too Many Weak Spots', *Foreign Policy*, 7 August 2023.

85 See Moller, 'Building the Airplane While Flying'.

86 See 'Landsbergis on Ukraine's NATO Invitation Declaration Failing to Live Up to Expectations: Vilnius Is Just a Bridge to Washington', Lrytas.lt, 13 July 2023, https://www.lrytas.lt/english/politics/2023/07/13/news/landsbergis-on-ukraine-s-nato-invitation-declaration-failing-to-live-up-to-expectations-vilnius-is-just-a-bridge-to-washing-27687318.

87 See John Deni, 'NATO Summit Could Have Been Historic. Instead, It Mostly Kicked the Can Down the Road', *Breaking Defense*, 14 July 2023, https://breakingdefense.com/2023/07/nato-vilnius-summit-could-have-been-historic-instead-it-mostly-kicked-the-can-down-the-road/.

The Primitivisation of Major Warfare

Lukas Milevski

In an interview in February 2023 about the ongoing Russian invasion of Ukraine, American General David Petraeus claimed that, 'with a few exceptions, Ukraine is not the future of warfare', adding that 'in large measure, it is what we would have seen had the Cold War turned hot in the mid-1980s – with largely Cold War weapons systems (albeit with some modernization)'. The exceptions he identified included drones and fire-and-forget missiles, which after initial targeting and launch fly to the target without further input from the operator. He further asserted that any future great-power war would have all this and more, and at higher levels of technological capability and sophistication.[1] Such comments follow many other technological visions of future warfare, most of which have been American.

These visions may be magnificent, but they do not reflect actual warfare, let alone major warfare. Warfare consumes and destroys, both through enemy action and through countering enemy action, and major warfare does so at rates that Western militaries have not experienced for decades. Yet the implications of such consumption and destruction are rarely considered when anticipating the warfare of the future. For small militaries, the danger of the simple attrition and destruction of their military capabilities is clear. Medium and larger militaries face a different problem: not attrition

Lukas Milevski is an assistant professor at the Institute for History at Leiden University, where he teaches strategic studies. He has published two books with Oxford University Press: *The Evolution of Modern Grand Strategic Thought* (2016) and *The West's East: Contemporary Baltic Defense in Strategic Perspective* (2018).

Survival | vol. 65 no. 6 | December 2023–January 2024 | pp. 119–136 https://doi.org/10.1080/00396338.2023.2285607

and destruction, but attrition and primitivisation. Through consumption and destruction, major warfare can turn the military organisations involved into more primitive versions of themselves. This is a multidimensional challenge for militaries and their support systems, touching on concerns ranging from defence-industrial capacity to force employment and strategy.

Sustained major warfare primitivises militaries

What does it mean to say that major warfare primitivises militaries? To be primitive is to be less advanced, usually technologically but often also socially or organisationally. Major warfare, a phenomenon with which the West had little engagement, intellectually or actually, between the end of the Cold War and the second Russian invasion of Ukraine in 2022, has the power to primitivise militaries. The stresses of sustained major warfare, particularly but not exclusively as imposed by battle, erode the involved military organisations technologically, socially and organisationally. Militaries as a whole, and specific formations in particular, may become less technologically advanced, less socially cohesive and less organisationally effective as a result of engaging in sustained campaigning against a major opponent, ultimately resulting in declining military effectiveness.

The social and organisational dimensions of primitivisation are likely to have affected armies since times immemorial, as they pertain primarily to the personal and professional relationships among individuals within organisations. The primitivisation of social ties can undermine the group cohesion generally understood to be required for soldiers to fight effectively on the battlefield. The sources of such cohesion remain debated, but may include personal ties among the so-called primary group, emotional ties to professional or other identities, and a group orientation toward task completion.[2] Sustained major warfare threatens social bonds, particularly within front-line units, through sheer attrition. The primary group may be destroyed, the sense of belonging to a particular group which should not be shamed through poor performance may be lost, and the sense that tasks can be plausibly completed erased.

Attrition affecting front-line units affects not only their own tactical and operational performance, but also that of their parent formations, thus transforming social primitivisation into organisational primitivisation. The loss of leaders and other specialists performing particular duties does not merely affect the social dimension of the organisation, but also impedes its overall functionality as leaders and other specialists are replaced by those who are less well trained, less experienced or less competent. Notably, while this loss of social and ultimately organisational cohesion can be expected to negatively affect the unit's tactical performance, it also decreases the chance of mass disobedience to orders. Disobedience also requires cohesion.[3] Primitivised formations may have lost some degree of effectiveness, but they are also less likely to pose a threat to their own government.

By contrast, the technological dimension has become a peculiar feature of *modern* major war as technology has become sufficiently complex to limit the manufacture of particular weapons systems. As equipment becomes more complex, it becomes more expensive; as both complexity and cost escalate, so too do production time and difficulty. The result is fewer units produced. This is as true of ordnance and munitions as it is of tanks and aircraft. If complex equipment is deployed and either consumed or destroyed on the battlefield, it is more difficult to replace than less complex equipment, which may then replace it. In this sense as well, militaries that sustain attrition in major operations can become more technologically primitive over time.

Crucially, the primitivisation of any armed force is not a matter only of its losses in the field and the significance of those losses for the immediate tactical–operational effectiveness of the relevant formations. Ideally, military power should be durable; the forces employed in war should survive in strategically useful condition through to the end of the war. This requires sustainment, over an undeterminable longer term, to replace both human and equipment losses. Yet as the equipment used by soldiers, and the training required to perform effectively on and off the battlefield, become more sophisticated, sustained major warfare necessarily becomes more difficult for any particular military organisation. Primitivisation also pertains to defence-industrial, procurement and personnel policies. Circumstance-appropriate policies, together with the infrastructure to implement them, may ameliorate primitivisation, whereas inappropriate policies and insufficient infrastructure will certainly encourage it.

Two modern examples demonstrate the full breadth of primitivisation in major warfare: the Wehrmacht on the Eastern Front during the Second World War and the Russian army in Ukraine today. Omer Bartov, in discussing the barbarisation of the Wehrmacht in the Soviet Union, depicted how staggering attrition hollowed out German formations, to the point that at least some divisions, such as the 12th Infantry Division, suffered more casualties over the course of the war than there were men present in its ranks during the initial invasion in 1941. Front-line German units could not hold continuous positions, battalion commanders floated around without battalions to command, companies were led by young and inexperienced officers rather than experienced non-commissioned officers, and increasing numbers of non-combat troops and poorly trained replacements were pushed into the fight.[4] As both social units and organisations, German formations were gradually broken down by the demands of sustained major warfare. This attrition afflicted the Wehrmacht technologically as well, a process which Bartov described as 'demodernisation'. The Wehrmacht's modern elements were concentrated into a few armoured divisions, which throughout the war were repeatedly attrited to the point that much of the time they could no longer honestly be described as armoured divisions.[5] Ironically, just as this multidimensional process of primitivisation began afflicting the Wehrmacht in the east from winter 1941–42 onward, its (defensive) combat power improved.[6] Certain consequences of primitivisation can be ameliorated, if not truly solved, through influences such as ideology – as was the case with the Wehrmacht, for which increasing ideological ferocity was able partly to compensate for qualitatively and quantitatively deteriorating forces and technology on the battlefield.

Russia has suffered similarly in Ukraine. As leaks from the US Department of Defense in early 2023 showed, Russia's *spetsnaz* (special-forces) brigades had already been devastated by the war to that point. Three brigades were believed to have suffered an astonishing 90–95% attrition rate, with one seemingly so ruined that, unlike the others, it could not be tracked returning to garrison in southern Russia from Ukraine.[7] Similarly, by the time of its involvement attacking Vuhledar in early 2023, Russia's 155th Naval Infantry Brigade had been substantially destroyed perhaps eight times because of the repeated use of poor tactics.[8] Although it is more difficult to assess Russia's contemporary military strength than Germany's in the 1940s, it seems probable that the Russian units that have suffered so much have been greatly primitivised, socially, organisationally and technologically. Indeed, Russian tactical adaptations seem to point to this conclusion, as Russian forces are increasingly distinguished as 'line', 'assault' and 'specialised'. The line units comprise poorly trained, recently mobilised men, soldiers from the two so-called separatist republics, and conscripted convicts, whose primary purposes are to hold ground and die. This focusing of attrition and primitivisation onto the line infantry has in turn enabled Russia to at least partially rebuild its relatively elite units for major actions or specialised functions, such as conducting assaults and artillery spotting.[9]

Russian units have been greatly primitivised

The primitivisation of the Russian army in Ukraine was most clearly visible, from an open-source perspective, in the pattern of engagements revealed in the many photos and especially videos of combat published over the course of the war thus far. Early Russian tactical behaviour emphasised armoured vehicles in substantial quantities, including actions from Bucha to Brovary, Bilohorivka and the Russian rout arising from the Kharkiv counter-offensive. The consequences of the staggering tally of Russian vehicular losses up to their withdrawal over the Dnipro River and the liberation of Kherson were made apparent after the appointment of General Sergey Vladimirovich Surovikin as commander of all Russian forces in Ukraine in early October 2022. Surovikin's tenure as overall commander coincided with a generally more defensive Russian posture as Moscow sought to avoid further substantial losses of territory. The Russian army still attacked, most notably toward and in Bakhmut, but the available footage of Surovikin's limited offensives revealed a disproportionately infantry-based force. Armoured vehicles appeared in video evidence primarily as taxis bringing infantry to, and then disgorging them upon, the battlefield before skedaddling as quickly as they could. In other words, if the videos are at all representative, the Russian army had been primitivised by November 2022 to the extent that armoured vehicles seemingly became, at least temporarily, too precious to lose in battle. This state of affairs led the German reporter Julian Röpcke to assert that 'the last three months have shown that Ukraine's strategy of "killing as many Russians as possible to stop them" has not worked', though he evidently failed to recognise the degree to which this was not at all Ukraine's choice but a reality apparently forced upon it by changes in Russia's tactics and force employment.[10]

Surovikin was replaced by the Russian Chief of Staff Valery Gerasimov in January 2023, though he carried on as the latter's deputy. A near-immediate change of tactics followed. Apparently belying its general primitivisation, the Russian army again threw machines into the line of fire. Scenes resulted at Vuhledar, Avdiivka and Marinka that were reminiscent of the armoured apocalypse at Bilohorivka a year earlier. In a plausible attempt to save machines in favour of losing mostly soldiers, in April 2023 the Russians switched from trying to encircle Bakhmut to urban fighting and squeezing the Ukrainians out. The primary outcome of Russia's winter offensive under Gerasimov's leadership was temporarily to re-accelerate the primitivisation of the army that Surovikin had sought slowly and partially to address. Despite Gerasimov's detrimental impact on at least some Russian formations (most notably the 155th Naval Infantry, which suffered heavily at Vuhledar), some observers have noted that Russia is beginning to re-equip certain battered units with brand-new equipment.[11] The Russian experience may yet demonstrate that primitivisation may be a partially ameliorable phenomenon for select formations even as others primitivise further, echoing the Wehrmacht's experience on the Eastern Front.

Ukraine's summer 2023 counter-offensive had, by the time of writing, been conducted in a slow and methodical manner, owing to a desire to avoid human casualties and material losses. Such a humane approach necessarily springs from multiple considerations, but among them is probably a concern about primitivisation. The Ukrainian army has so far been able not only to avoid primitivisation but actually to increase its average technological and perhaps organisational level as a result of Western aid, whether in the form of heavy equipment or training. Yet such Western aid remains limited compared to the actual demands of major warfare, resulting in a comparatively modern and sophisticated force concentrated in a few brigades – much like the Wehrmacht or the Russian army – yet which might still easily suffer major losses and therefore experience primitivisation due to poor luck, carelessness and the like.

Primitivisation is not a definitive process, even in the short term during wartime; it can be ameliorated by emphasising other factors, such as ideology, which can provide new reasons not only to continue fighting, but to fight even harder. Another key coping mechanism, seen in the German, Russian and indeed Ukrainian examples, is the creation of a two-level force, with modern equipment and sometimes better-trained or otherwise privileged soldiers concentrated in particular units – German panzer divisions, Russian airborne divisions, the new Western-armed Ukrainian brigades – while the rest of the force makes do either with increasingly less or increasingly older, less reliable equipment. Primitivisation also affects force employment tactically and operationally, with an emphasis on preserving the modern forces in particular when possible and therefore using them primarily as reserves to put out fires or to conduct particular offensive operations that less modern forces may not be able to achieve on their own. Primitivisation may also be associated with defence; once primitivised, both the Wehrmacht and the Russian army in Ukraine predominantly fought on the defensive, with substantial offensive actions such as the major Russian attacks at Avdiivka in October 2023 proving to be accelerants of further primitivisation.

Primitivisation, campaigning and Western militaries

Other than in the instances already described, the West has not had to consider the prospect of the full-spectrum (social, organisational and technological) primitivisation of its armed forces for decades, perhaps not since the British retreat from the beaches of Dunkirk. A major exception may be the US Army during the Vietnam War, where the unpopularity of the war combined with the staffing policies implemented by the army led to the constant rotation of personnel through units such that the social aspect of military organisation suffered, with drug abuse or the fragging of officers becoming rife within some units at certain times.

Having mainly confronted foes that were both militarily inferior and geographically distant since the end of the Cold War, the West as a whole has been slimming down its military and defence establishments for years. In recent decades, the emphasis has increasingly been on professionalism and high technology, resulting in a comparatively low mass of soldiers and major weapons systems. The Revolution in Military Affairs and associated concepts thrilled many military specialists, often leading to fantastical strategic thinking. David Deptula pronounced that developments such as effects-based operations meant that the 'character of warfare is changing and the degree of that change is considerable – analogous to the difference in world views between Ptolemy and Copernicus'.[12] Max Boot praised the resulting 'new style of warfare that eschews the bloody slogging matches of old'.[13] The underlying assumption has been that technology can not only solve tactics and strategy, but do so at minimal cost to oneself – and even to the enemy.

To this day, Western visions of future war tend to emphasise technology. This is particularly true of American visions, with the other NATO allies tagging along to some degree, even if only out of necessity for Alliance interoperability. At the 2019 Mad Scientist Conference at the University of Texas at Austin, for example, Robert Work, one-time US deputy secretary for defense, presented a vision for 'algorithmic warfare', which he claimed will be

> characterized by combat operations transformed by universal digitization and widespread use of machine intelligence in both systems at rest and systems in motion, leading to new forms of *human–machine collaboration* and *human–machine* and *machine–machine combat teaming*, and the more powerful *collaborative human–machine battle networks* they enable.

He urged military leaders to 'NOT pursue optionally manned combat systems except for legacy platforms that commanders are willing to lose'. Instead, he suggested they should 'pursue optionally teleoperated robotic combat systems as a bridge to better autonomous control systems'.[14]

Such lofty technological fantasies implicitly ignore the enemy and its capability to do harm to one's own military, generally because the West's wars since the end of the Cold War have been so militarily lopsided. Yet to assume that this will continue into the future is excessively optimistic; any good reading of history demonstrates that such strategic optimism is rarely justified.[15] The general belief that higher technology minimises losses may have some merit, but must still be critically examined. High technology will not and cannot altogether preclude the possibility of losses in major future wars that may trigger primitivisation.

Western (and especially American) expectations about technology are premised on the experience of an immature military revolution. Perceptions of a supposed precision-strike revolution have been coloured by the Western experience of precise warfare against woefully unprepared enemies in Iraq in 1991 and 2003, Serbia during the wars surrounding the collapse of Yugoslavia, Afghanistan in 2001, Libya in 2011, and protracted insurgencies in Iraq and Afghanistan. There has not yet been an instance of symmetrical precise warfare, though Ukraine is arguably adopting aspects of such warfare as the West supplies it with certain classes of precise munitions. John Maurer has suggested that the tried-and-failed British concept of 'broken-backed warfare' from the early days of the atomic era may be appropriate for thinking through the strategic problems of precise warfare among peers. According to this logic, mass precision munitions will disrupt but not conquer, and so are unlikely to coerce; precision arsenals will deplete; and the surviving conventional militaries on both sides will ultimately still have to engage each other directly.[16] In imagining such an essentially primitivised strategic future, Maurer also makes a crucial point about the limitations of our engagement with precision warfare to date: it has been too asymmetrical to draw firm lessons from.

In addition to being technologically asymmetrical, Western experience since the end of the Cold War has tended to involve limited interventions against sometimes staggeringly incompetent or otherwise relatively incapable adversaries. Such incompetence can magnify the impact of high technology, especially when that technology is used skilfully. This is Stephen Biddle's argument about the Gulf War. Technology alone cannot explain the disproportionately asymmetrical result of that conflict; the Iraqis also made outrageous tactical mistakes, and coalition forces were skilled enough to take appropriate advantage.[17] Such mistakes were not restricted to the battlefield: the Iraqis allowed the United States to build up its forces in Saudi Arabia unmolested. Similarly, during the break-up of Yugoslavia, Serbia had no ability to impose its will on NATO, except by attacking its own neighbours. Libya too had no opportunity to upset the Western intervention in 2011. Thus, with the exception of the insurgencies in Iraq and Afghanistan, the West has largely been able to determine the main pattern of recent operations with little or no interference. As a result, the effectiveness of high technology was easily maximised from the beginning of hostilities. Such circumstances are unlikely to be present in the major wars of the imaginable future.

Instead, such wars are likely to be alliance-centric defensive wars, possibly involving the defence of Europe against Russian aggression or Taiwan against Chinese predation. These are hypothetical wars which, for the West, would start when the *enemy* is ready, not the West. Western participants will have to react, defend and counter-attack. This presents different tactical, operational and strategic challenges than do discretionary interventions in which the West can generally act when ready, and usually from a distance, a strategic advantage that translates into a tactical advantage. The character of both defensive and offensive battles in future major wars is likely to differ from this kind of experience, raising questions about the fitness of Western, and especially European, militaries to wage them.

Firepower can kill but not conquer

To mount an effective defence in future major wars, Western militaries, especially armies, will have to get in the way and stay there. High technology may put some Western artillery on the periphery of, or sometimes even beyond, an adversary's own artillery range, but that will only partially insulate Western artillery from attack. The further forward any formation's subunits are, the more subject they will be to fire and, therefore, to losses, whether human or material. When counter-attacking, Western militaries will have to go out into the open and close with the enemy, perhaps over prepared ground against fortifications and minefields. If the enemy stands and fights, something which should be expected, Western forces will have to engage in close-quarters combat to liberate stubbornly defended ground from occupying troops. Firepower can kill and disrupt, but not conquer.

Human and material losses will result that high technology will be able only partly to prevent or mitigate – especially in land forces, which are usually required to make and maintain contact with the enemy. Yet the alternative to absorbing casualties may be tactical failure. An overemphasis on force protection may undermine a force's ability to fight and, ultimately, win. Western military power, and land power in particular, has oscillated since the end of the Cold War between heroic and post-heroic modes of engagement. Major wars are almost inevitably heroic, yet heroism usually comes at a cost.[18] The West's experience of casualties and material losses since 1990 is unlikely to reflect the battlefields of future major wars.

Christopher Lawrence has analysed the relationship between force size and average daily casualty rates for American forces during the Second World War, finding that companies (about 200 personnel) averaged 21% casualties per day, battalions (800) 9.5% and brigades (3,000) 2.6%.[19] If average daily casualty rates in major future warfare are even a substantial fraction of Lawrence's figures, one wonders how long Europe's readily deployable forces might last on campaign. This is a particularly pressing question given that casualties will inevitably be highest among front-line forces, which themselves represent only a limited portion of larger formations. Historically, the combat worthiness of a battalion or even a brigade can be run down relatively quickly in intense fighting, even as most of the rest of the formation continues to function.

Western but non-American militaries may be both too slimmed down and too technologically complex to sustain the sorts of losses which major future warfare may impose without suffering primitivisation. This is particularly true in the context of hypothetical wars against Russia or China, with their mass armies. Jack Watling of the Royal United Services Institute has observed that, in terms of artillery, the British army is 'comprehensively outgunned and outranged' by the Russian army. It appears that any single standard Russian motor-rifle brigade can be expected to field more organic heavy firepower than the entire British army combined.[20] Other major European armies are not in significantly better condition artillery-wise relative to potential major foes, especially given their contributions to the Ukrainians, which have substantially, albeit temporarily, decreased many countries' artillery parks. For example, France has donated 30 CAESAR self-propelled howitzers of the 76 it had at the beginning of 2022, and

Germany 14 of its 121 PzH 2000s.[21] Despite the artillery losses it has suffered in Ukraine, Russia can still deploy artillery, however technologically inferior, in overwhelming numbers against such comparatively small European artillery forces. The story is similar for personnel and also, albeit to a lesser extent, for heavy armour.

The end result in tactical terms is likely to be that, whether on the defensive or offensive, superior hostile firepower will inflict casualties, even if Western forces ultimately win the battle. European forces in particular simply may not have the available firepower, whether tubes or munitions, to engage all relevant targets before they become a direct threat. The role airpower could play is unclear. Western airpower is certainly more potent than any adversary's, both technologically and tactically, but Western militaries are still unlikely to have the near-perfect freedom in the skies which they have enjoyed for decades, particularly before the US Air Force gets involved to suppress or destroy hostile ground-based air defence. Moreover, ammunition is even more important for airpower than ground-based firepower. European air forces largely ran out of munitions less than a month into the intervention in Libya in 2011.[22] US ordnance stocks were severely challenged by the campaign against the Islamic State.[23] Any warfare against a major hostile power would represent a far more target-rich environment than Libya or Islamic State territory. Yet this represents another key aspect of primitivisation: not only can artillery and air forces be expected to fire or release dumb shells or comparatively primitive bombs after having unleashed their full precision stockpiles, but ammunition usage is also likely to skyrocket and deplete ammunition stockpiles even faster.

Moreover, European forces cannot afford to take losses, because each loss would represent a proportionally larger amount of available firepower, personnel or other military capability as compared to similar losses by their massed adversaries. Due to its relatively sclerotic defence industry, Russia has had difficulty replenishing losses on the front line in Ukraine and has often done so with comparatively ancient equipment drawn from deteriorating Soviet stockpiles. Yet non-American Western militaries may not have the industrial capacity or the stockpiled resources to achieve even this much.[24] Western, and especially non-American, militaries represent the high-tech yet fragile sharp ends of insufficient defence-industrial and logistical systems, especially when matched against the lower-technology and less fragile ends of the not quite as insufficient systems of rival powers.

Countering primitivisation

There is no doomsday warning here that Russia can, let alone will, conquer Europe. Even against no opposition, Russia would have nearly insuperable trouble sustaining a military advance beyond immediately neighbouring countries.[25] Yet taking primitivisation seriously is necessary to further the aim of improving resilience. The prospect of the primitivisation of Western armed forces in a future major war has widespread implications for defence-industrial, procurement and even personnel policies, as well as for force design. These implications have been thrown into stark relief by Russia's 2022 invasion of Ukraine.

The West is not ready for what some have called industrial warfare. Even the US is not ready, having made defence-industrial and procurement choices that have, at the very least, increasingly minimised certain ammunition types.[26] Even without any losses, Western forces will find themselves primitivised by having to use dumb and imprecise munitions after expending all their precise ammunition. The United States is taking steps to remedy this problem, but Europe is struggling to follow suit. Ammunition has been a major focus of the Western angst brought on by Russia's invasion, yet the same problem is present for all equipment. Europe cannot build artillery or tanks at the requisite scale or speed to sustain major warfare.[27] The US is better placed, having maintained huge stocks, but may find it challenging to sustain the materiel side of a major war as well. Countries concerned by technological primitivisation have two main alternatives: 1) develop the industrial might to sustain intense, long-duration, high-tech warfare; or 2) be prepared to revert to less high-tech warfare employing older stockpiles of military equipment, or have the industrial capacity to build less advanced equipment at scale. The US is broadly capable of embracing both options in time, whereas Europe is currently capable of neither.

Yet even if the industrial capacity is present to produce high-tech equipment at scale, without the trained personnel to operate it, militaries will suffer primitivisation all the same. Virtually all Western militaries are concerned about force levels, though it has been suggested that such concerns are overblown, at least in the United States.[28] Western visions of future warfare tend to assume low casualties in the same way that they assume low material losses, in part because technology is expected to allow far fewer servicemembers to be in any danger at all, let alone lethal danger. Yet casualties in major warfare will occur, which will have both short- and long-term consequences for deployed formations that will need to cope with losses in the immediate tactical and operational circumstances, and to replace losses over the course of the campaign. Extensive attrition may lead to social and ultimately organisational primitivisation, causing the formation to become less effective.

Some services within Western militaries have been restructuring over the past few years to embrace new visions of future warfare defined by particular foes and particular technologies. The US Marine Corps, for example, has been undergoing a controversial force redesign aimed at countering China and embracing new technologies. The redesign includes reducing infantry and direct-support capabilities in favour of technology.[29] Such capabilities would no doubt be useful, perhaps necessary, in a conflict against China. Yet they will also make the corps more susceptible to primitivisation in any scenario involving human and material losses, which it would have difficulty replacing. A force that is designed around high technology alone, and that cannot function in the intended operational space without it, may be little more than a glass cannon.

Operationally, it appears likely that either the prospect or reality of primitivisation will slow down offensive operations. The mere prospect of primitivisation will haunt commanders on the attack, leading them to prioritise force protection as much as possible without abandoning the mission, although the mission's timetable will change, as has been seen in Ukraine's summer 2023 counter-offensives. Actually primitivised armed forces will have little choice but to move more slowly, as they will have already burned through their capability for major mechanised offensives, as appears to be the case for the Russian army in Ukraine. With primitivisation slowing offensives, they are likely to be less strategically and politically decisive, and therefore the war will go on.

Defensive operations will also be more difficult, even with slower offensives. Commanders are likely to be loath to risk their high-tech equipment in mundane defensive operations, which would necessarily increase the risk of primitivisation, and so may pull back relatively elite and well-equipped units to act as reserves. The Wehrmacht displayed this force-employment pattern on the Eastern Front, as have both Russia and Ukraine in their ongoing war. Yet the very act of presenting such a defence may give hope to each side that offensives may succeed, possibly very rapidly (as actually occurred on the Kharkiv front in early autumn 2022), thus bolstering the political will to fight.

*   *   *

Primitivisation is an under-recognised problem for modern militaries, the greatest example of which prior to 2022 was seen on the Eastern Front during the Second World War. Involving much more than a simple incapacity to manufacture enough tanks or ammunition, it is a multidimensional challenge to which Western militaries and their governments do not have real answers. Meeting this challenge will require a wide range of industrial and operational responses. It should also moderate the excessive technological optimism that has distorted Western defence thinking for at least the last 30 years.

Notes

1   Peter Bergen, 'Gen. David Petraeus: How the War in Ukraine Will End', CNN, 14 February 2023, https://edition.cnn.com/2023/02/14/opinions/petraeus-how-ukraine-war-ends-bergen-ctpr/index.html.

2   See Anthony King, 'On Cohesion', in Anthony King (ed.), *Frontline: Combat and Cohesion in the Twenty-first Century* (Oxford: Oxford University Press, 2015), pp. 3–23.

3   See Tarak Barkawi, 'Subaltern Soldiers: Eurocentrism and the Nation-state in the Combat Motivation Debates', in King, *Frontline*, pp. 27–8.

4   Omer Bartov, *The Eastern Front 1941–45: German Troops and the Barbarisation of Warfare* (New York: Palgrave Macmillan, 1986), ch. 1.

5   Omer Bartov, *Hitler's Army: Soldiers, Nazis, and War in the Third Reich* (Oxford: Oxford University Press, 1992), ch. 1.

6   *Ibid.*, p. 33.

7   See Alex Horton, 'Russia's Commando Units Gutted by Ukraine War, U.S.

Leaks Show', *Washington Post*, 14 April 2023, https://www.washingtonpost.com/national-security/2023/04/14/leaked-documents-russian-spetsnaz/.

8   See Alia Shoaib, 'An Elite Russian Brigade of 5,000 Soldiers Has Been Destroyed and Reformed as Many as 8 Times After Heavy Losses, Report Says', *Business Insider*, 26 March 2023, https://www.businessinsider.com/same-russian-brigade-destroyed-and-reformed-8-times-report-2023-3?r=US&IR=T.

9   See Jack Watling and Nick Reynolds, 'Meatgrinder: Russian Tactics in the Second Year of Its Invasion of Ukraine', Royal United Services Institute Special Report, May 2023, pp. 3–5.

10 Julian Röpcke (@JulianRoepcke), post to X, 7 March 2023, https://twitter.com/JulianRoepcke/status/1633028601938362368.

11 See Naalsio (@naalsio26), post to X, 22 June 2023, https://twitter.com/naalsio26/status/1671626465996046338.

12 David A. Deptula, *Effects-based Operations: Change in the Nature of Warfare* (Arlington, VA: Aerospace Education Foundation, 2001), p. 17.

13 Max Boot, 'The New American Way of War', *Foreign Affairs*, vol. 82, no. 4, July–August 2003, p. 42.

14 Robert O. Work, 'AI and Future Warfare: The Rise of Robotic Combat Operations', Mad Scientist Conference, University of Texas at Austin, 24 April 2019, emphasis in the original.

15 See Lawrence Freedman, *The Future of War: A History* (New York: PublicAffairs, 2017).

16 John D. Maurer, 'The Future of Precision-strike Warfare: Strategic Dynamics of Mature Military

Revolutions', *Naval War College Review*, vol. 76, no. 2, Spring 2023, pp. 13–37.

17 Stephen Biddle, 'Victory Misunderstood: What the Gulf War Tells Us About the Future of Conflict', *International Security*, vol. 21, no. 2, Autumn 1996, pp. 139–79.

18 See Lukas Milevski, 'Variable Heroism: Landpower in US Grand Strategy Since 9/11', in Jason Warren (ed.), *Landpower in the Long War: Projecting Force After 9/11* (Lexington, KY: University Press of Kentucky, 2019), pp. 15–31.

19 Christopher A. Lawrence, *War by Numbers: Understanding Conventional Combat* (Lincoln, NE: Potomac Books, 2017), p. 147.

20 Jack Watling, 'The Future of Fires: Maximising the UK's Tactical and Operational Firepower', RUSI Occasional Paper, November 2019, pp. 1–2.

21 See Stijn Mitzer, Jakub Janovsky and Joost Oliemans, 'Answering the Call: Heavy Weaponry Supplied to Ukraine', *Oryx*, 11 April 2022 (regularly updated; accessed 11 August 2023), https://www.oryxspioenkop.com/2022/04/answering-call-heavy-weaponry-supplied.html; and IISS, *The Military Balance 2022* (Abingdon: Routledge for the IISS, 2022), pp. 105, 110.

22 See Karen DeYoung and Greg Jaffe, 'NATO Runs Short on Some Munitions in Libya', *Washington Post*, 15 April 2011, https://www.washingtonpost.com/world/nato-runs-short-on-some-munitions-in-libya/2011/04/15/AF3O7ElD_story.html.

23 See John Q. Bolton, 'The More Things Change … Russia's War in Ukraine Mirrors the Past as Much as It Shows the Future', *Military Review*, July 2023, https://www.armyupress.

army.mil/Journals/Military-Review/
Online-Exclusive/2023-OLE/
The-More-Things-Change/.

24 See Alex Vershinin, 'The Return
    of Industrial Warfare', RUSI
    Commentary, 17 June 2022, https://
    rusi.org/explore-our-research/
    publications/commentary/
    return-industrial-warfare.

25 See Ben Connable et al., *Russia's Limit of
    Advance: Analysis of Russian Ground Force
    Deployment Capabilities and Limitations*
    (Santa Monica, CA: RAND, 2020).

26 See Vershinin, 'The Return of
    Industrial Warfare'.

27 See Hannah Aries, Bastian Giegerich
    and Tim Lawrenson, 'The Guns of
    Europe: Defence-industrial Challenges
    in a Time of War', *Survival*, vol. 65, no.
    3, June–July 2023, pp. 7–24.

28 See Stefan Borg, 'Meeting the US
    Military's Manpower Challenges',
    Parameters, vol. 52, no. 3, Autumn
    2022, pp. 97–109.

29 US Marine Corps, 'Force Design 2030',
    March 2020, p. 2.

Slouching Towards a Nuclear Gomorrah

Anonymous

The global nuclear order that took shape in the decades following the advent of nuclear weapons today faces acute pressures that threaten its near-term viability, much less its solvency, over the next decade or more. The main pillars of this order – the prevention of nuclear war, non-proliferation of nuclear weapons and sharing of peaceful nuclear technology – stand on a foundation of international practices, both formal and tacit, that appears increasingly unstable. Although prognostications of its collapse are as old as the nuclear order itself, a confluence of factors may soon set in motion stresses too forceful for the order to withstand. Even if wholesale tragedy is averted, a new nuclear paradigm may emerge that is unrecognisable, with grim implications for international peace and prosperity.

The world nuclear order was built, partly by design and partly by improvisation, over generations. Consisting of treaties, political commitments, voluntary norms and international law, it has imposed a degree of stability on the nuclear era that was feared impossible at its dawning. Key elements of the order include, above all, respect for the nuclear taboo (that is, the non-use of nuclear weapons in conflict); near-universal compliance with a moratorium on nuclear-explosive testing; the non-proliferation of nuclear weapons and related technologies beyond the five recognised nuclear

The author is a career member of the US government's Senior Executive Service with responsibility for national-security matters.

Survival | vol. 65 no. 6 | December 2023–January 2024 | pp. 137–158 https://doi.org/10.1080/00396338.2023.2285608

powers; extended-deterrence arrangements to maintain strategic stability and dissuade proliferation; arms-control agreements and verification measures; the right to harness civil nuclear technology under International Atomic Energy Agency (IAEA) safeguards; strict regulatory control of nuclear material; and collective action to prevent nuclear terrorism.

Russia's potential employment of nuclear weapons in Ukraine is only the most pressing of a range of looming threats to the nuclear order. The actual use of nuclear weapons in armed conflict would deeply affect the strategic calculus of every nuclear-armed state, with ominous prospects for the durability of nuclear deterrence. Even short of use, the influence these weapons have already exerted in Ukraine has been enormous. Russia's nuclear deterrent made direct Western military intervention in the conflict unfathomable from the start, a lesson that could whet interest in nuclear weapons among states in Asia, the Middle East and elsewhere. Further, the nuclear-modernisation programmes of the five recognised nuclear-weapons states have confirmed the unseriousness of their nominal commitment to disarmament – a core element of the grand bargain that gave rise to the Treaty on the Non-Proliferation of Nuclear Weapons (NPT) to begin with. For all intents and purposes, the world has abandoned this ideal, and exasperation with the fiction of disarmament could ultimately signal the death of the treaty altogether.

The world has abandoned the disarmament ideal

Even if the NPT continues to limp along, ever more toothless, the broader strategic nuclear-stability regime is increasingly rickety. Global cooperation to limit arms racing has all but ceased. The incentives and penalties that slowed the spread of nuclear weapons for half a century are losing their potency. Competition to service the burgeoning global nuclear-energy sector promises to reward vendors whose commitment to non-proliferation is pliable. The allure of profit and influence will probably, over time, supersede the abstract virtue of non-proliferation, increasing the likelihood that material from civil nuclear programmes will be diverted for military purposes. Likewise, cooperation to prevent nuclear terrorism has atrophied.

Focused and lavishly funded from the collapse of the Soviet Union in the 1990s to the Nuclear Security Summit process of the 2010s, the resumption of great-power competition and emergence of new strategic threats has eclipsed attention to non-state nuclear threats.

An unmistakable sense is forming that the centre cannot hold as its defenders dwindle. China, India and Russia, accounting for more than a third of the world's population, each hunger for a new international system to replace the one prescribed and dominated by the West. On the eve of Russia's invasion of Ukraine, Chinese President Xi Jinping and Russian President Vladimir Putin issued a lengthy joint statement noting the 'transformation of the global governance architecture and world order'.[1] Their governments will not be reliable champions of a nuclear order that has been a potent source of the West's global authority, which they wish to undercut.

Absent consensus among the major powers on the basic desirability of the nuclear order, leaving aside any commitment to its care and nourishment, the nuclear landscape of the near future will be bleak. At the least, it may feature a world in which nuclear-weapons use is not only *not* unthinkable, but actively integrated into war-fighting doctrine, with half again as many states in possession of these weapons; a world in which the distinction between the nuclear haves and have-nots is jettisoned, giving licence to develop nuclear weapons to any state with the technical means to do so; and a world in which the decades-long trend of improving nuclear-material security is reversed, affording stateless fanatics access to arms once possessed and controlled only by governments.

US policymakers have neither accepted the potential for the nuclear order to collapse nor made a concerted study of options for forestalling this eventuality, if they exist at all. Although the 2022 Nuclear Posture Review contains no glaring accelerants to speed the immolation of the order, the Strategic Posture Commission's recent report points to a more foreboding future, with its unabashed longing for a nuclear build-up.[2] Notably lacking among senior leaders is any vision for a new grand bargain to address the central pressures on the nuclear order: the perishability of the arrangement in which nuclear weapons are permitted to some states but not others, and the failure to make good on widely sharing the benefits of peaceful nuclear energy. Nor has the United States evinced any appetite for concessions, in the form of major changes to its strategic posture, that might make a renewed compact palatable to the most likely agents of the order's disintegration.

The demise of nuclear arms control

By their very nature, treaties are meant to evoke a sense of permanence. Yet many arrangements to keep peace between the great powers have been surprisingly short-lived. The Washington Naval Treaty, signed in 1922, sought to prevent a naval arms race among the victors of the First World War by limiting construction of capital ships. However, French and Italian violations occurred throughout the 1920s and 1930s, and each of the warring powers had amassed impressive fleets by the outbreak of the Second World War.[3] Similarly, violations of the Treaty of Versailles, also meant to preserve peace after the First World War, began less than a year after its signing with Germany's reintroduction of troops to the Rhineland. By 1935, the treaty had effectively collapsed under the weight of Germany's rearmament.[4] The half-lives of these treaties caution against taking for granted the durability of instruments for stabilising nuclear competition. The few nuclear agreements that survive have well outlasted empirical treaty 'lifespans' already.

Long before Russia's invasion of Ukraine, the nuclear arms-control regime that had assuaged strategic instability for decades appeared in danger of total implosion. Beginning with the termination of the Anti-Ballistic Missile Treaty in 2002, the regime sustained further blows with the scuttling of the Iran nuclear deal in 2018, the Intermediate-Range Nuclear Forces Treaty in 2019 and the Treaty on Open Skies in 2020.[5] Then, in early 2023, Putin announced that Russia would suspend participation in the New Strategic Arms Reduction Treaty (New START).[6] Although the Biden administration had signalled its willingness to negotiate a 'new arms control framework' with Russia upon the expiration of New START in 2026, its specification of the need for 'a willing partner operating in good faith' implicitly concedes the dim prospects for cooperation with Moscow.[7] Indeed, Russia's withdrawal from the Comprehensive Nuclear-Test-Ban Treaty (CTBT) in late 2023 is further grounds for pessimism.[8] Nor is there any reasonable possibility of a multilateral arms-control agreement with China, whose foreign ministry has repeatedly scoffed at the notion.[9]

What remains of nuclear arms control is effectively the CTBT, the Outer Space Treaty, the Partial Nuclear Test Ban Treaty, the Threshold Test Ban Treaty and the NPT. The CTBT, adopted by the United Nations General Assembly in 1996 but never having entered into force, has settled into an unenforceable global norm against nuclear-explosive testing. Although observed since 1998 by every state except North Korea, this norm would almost certainly not survive a resumption of testing by any of the nuclear-weapons states. The NPT is perhaps even more endangered, having become a vessel into which various parties have poured their disenchantment with not only the nuclear order but also the broader international system.

The obsolescence of the NPT

Often described as the 'cornerstone' of the non-proliferation regime, the NPT was a remarkable achievement when it entered into force in 1970. Just ten years earlier, pervasive gloom had taken hold that any potentate or junta that wanted a nuclear weapon would have one. Recall presidential candidate John F. Kennedy's warning in 1960 that, because of scientific advances, '10, 15, or 20 nations will have a nuclear capacity … by the end of the presidential office in 1964'.[10] That so few states ultimately obtained nuclear weapons was due in large part to the social compact at the heart of the NPT. Under this agreement, the number of nuclear-weapons states would be capped at the five countries that already possessed them, which pledged to 'pursue negotiations in good faith' to dismantle their arsenals. In exchange, the non-weapons states would agree not to develop nuclear weapons, and the fruits of nuclear technology would be available to all.[11] Although the treaty sanctified hypocrisy at its most base, the alternative was far worse, and the devil's bargain was, after all, only meant to be temporary.

More than 50 years later, the gulf between the early promise of the NPT and the present reality is vast. Almost half of the world's nuclear-armed states remain outside the treaty, and, with the exception of North Korea, the outliers are hardly international pariahs. More than one enjoys close cooperation with the United States. Meanwhile, like prehistoric scorpions suspended in amber, the recognised nuclear powers are unmoved to honour their pledge to disarm – all five are presently in the midst of sweeping upgrades to their nuclear arsenals – even as they jealously guard access to nuclear technology.

The United States has embarked on a multiyear 'life extension' process to refurbish five classes of nuclear warheads, and recently showcased a new strategic bomber.[12] In 2021, the United Kingdom reversed an earlier pledge to reduce the ceiling of its nuclear arsenal, raising the cap from 180 warheads to 'no more than 260', a 44% increase.[13] France has begun developing a third-generation ballistic-missile submarine, as well as a new submarine-launched ballistic missile.[14] More ominously, Russia and China continue to unveil exotic nuclear systems. In 2018, Putin announced the development of six new weapons, among them the nuclear-powered *Burevestnik* cruise missile and the *Poseidon* underwater nuclear drone.[15] Following suit in 2021, Beijing tested a hypersonic Fractional Orbital Bombardment System and was discovered to have been building scores of intercontinental ballistic-missile (ICBM) silos in its western desert.[16]

Fairly or unfairly – the global security environment is admittedly daunting – frustration with the five recognised nuclear-weapons states among many non-weapons states is visceral. The reaction to the AUKUS submarine deal, under which the United States and United Kingdom will assist Australia in developing nuclear-powered submarines, is instructive in this regard.[17] Although much opposition to the deal centres on non-proliferation concerns – namely, that the precedent might allow a country to develop a clandestine nuclear weapon under the guise of a nuclear-submarine programme – the more significant objection stems from what is seen as its inherent hypocrisy. As Harshit Prajapati notes, AUKUS 'exposes Washington's double standards for allowing Australia to acquire [nuclear-powered submarines] while taking a hard line against the Iranian nuclear program' and 'demonstrates that it is comfortable bending the nuclear non-proliferation regime to suit its preferences'.[18] As the deal is implemented, Washington will have to contend with perceptions of inequity among the nuclear have-nots, a pointed expression of which is the multinational diplomatic effort to abolish nuclear weapons.

It is difficult to say whether the Treaty on the Prohibition of Nuclear Weapons – informally known as the 'Ban Treaty' – is driven more by genuine fear and loathing of these weapons or the perceived insincerity of the nuclear-armed states. In either case, the movement is gaining steam. When the Ban Treaty was considered in the UN General Assembly in 2017, 122 nations voted in favour, and the accord nominally entered into force in early 2021.[19] Although the United States and the other nuclear-weapons states did not even bother to vote, and the treaty's chances for achieving nuclear disarmament approach zero, the undercurrent propelling the effort may nonetheless have seismic consequences. Indeed, it could have the perverse effect of toppling the NPT itself, thereby making nuclear proliferation, and by extension the use of nuclear weapons, more rather than less likely. An extreme manifestation of discontent with the NPT could entail a critical mass of member states withdrawing from the treaty in protest over the nuclear-weapons states' failure to disarm. In this eventuality, the NPT could effectively collapse, giving opponents of nuclear weapons the ignominious distinction of having dismantled the principal mechanism to prevent their global spread.

In the near term, an even more dire threat to the NPT looms in the form of Russia's potential employment of nuclear weapons in Ukraine. Any such use by one of the recognised nuclear-weapons states would likely herald the effective dissolution of the treaty by signalling unmistakably to the non-weapons states that nuclear disarmament is a mirage. While their particular security considerations would govern the decision to pursue or forsake nuclear arms, the wish to avoid global opprobrium for violating the NPT would no longer be an inhibiting factor.

Shattering the nuclear taboo

In 1995, as part of an effort to indefinitely extend the NPT, the five recognised states adopted 'negative security assurances' pledging not to use or threaten to use nuclear arms against non-nuclear-weapons states in good standing with the treaty.[20] Russia has violated this commitment many times over. Even before the present crisis, Moscow was ostentatious in its nuclear posturing, simulating a nuclear attack on Sweden in 2013, among other provocations.[21] Since Russia's invasion of Ukraine in 2022, the Kremlin's nuclear rhetoric has done further violence to the nuclear taboo. Putin has intently stoked the fear of nuclear war, cautioning the West that its intervention in Ukraine would result in 'consequences greater than any you have faced in history'.[22] As Russia's fortunes on the battlefield waned, its nuclear warnings became even more pronounced, with repeated allusions to the use of nuclear weapons. The ramifications of such use would be difficult to overstate.

Notwithstanding the initial horror over such an occurrence, a counter-intuitive outcome might ultimately arise. Because the destructiveness of a tactical nuclear weapon in particular would fall short of common conceptions of nuclear annihilation, the prevailing attitude towards the attack could be one of relative passivity. The upshot might thus be a diminished fear of nuclear weapons and consequently a heightened likelihood of their use in future conflicts. The nuclear-armed states might in turn modify their nuclear-use doctrine to emphasise pre-emption rather than deterrence by threat of retaliation. Evidence of such doctrinal shifts exist even without the catalyst of a Russian nuclear strike in Ukraine; in September 2022, North Korea's ersatz legislature passed a 'law' authorising the employment of nuclear weapons 'automatically and immediately' in the event of an imminent strike against the Kim Jong-un regime.[23] In tandem with doctrinal changes, new offensive capabilities could be developed, such as missiles with enhanced accuracy and earth penetration for counterforce strikes. Together with a more liberal threshold for employment, these systems could drive a paradigm shift whereby nuclear weapons were perceived as standard war-fighting tools rather than as political instruments.

Events seem to affirm the deterrent value of nuclear weapons

Russia's nuclear employment could also transform perceptions of the attractiveness of nuclear weapons. Were a strike in Ukraine seen as ushering in a new era in which nuclear weapons were wielded more promiscuously, several latent nuclear states might feel pressure to cross the nuclear threshold and field their own deterrent forces. Even before the Russo-Ukrainian war, events over the last three decades would seem to affirm the deterrent value of nuclear weapons and the inadvisability of eschewing them. North Korean leader Kim Jong-un is openly contemptuous of Iraq's and

Libya's decisions to discontinue their nuclear programmes, which he evidently believes left them vulnerable to the West's assaults.[24] Likewise, while Ukraine never assumed operational control of the nuclear warheads it inherited from the Soviet Union, Ukrainian leaders have since expressed seller's remorse at having relinquished them.[25]

Polling in 2023 showed that two-thirds of South Koreans favour an indigenous nuclear deterrent.[26] South Korea's growing ballistic-missile programme and long-standing interest in uranium enrichment and reprocessing technology suggest a 'hedging' strategy that would enable it to develop nuclear weapons relatively quickly. In early 2023, South Korean President Yoon Suk-yeol asserted for the first time that his country would consider developing its own nuclear weapons in response to North Korea's rising nuclear threat.[27] Even Japan's long-standing hostility towards nuclear weapons appears to be softening. While public opposition remains strong – polling indicates roughly 75% of Japanese support Japan's signing of the Ban Treaty – Japanese politicians' musings about obtaining the bomb have become decidedly more mundane.[28] The late former prime minister Abe Shinzo's 2016 remark that Japan's constitution did not explicitly prohibit a nuclear deterrent did not prompt a widespread outcry; once upon a time it would have.[29] Outside of Asia, some fear that Germany or Sweden too could conclude that nuclear weapons were necessary for self-defence against Russia.[30]

Iran's nuclear ambitions have provoked anxiety for more than 30 years. While the US intelligence community continues to judge that Iran is not undertaking the key activities necessary to develop a nuclear weapon, suspicions persist that its leaders secretly covet the bomb.[31] Even if Iran ultimately does not develop a nuclear arsenal, its behaviour illuminates the weaknesses of a non-proliferation regime, offering a road map to attaining the bomb by way of a civil programme with a weak but legal peaceful-uses justification. Should Tehran obtain a nuclear weapon, Saudi Arabia would almost certainly follow suit. In 2023, Crown Prince Muhammad bin Salman, its de facto ruler, averred that while Saudi Arabia was 'concerned of any country getting a nuclear weapon', if Iran did so Saudi Arabia 'will have to get one'.[32] Elsewhere in the region, Turkiye might find such weapons attractive not only for the security they offer but also as an expression of discontent with its per-ceived treatment as a second-class citizen. Turkish President Recep Tayyip Erdoğan declared in 2019 that 'some countries have missiles with nuclear warheads, not one or two. But we can't have them. This, I cannot accept.'[33]

Although Russia's use of nuclear weapons in Ukraine could accelerate the global proliferation of nuclear weapons, it is important to note that this event is hardly a necessary catalyst. Each of the most likely proliferant states may arrive at the desirability of these weapons irrespective of the endgame in Ukraine. And the ability of the non-proliferation regime to forestall a cascade of new nuclear nations may be compromised regardless of which side prevails in that conflict.

Nuclear terrorism

Among the potential drivers of nuclear disorder, perhaps the only close competitor to Russia's use of a nuclear weapon in Ukraine, would be an act of nuclear terrorism. Even in this domain, there is a potential nexus to Russia. Siegfried Hecker, former director of Los Alamos National Laboratory, noted in the aftermath of Russia's invasion that, despite past US–Russia cooperation on nuclear-material security, 'now we must be concerned about Russia committing nuclear or radiological terrorism'.[34] The non-occurrence of a terrorist nuclear attack in the more than 20 years since 9/11 has led to some degree of complacency about the non-state threat. Once-formidable groups such as al-Qaeda and the Islamic State have been diminished to the point of manageability. Nevertheless, the global stockpile of fissile material is sufficient to produce more than 200,000 nuclear weapons, and it is unduly optimistic to believe extremists will never gain access to even a single weapon's worth of this material. Further, access to technology that may enable non-state nuclear capabilities is increasingly difficult to restrict. Dual-use manufacturing technologies continue to multiply, and novel uranium-enrichment processes are becoming more feasible. By enabling the localised manufacture of critical bomb ingredients, tell-tale signatures of a weapons programme can be reduced, thwarting traditional means of detection.

Even if the source of the material used in a terrorist nuclear attack were far removed from the civil nuclear sector, in the aftermath of such an event one could imagine a global backlash against all things nuclear, including commercial nuclear energy. In addition to halting the construction of new reactors around the world, demands could intensify to dispose of and further restrict access to nuclear fuels. Stifling peaceful uses of nuclear technology would have a wide range of unfortunate effects, not least that of curtailing a major source of carbon-free energy just as the climate crisis became a matter of existential peril for the planet.

A grand call to purpose

Although not without its hazards, the nuclear order has provided a level of stability whose absence would be felt worldwide. Consequently, buttressing the order is the collective responsibility of every nation, even as certain leading actors should be expected to play a disproportionate role in forestalling its demise. Chief among these is the United States, not only as one of the architects of the original order but also as an agent of many of the strains that presently beset it. To fulfil this responsibility, the United States must signal its willingness to negotiate meaningful, even radical, changes to its nuclear posture, non-proliferation policy and approach to civil nuclear energy in exchange for global buy-in to a new strategic-stability paradigm. Only dramatic reforms will be sufficient to overcome the scepticism of the nuclear have-nots and revitalise a global commitment to a new, equitable and sustainable nuclear order. Equally important will be to address Russia's and China's perceptions of insecurity stemming from the US missile-defence posture and nuclear-use doctrine.

Reinvigorating the global nuclear order cannot succeed without an American repudiation of strategic missile defence, which is a major source of China's and Russia's nuclear neuralgia. When Putin unveiled the new *Burevestnik* and *Poseidon* nuclear-weapons systems in 2018, he pointedly noted their necessity to defeat US missile defences, adding that if a means to counter the new Russian weapons somehow materialised, 'our boys will think of something new'.[35] Likewise, China's leaders have not forgotten that the original pretext for the United States' 1967 decision to deploy an anti-ballistic-missile system was not to counter the Soviet missile threat but rather to blunt China's emerging nuclear capability.[36]

US leaders take pains to emphasise that the current incarnation of the system is not oriented against either country. The 2022 Missile Defense Review insists the US Ground-Based Midcourse Defense system 'is neither intended for, nor capable of, defeating the large and sophisticated ICBM, air-, or sea-launched ballistic missile threats from Russia and [China]' but rather is designed 'to address ballistic missile threats from states like North Korea and Iran'.[37] Beijing and Moscow are understandably sceptical of these assurances, in part because the representations of US officials so often cut against them. Former US national security advisor John Bolton, for instance, recently called for a 'far more ambitious' missile-defence system geared towards not only rogue states but also China and Russia.[38]

Rejecting strategic defences would pay immense dividends

The Pentagon manifests a curious schizophrenia where China's nuclear arsenal is concerned, wringing its hands over Beijing's nuclear build-up while simultaneously championing the very system most responsible for its perception of insecurity. The US Strategic Command (STRATCOM), for example, proclaimed in 2020 that 'missile defense has gone from theoretical to a proven military capability in the 21st century, and the Missile Defense Agency is looking to extend those capabilities against new threats'.[39] The very next year, the Pentagon's annual report to Congress on China's military predicted that China 'likely intends to have at least 1,000 warheads by 2030'.[40] This is an almost cartoonish exemplar of the classic security dilemma, wherein China's nuclear build-up is the source of anxiety to US military planners who are oblivious to their authorship of the negative feedback loop.

In truth, there has long been a Potemkin quality to the Pentagon's professions of the system's effectiveness, and one senses that its advocates are robotically reciting the party line. In response to the 2020 boast about the programme's maturation, scholar Jeffrey Lewis tartly observed that 'almost no one at STRATCOM believes this'.[41] Rejecting strategic defences and restricting anti-missile technology to theatre systems would not only pay immense dividends to global stability but in all likelihood would be quietly welcomed by Pentagon budgeters.

Allaying Russia's and China's fears that the United States is pursuing nuclear primacy – that is, the ability to wholly eliminate an adversary's strategic deterrent in a pre-emptive attack – would require changes to the US nuclear posture. In this regard, a debate has raged for decades in US policy circles about the virtues and demerits of a 'no first use' pledge, by which the United States would forswear the pre-emptive use of nuclear weapons and commit to employing them only in retaliation against a nuclear attack. A semantic younger sibling of this policy is the 'sole purpose' formulation, which then-presidential candidate Joe Biden articulated when he declared that 'the sole purpose of the US nuclear arsenal should be deterring – and, if necessary, retaliating against – a nuclear attack'.[42] Despite hopes in the arms-control community that Biden's campaign rhetoric would be codified in the administration's Nuclear Posture Review, the document contained neither a no-first-use pledge nor a sole-purpose affirmation.[43] Such a commitment would be a necessary starting point for conveying the United States' sincerity that its nuclear deterrent is just that – a defensive capability rather than an offensive one.

Rhetorical and doctrinal changes would have to be followed by a concrete reorientation of the nuclear posture away from offensive capabilities. In recent decades, the US military has pursued numerous systems with clear first-strike implications, including increasingly accurate conventional munitions to destroy command-and-control nodes, stealth aircraft to penetrate advanced air defences and space-based platforms to target mobile nuclear systems. Advances in networked ground sensors, signals intelligence to provide geolocation and long-loiter uncrewed aerial systems have improved the United States' ability to locate and destroy mobile missiles in particular – generally understood to be second-strike platforms.[44] Emphasis on these capabilities cannot help but reinforce Moscow's and Beijing's paranoia. While some have clear roles in conventional warfare and thus cannot be eliminated out of hand, formally disassociating them from nuclear war fighting is necessary to assuage fears of their pre-emptive potential.

Naturally, proposals to negotiate away military capabilities that bestow strategic advantages to the United States would be hotly contested, potentially along partisan lines. There is, however, notable precedent for such a course.

At the end of the Cold War in 1991, then-president George H.W. Bush unilaterally initiated the elimination of several classes of tactical nuclear weapons without reciprocal measures by Russia.[45] Only such a sweeping gesture would be enough to sway doubting governments of the United States' genuineness in pursuing a new and even-handed nuclear order.

A new nuclear order

Having signalled its willingness to entertain unprecedented concessions in the nuclear realm, the United States should then adopt as a central pillar of its national-security and foreign policies the ambition to midwife a fresh consensus on global nuclear policy with two overriding objectives. The first would be the prevention of a new strategic arms race among the nuclear powers, including those outside the NPT, and the cessation of further nuclear proliferation. The second would be a recommitment to sharing the fruits of peaceful nuclear technology, especially in the Global South, as part of a worldwide campaign to meet rising energy needs while simultaneously combatting the climate crisis.

The first objective, while falling short of the abolitionist vision of Ban Treaty adherents, is as much as can be reasonably achieved in the present geopolitical environment. In the foreseeable future, a plausible outcome would be a world in which the number of extant nuclear weapons were sufficient to deter major conflict but not so great that a failure of deterrence would end life as we know it on the planet. Presented with a choice between an achievable half measure and the grim destination towards which the world is presently slouching, all but the most fanatic abolitionists would likely acquiesce to the former.

On the practical level, a new arms-control framework would be required. A notional target for multilateral nuclear-arms limitations might include a cap of no more than 1,000 weapons for the five recognised nuclear-weapons states – to include non-strategic systems – and a fixed timetable for step-wise reductions to 500. The upper figure would require the United States and Russia to make substantial cuts to their existing stockpiles, but would accommodate the anticipated growth of China's arsenal over the coming decade.

Of course, one must not be naive about the prospect of Russia's appetite for arms-control negotiations while in the midst of a brutal war of attrition with the West. Putin may ostentatiously rebuff any American-led nuclear initiative, at least initially. Yet precisely because of the economic pressure from the Russia–Ukraine war, the Kremlin may be more eager to avoid a costly and futile arms race with the United States than is commonly supposed. Further, its reaction to a genuine overture to forgo strategic missile defences is difficult to predict. At the very least, Moscow's refusal would entrench its status as a pariah state, which itself may be useful in managing its misbehaviour. A more promising possibility, however, is that laying the conceptual groundwork for a new strategic-stability regime may nonetheless bear fruit in a not-distant future.

Likewise, the non-recognised states that possess nuclear weapons would be called upon to freeze the size of their stockpiles, with customised incentives for each to do so. North Korea, for example, hungers for recognition as a nuclear power, which the United States and its allies could easily extend, along with a treaty ending the Korean War, at little strategic cost.[46] Similarly, permitting the accession of India and Pakistan to the Nuclear Suppliers Group would remove a perennial irritant to both governments and encourage New Delhi and Islamabad to become more responsible nuclear actors.

A new multilateral arms-control framework should also stipulate a number of measures for reducing nuclear tensions and closing off potential new avenues for arms races. In particular, the adoption of no-first-use pledges should be the *sine qua non* condition of participation. The putative nuclear powers should also pursue agreement to disallow testing of space-based nuclear-weapons systems, strengthening the celestial restrictions already in place in the Outer Space Treaty and Partial Nuclear Test Ban Treaty. Novel nuclear-weapons systems and delivery vehicles must be proscribed, and provisions for an intrusive inspections regime would naturally be required.

Although individual nuclear states may recoil at one or more of these provisions, a bold proposal to reduce the threat of global nuclear war should be grounds for genuine optimism among those frustrated with the nuclear powers' intransigence. Still, attention to nuclear weapons would also have to be paired with action to share civil nuclear technology, both as a symbol of nuclear equity and as a tangible inducement to cooperation. In 1953, US president Dwight D. Eisenhower proposed to share nuclear technology with developing nations for humanitarian purposes, pledging to 'find the way by which the miraculous inventiveness of man shall not be dedicated to his death, but consecrated to his life'.[47] A new nuclear order requires a similar embrace of peaceful nuclear energy – not merely a more permissive stance towards civil nuclear expansion but also the extension of technical assistance and financing to facilitate it. Notwithstanding the security implications now understood to have arisen from Eisenhower's initiative, the risks of a modern Atoms for Peace programme must be weighed against the dangers of inaction.[48] The potential collapse of the nuclear order and the climate crisis are immediate perils. Forgoing an effort that would ameliorate both simply to avoid a theoretical and eminently manageable security challenge, which may materialise anyway, would surely be incomprehensible to future generations.

Cost reductions in building nuclear reactors, particularly Small Modular Reactor units, have coincided with urgent and growing energy needs worldwide, particularly in the developing world. A range of humanitarian applications is now imaginable in light of advances in safe, affordable nuclear power, such as dotting the coastlines of the Global South with inexpensive modular reactors to desalinate seawater for agriculture on a grand scale, ensuring that food supplies keep pace with population growth. With almost three billion people worldwide still cooking meals on makeshift stoves fuelled by crop waste, wood, coal and animal dung, the allure of widespread carbon-free electricity should supersede any squeamishness about the creeping proliferation of nuclear weapons.[49]

A new peaceful nuclear-energy initiative would naturally have to resolve the complexities that bedevilled previous efforts such as the Global Nuclear Energy Partnership, not least the implicit reinforcement of a nuclear caste system. Distinguishing between fuel-supplier states, which would provide uranium and take back spent fuel, and fuel-user nations, which would be discouraged from enriching and reprocessing nuclear fuel, is the sort of imperiousness that so irritates the nuclear have-nots. Although generous financing packages for nuclear newcomers might make the construct palatable in the near term, a more durable system would ultimately have to account for the ambitions of states that wish to master the nuclear-fuel cycle, under appropriate IAEA strictures, free of the disparaging gaze of self-appointed nuclear guardians. To reinforce the peaceful use of nuclear energy, the substantial subsidies provided to the nuclear industry through federal loans and grants should be focused on reactor technologies that can be licensed and deployed quickly with fuels that carry a low risk of theft and use in weapons.

The ultimate end of a novel multilateral arms-control agreement and a new framework for civil nuclear cooperation is the enactment of a rejuvenated NPT with a stable foundation. Such a treaty would register the reality of the nuclear landscape by acknowledging the present possessors of nuclear arms while setting less utopian objectives for global security than the chimera of nuclear abolition. The new treaty should empower the IAEA with a broader and more muscular mission in arms-control verification, giving non-nuclear member states a tangible role in arbitrating the behaviour of the nuclear powers. This enhanced IAEA would require a new commitment from member states to provide the resources, facility access and personnel required for the agency to succeed in its verification mission.

A new NPT would require acknowledgement that member states that have mastered the nuclear-fuel cycle are 'hedge states' – nations that possess the material and technology to build nuclear weapons but choose not to do so. It will not be possible to verify that such countries cannot sprint to develop the bomb in relatively short order. Provisions of the new NPT would need to account for this reality by providing for invasive inspections and eliciting new commitments to non-proliferation and robust security around nuclear facilities to ensure weapons-useable materials remain under state control. Although this arrangement would extend the inequity of codifying privileges to some states that are not enjoyed by all, expanding the number of the former while cleaving more closely to the spirit of the original treaty by advancing civil nuclear energy for the latter could be sufficient to secure its ratification.

*   *   *

The case made here for the looming collapse of the nuclear order could be overstated, and despair unwarranted. Several eminent scholars have pointedly dismissed concerns that the present threats to the order are especially grave, arguing that even the most likely agents of disruption – Russia and China – can ultimately be relied upon to fortify the extant system.[50] Yet an event that is at once low-probability and high-consequence may entail enormous risk, so the danger of the order's disintegration should be considered quite grave. The implications would be so calamitous and far-reaching as to merit extraordinary attention to the mere possibility of its occurrence.

At this juncture, due focus appears to be lacking. Nuclear policymaking is too often seen as a niche functional activity rather than a broadly based one central to the world order. Moreover, there is scant evidence of the political and diplomatic creativity that once birthed the near miracle of the nuclear order in the first place – no 'Nixon goes to China' moment that might catalyse a major pivot in international nuclear cooperation appears to be in the offing. A more useful intellectual exercise than cataloguing the reasons a new order cannot be erected would be to imagine the strife and insecurity of a world a decade or two hence without one at all.

Notes

1   President of Russia, 'Joint Statement of the Russian Federation and the People's Republic of China on the International Relations Entering a New Era and the Global Sustainable Development', 4 February 2022, http://en.kremlin.ru/supplement/5770.

2   See, respectively, US Department of Defense, '2022 Nuclear Posture Review', October 2022, https://media.defense.gov/2022/Oct/27/2003103845/-1/-1/1/2022-NATIONAL-DEFENSE-STRATEGY-NPR-MDR.PDF; and Madelyn R. Creedon et al., 'America's Strategic Posture: The Final Report of the Congressional Commission on the Strategic Posture of the United States', October 2023, https://armed-services.house.gov/sites/republicans.

armedservices.house.gov/files/Strategic-Posture-Committee-Report-Final.pdf.

3   See Robert Gordon Kaufman, *Arms Control During the Pre-nuclear Era: The United States and Naval Limitation Between the Two World Wars* (New York: Columbia University Press, 1990).

4   See Klaus P. Fischer, *Nazi Germany: A New History* (New York: Continuum, 1995), p. 408.

5   See, respectively, Terence Neilan, 'Bush Pulls Out of ABM Treaty; Putin Calls Move a Mistake', *New York Times*, 13 December 2001, https://www.nytimes.com/2001/12/13/international/bush-pulls-out-of-abm-treaty-putin-calls-move-a-mistake.html; Mark Landler, 'Trump

Abandons Iran Nuclear Deal He Long Scorned', *New York Times*, 8 May 2018, https://www.nytimes.com/2018/05/08/world/middleeast/trump-iran-nuclear-deal.html; Shannon Bugos, 'US Completes INF Treaty Withdrawal', *Arms Control Today*, September 2019, https://www.armscontrol.org/act/2019-09/news/us-completes-inf-treaty-withdrawal; and Kingston Reif and Shannon Bugos, 'US Completes Open Skies Treaty Withdrawal', *Arms Control Today*, December 2020, https://www.armscontrol.org/act/2020-12/news/us-completes-open-skies-treaty-withdrawal.

6   See Mary Ilyushina, Robyn Dixon and Niha Masih, 'Putin Says Russia Will Suspend Role in New START Nuclear Accord with US', *Washington Post*, 21 February 2023, https://www.washingtonpost.com/world/2023/02/21/putin-speech-ukraine-state-of-nation/.

7   White House, 'President Biden Statement Ahead of the 10th Review Conference of the Treaty on the Non-Proliferation of Nuclear Weapons', 1 August 2022, https://www.whitehouse.gov/briefing-room/statements-releases/2022/08/01/president-biden-statement-ahead-of-the-10th-review-conference-of-the-treaty-on-the-non-proliferation-of-nuclear-weapons/.

8   See Filipp Lebedev and Mark Trevelyan, 'Russia Passes Law Pulling Ratification of Nuclear Test Ban Treaty', Reuters, 25 October 2023, https://www.reuters.com/world/europe/russian-upper-house-approves-de-ratification-nuclear-test-ban-treaty-2023-10-25.

9   See David E. Sanger, William J. Broad and Chris Buckley, '3 Nuclear Superpowers, Rather Than 2, Usher in a New Strategic Era', *New York Times*, 19 April 2023, https://www.nytimes.com/2023/04/19/us/politics/china-nuclear-weapons-russia-arms-treaties.html.

10 'Transcript: Senator John F. Kennedy and Vice President Richard M. Nixon, Third Joint Radio–Television Broadcast, 13 October 1960', available from the John F. Kennedy Presidential Library and Museum, https://www.jfklibrary.org/archives/other-resources/john-f-kennedy-speeches/3rd-nixon-kennedy-debate-19601013.

11 See 'Treaty on the Non-Proliferation of Nuclear Weapons', available from the United Nations Office for Disarmament Affairs, https://disarmament.unoda.org/wmd/nuclear/npt/text/.

12 United States Senate Committee on Armed Services, 'Testimony of Secretary of Energy Jennifer Granholm and Under Secretary for Nuclear Security Jill Hruby Before the Senate Committee on Armed Services', 19 May 2022, https://www.armed-services.senate.gov/imo/media/doc/5.19.22%20SASC%20Secretary%20Granholm%20and%20NNSA%20Hruby%20Testimony.pdf.

13 HM Government, 'Global Britain in a Competitive Age: The Integrated Review of Security, Defence, Development and Foreign Policy', March 2021, p. 76.

14 See Timothy Wright and Hugo Decis, 'Counting the Cost of Deterrence: France's Nuclear Recapitalisation', International Institute for Strategic

Studies, Military Balance Blog, 14 May 2021, https://www.iiss.org/online-analysis//military-balance/2021/05/france-nuclear-recapitalisation.

15 See Joseph Trevithick, 'Russia Releases Videos Offering an Unprecedented Look at Its Six New Super Weapons', *Drive*, 19 July 2018, https://www.thedrive.com/the-war-zone/22270/russia-releases-videos-offering-an-unprecedented-look-at-its-six-new-super-weapons.

16 See Jeffrey Lewis, 'China's Orbital Bombardment System Is Big, Bad News – but Not a Breakthrough', *Foreign Policy*, 18 October 2021, https://foreignpolicy.com/2021/10/18/hypersonic-china-missile-nuclear-fobs/; and Joby Warrick, 'China Is Building More than 100 New Missile Silos in Its Western Desert, Analysts Say', *Washington Post*, 30 June 2021, https://www.washingtonpost.com/national-security/china-nuclear-missile-silos/2021/06/30/0fa8debc-d9c2-11eb-bb9e-70fda8c37057_story.html.

17 See Nick Childs, 'The AUKUS Anvil: Promise and Peril', *Survival*, vol. 65, no. 5, October–November 2023, pp. 7–24.

18 Harshit Prajapati, 'Bad Precedent: Has AUKUS Torpedoed the Nuclear Nonproliferation Regime?', *National Interest*, 28 August 2022, https://nationalinterest.org/blog/buzz/bad-precedent-has-aukus-torpedoed-nuclear-nonproliferation-regime-204472.

19 See Rebecca Davis Gibbons, 'The Humanitarian Turn in Nuclear Disarmament and the Treaty on the Prohibition of Nuclear Weapons', *Nonproliferation Review*, vol. 25, nos 1–2, July 2018, pp. 11–36.

20 See 'US Negative Security Assurances at a Glance', *Arms Control Today*, March 2018, https://www.armscontrol.org/factsheets/negsec.

21 See Armin Rosen, 'NATO Report: A 2013 Russian Aerial Exercise Was Actually a "Simulated Nuclear Attack" on Sweden', *Business Insider*, 3 February 2016, https://www.businessinsider.com/nato-report-russia-sweden-nuclear-2016-2.

22 Uri Friedman, 'Putin's Nuclear Threats Are a Wake-up Call for the World', *Atlantic*, 15 March 2022, https://www.theatlantic.com/ideas/archive/2022/03/putin-nuclear-weapons-system-presidential-power/627058/.

23 See Min Joo Kim, 'North Korea Codifies Right to Launch Preemptive Nuclear Strikes', *Washington Post*, 9 September 2022, https://www.washingtonpost.com/world/2022/09/09/north-korea-nuclear-weapons-kim-jong-un/.

24 See Mark McDonald, 'North Korea Suggests Libya Should Have Kept Nuclear Program', *New York Times*, 24 March 2011, https://www.nytimes.com/2011/03/25/world/asia/25korea.html.

25 See William J. Broad, 'Ukraine Gave Up a Giant Nuclear Arsenal 30 Years Ago. Today There Are Regrets', *New York Times*, 5 February 2022, https://www.nytimes.com/2022/02/05/science/ukraine-nuclear-weapons.html.

26 Connor Echols, 'A Supermajority of South Koreans Want Nukes: Polls', *Responsible Statecraft*, 7 March 2023, https://responsiblestatecraft.org/2023/03/06/a-supermajority-of-south-koreans-want-nukes-polls/.

27 See S. Nathan Park, 'South Korea Floats Building Nukes amid US Neglect', *Responsible Statecraft*, 23 January 2023, https://responsiblestatecraft.org/2023/01/23/south-korea-floats-building-nukes-amid-us-neglect/.

28 See Jonathon Baron, Rebecca Davis Gibbons and Stephen Herzog, 'Japanese Public Opinion, Political Persuasion, and the Treaty on the Prohibition of Nuclear Weapons', *Journal for Peace and Nuclear Disarmament*, vol. 30, no. 2, December 2020, pp. 299–309.

29 See Justin Ryall, 'Shinzo Abe's Government Insists Japanese Constitution Does Not Explicitly Prohibit Nuclear Weapons', *South China Morning Post*, 4 April 2016, https://www.scmp.com/news/asia/east-asia/article/1933540/shinzo-abes-government-insists-japanese-constitution-does-not.

30 See Kartike Garg and Rahul Jaybhay, 'After Ukraine, Will More Countries Want Nukes?', *National Interest*, 10 July 2022, https://nationalinterest.org/blog/buzz/after-ukraine-will-more-countries-want-nukes-203474.

31 See Office of the Director of National Intelligence, '2022 Annual Threat Assessment of the US Intelligence Community', February 2022, https://www.dni.gov/files/ODNI/documents/assessments/ATA-2022-Unclassified-Report.pdf.

32 Quoted in Julian Borger, 'Crown Prince Confirms Saudi Arabia Will Seek Nuclear Arsenal if Iran Develops One', *Guardian*, 21 September 2023, https://www.theguardian.com/world/2023/sep/21/crown-prince-confirms-saudi-arabia-seek-nuclear-arsenal-iran-develops-one.

33 Quoted in Mark Hibbs, 'Scratching Erdogan's Nuclear Itch', Carnegie Endowment for International Peace, 22 October 2019, https://carnegieendowment.org/2019/10/22/scratching-erdogan-s-nuclear-itch-pub-80178.

34 Quoted in John Mecklin, 'Siegfried Hecker: Putin Has Destroyed the World Nuclear Order. How Should the Democracies Respond?', *Bulletin of the Atomic Scientists*, 21 April 2022, https://thebulletin.org/2022/04/siegfried-hecker-putin-has-destroyed-the-world-nuclear-order-how-should-the-democracies-respond/.

35 Quoted in Neil MacFarquhar and David E. Sanger, 'Putin's "Invincible" Missile Is Aimed at US Vulnerabilities', *New York Times*, 1 March 2018, https://www.nytimes.com/2018/03/01/world/europe/russia-putin-speech.html.

36 See, for example, Morton H. Halperin, 'The Decision to Deploy the ABM: Bureaucratic and Domestic Politics in the Johnson Administration', *World Politics*, vol. 25, no. 1, October 1972, pp. 62–95.

37 US Department of Defense, '2022 Missile Defense Review', October 2022, p. 6, https://media.defense.gov/2022/Oct/27/2003103845/-1/-1/1/2022-NATIONAL-DEFENSE-STRATEGY-NPR-MDR.PDF.

38 See John Bolton, 'Missile Defense Is More Urgent Than Ever', *Wall Street Journal*, 13 November 2022, https://www.wsj.com/articles/missile-defense-is-more-urgent-than-ever-national-security-russia-china-iran-north-

korea-icbm-hypersonics-rogue-state-11668349181.

39 See United States Strategic Command (@US_STRATCOM), post to X, 11 July 2020, https://twitter.com/US_STRATCOM/status/1281965335944495105.

40 Office of the Secretary of Defense, 'Annual Report to Congress: Military and Security Developments Involving the People's Republic of China, 2021', 3 November 2021, https://media.defense.gov/2021/Nov/03/2002885874/-1/-1/0/2021-CMPR-FINAL.PDF.

41 Jeffrey Lewis (@ArmsControl Wonk), post to X, 29 May 2022, https://twitter.com/ArmsControlWonk/status/1530979506927939587.

42 Joseph R. Biden, Jr, 'Why America Must Lead Again', *Foreign Affairs*, vol. 99, no. 2, March–April 2020, p. 75.

43 See Daryl G. Kimball, 'Biden Policy Allows First Use of Nuclear Weapons', *Arms Control Today*, April 2022, https://www.armscontrol.org/act/2022-04/news/biden-policy-allows-first-use-nuclear-weapons.

44 See Austin Long and Brendan Rittenhouse Green, 'Stalking the Secure Second Strike: Intelligence, Counterforce, and Nuclear Strategy', *Journal of Strategic Studies*, vol. 38, nos 1–2, January 2015, pp. 38–73.

45 See George Bush, 'Address to the Nation on Reducing United States and Soviet Nuclear Weapons', 27 September 1991, available from the American Presidency Project, University of California at Santa Barbara, https://www.presidency.ucsb.edu/documents/address-the-nation-reducing-united-states-and-soviet-nuclear-weapons.

46 See Toby Dalton and Ankit Panda, 'US Policy Should Reflect Its Own Quiet Acceptance of a Nuclear North Korea', Carnegie Endowment for International Peace, 15 November 2022, https://carnegieendowment.org/2022/11/15/u.s.-policy-should-reflect-its-own-quiet-acceptance-of-nuclear-north-korea-pub-88399.

47 Dwight D. Eisenhower, 'Atoms for Peace', Speech to the UN General Assembly, 8 December 1953, available from the International Atomic Energy Agency, https://www.iaea.org/about/history/atoms-for-peace-speech.

48 See Matthew Fuhrmann, *Atomic Assistance: How 'Atoms for Peace' Programs Cause Nuclear Insecurity* (Ithaca, NY: Cornell University Press, 2012).

49 See World Health Organization, 'WHO Publishes New Global Data on the Use of Clean and Polluting Fuels for Cooking by Fuel Type', 20 January 2022, https://www.who.int/news/item/20-01-2022-who-publishes-new-global-data-on-the-use-of-clean-and-polluting-fuels-for-cooking-by-fuel-type.

50 See, for example, Alexander K. Bollfrass and Stephen Herzog, 'The War in Ukraine and Global Nuclear Order', *Survival*, vol. 64, no. 4, August–September 2022, pp. 7–32.

China's Legal Diplomacy

Lynn Kuok

China is engaging in a broad and systematic effort to align its legal capabilities with its strategic goals in the South China Sea and the Taiwan Strait, and may seek to do so outside of Asia in places as far afield as the Arctic and Antarctic. While its assertive 'wolf-warrior diplomacy' has received considerable attention, its legal diplomacy has largely gone under the radar. Despite their insistence on the importance of a rules-based international order, the United States and other Western powers have been less proactive and methodical in their use of international law.

There is, of course, nothing inherently problematic about using international law to achieve strategic ends, especially when compared to alternatives like the use of force. Beijing's bolstering of its international legal capacity, moreover, is understandable given its late start to developing such capabilities, which had been sorely missing given the country's initial absence from and unfamiliarity with the international institutions in which the conduct of international legal policies and practice take place, such as the United Nations and the World Trade Organization.[1] But to the extent that China is seeking to reshape and, in some cases, fill gaps in international law, governments that care about the rule of law as we know it today, or that are concerned about China's intentions and ultimate goals, should be alert to Chinese behaviour.

Lynn Kuok is IISS Shangri-La Dialogue Senior Fellow for Asia-Pacific Security and co-editor of the IISS's *Asia-Pacific Regional Security Assessment*.

Survival | vol. 65 no. 6 | December 2023–January 2024 | pp. 159–178 https://doi.org/10.1080/00396338.2023.2285610

China's evolving attitude

From the founding of the People's Republic of China in 1949 through to the start of the Reforming and Opening-up Policy in the late 1970s, China was 'highly critical' of the international legal order and had little engagement with international law. It adopted an approach of 'selective adaptation', whereby it refrained from substantially committing to or simply rejected international legal regimes, which it considered itself to have played at best a minor role in creating. Since the late 1970s, however, China has gradually embraced international legal regimes, adopting 'progressive compliance' and 'paper compliance' approaches.[2]

In 1996, Jiang Zemin, then Chinese president, warned at a meeting organised by the Central Committee of the Chinese Communist Party that China's relative ignorance about international law put it at a strategic disadvantage.[3] He called on China to become 'adept at using international law as a weapon to safeguard our national interests and national dignity, to uphold international justice, and to firmly grasp the initiative in international cooperation and struggle'.[4] This set in train two developments. In 1999, two Chinese military researchers published a book, *Unrestricted Warfare*, that repeatedly referenced the need to use law as a weapon to advance what they called 'legal warfare'.[5] In 2002, the People's Liberation Army (PLA) approved a regulation stipulating that the PLA avail itself of 'legal warfare', 'psychological warfare' and 'media warfare'.[6] Hu Jintao, Jiang's successor, in justifying the impending enactment of the Anti-Secession Law, which enshrined the policy of using military means to prevent Taiwan's secession, declared in December 2004 that 'the active use of legal weapons is an important means for us to contain the "Taiwan independence" secessionist forces and their activities and to promote the process of peaceful reunification of the motherland'.[7] In 2014, President Xi Jinping insisted that all countries 'jointly safeguard the authority and solemnity of international law and international order', 'oppose the distortion of international law, and oppose the violation of the legitimate rights and interests of other countries and the destruction of peace and stability in the name of "rule of law"'.[8]

Xi's 2014 speech, and a later one at the Boao Forum for Asia in 2021,[9] may have eschewed any language depicting law as a weapon, but there was little to indicate that China's view of international law and the purposes it serves had softened. Indeed, China's concerns about the international security environment have since become more acute. The US and China are engaged in intense competition, and international law is one arena in which the rivalry is playing out. Furthermore, China's leaders now believe that international law can play a key role in legitimising and advancing China's rise. Congyan Cai, a leading Chinese legal scholar, writing in 2019, indicated that he expected China to improve its record of compliance with international law. (In making this claim, he did not address Beijing's rejection of an international-tribunal ruling in a case the Philippines brought against China on the South China Sea.) He explained that it will not only have more resources and knowledge available to do so, but also 'may recognize that better compliance can enhance the legitimacy of its rise in the long run'. Cai also expected China to intensify its 'norm entrepreneurship'. As he put it: 'China not only seeks to better accommodate international law. It also seeks international law to better accommodate China.'[10]

China's legal diplomacy does not operate in a vacuum, of course, and is part of a broader effort to augment China's soft power. Success in that effort has been fitful and geographically uneven. It arguably peaked in 2008, when China hosted the Summer Olympics. Since then, China's attractiveness has diminished due to its increasing assertiveness in the South China Sea and over Taiwan, and, in the West, to its wolf-warrior diplomacy, ham-fisted response to the coronavirus pandemic, and perceptions of increasing cooperation with Moscow since Russia's invasion of Ukraine. Meanwhile, China has ramped up its practice of legal diplomacy in the security realm, most notably in the South China Sea, where Beijing's legal efforts have been at their most focused, sophisticated and sustained, and in the Taiwan Strait, where there has been a renewed emphasis on legal diplomacy as tensions there have once again increased.

The South China Sea

Beijing's concerted legal diplomacy has allowed it to exploit grey areas in the law to build on and militarise land features that are subject to competing claims to sovereignty, lay claim to economic rights in coastal states' exclusive economic zones (EEZs), and contest the lawful exercise of passage rights and freedoms of the seas by naval powers in the South China Sea. In this effort, China has deliberately kept its territorial and maritime claims ambiguous. China's first official reference to a controversial dashed line, which encompasses much of the South China Sea but for which Beijing has never provided coordinates, was in a submission on 7 May 2009 to the United Nations Commission on the Limits of the Continental Shelf. Beijing stated that 'China has indisputable sovereignty over the islands in the South China Sea and the adjacent waters, and enjoys sovereign rights and jurisdiction over the relevant waters as well as the seabed and subsoil thereof'.[11]

Beijing has not clarified what it is claiming by way of the dashed line. There are at least three different interpretations of the line: firstly, it could represent a claim of sovereignty over islands and to maritime zones generated from them in accordance with the United Nations Convention on the Law of the Sea (UNCLOS); secondly, the line might indicate a national boundary between China and neighbouring states; and thirdly, it could define a 'historic' claim over maritime space, which might be a sovereignty claim or a claim to a lesser set of rights to that space. Only the first interpretation could be consistent with the international law of the sea.

China has kept its claims ambiguous

China has taken advantage of the lack of legal clarity under general international law about the rights of occupying states on disputed land to build on and militarise contested features in the South China Sea. It continues to fortify Mischief Reef, which an international tribunal has since found to be a low-tide elevation within the Philippines' EEZ, even though the tribunal held that this was unlawful on the ground that coastal states have sovereign rights and jurisdiction over low-tide features in their EEZs.[12] Beijing has ignored the distinction between high-tide and low-tide features.

China has also encroached on coastal states' exclusive economic rights on nebulous and shifting legal grounds. Initially emphasising the dashed line and 'historic rights', more recently China has appeared to treat the groups of features in the South China Sea as single units from which maritime zones may be established.[13] It has pushed this argument despite the international tribunal's clear ruling that China, as a continental state, cannot draw archipelagic straight baselines (the starting points from which maritime zones are measured) around the Spratly Islands, which were the focus of the Philippines' case and the tribunal's decision, even if the conditions set out in UNCLOS on the use of archipelagic straight baselines were met.[14]

In addition, Beijing has pushed unsupportable interpretations of UNCLOS on passage and high-seas freedoms. It has denied that warships are entitled to innocent passage in its territorial seas without obtaining prior authorisation, citing domestic legislation.[15] The convention does not set out any such requirement. Beijing has also objected to the conduct of military exercises, including surveillance activities, in its EEZ, although it has not passed domestic legislation barring military activities in this zone. UNCLOS specifies that vessels enjoy in EEZs the same 'freedoms … of navigation and overflight … and other internationally lawful uses of the sea' as they do on the high seas, subject only to the obligation to pay 'due regard' to the rights and duties of the coastal state.[16] Military activities, including surveillance, are regarded by the majority of states as an internationally lawful use of the sea, and UNCLOS makes it clear that China's 'sovereign rights' to its EEZ are limited to the exploration, exploitation, conservation and management of living and non-living resources.[17] Live-fire exercises could conceivably damage Chinese resources, but short of such damage occurring, China has no basis for objecting to foreign military activities.

China has connected the outermost points of its coast and the outermost points of the outermost Paracel Islands, in the western part of the South China Sea, when the requirements under UNCLOS for doing so (a deeply indented coast, a fringe of islands, or being an archipelagic state) are not met. The default baselines under UNCLOS are normal baselines, which hug the coast, following its contours. The waters extending landward from straight baselines are internal, with the same legal character as land, requiring the coastal state's authorisation to enter and pass. China's use of straight baselines, rather than normal baselines, along its mainland coast and around the Paracel Islands effectively expands its maritime zones seaward and unlawfully seeks to convert waters landward of those straight baselines to internal waters. China appears to have objected to passage by American and British vessels near the Paracel Islands on this basis. China has also left open the possibility of drawing straight baselines around the Spratlys.[18]

Finally, China has rejected the July 2016 international-tribunal ruling in the Philippines' case against China on the basis that the tribunal had no jurisdiction to hear the case. Beijing argues that a court or tribunal constituted under UNCLOS has jurisdiction only to hear matters concerning the 'interpretation or application' of UNCLOS and that the tribunal ruled *ultra vires* by ruling on issues of sovereignty.[19] However, the tribunal ruled not on sovereignty over land features but rather on the status of features and their respective maritime entitlements. China's position has not been that it rejects international law, as critics sometimes maintain; rather, it claims that its positions are in keeping with and bolster international law.[20]

China set up the Collaborative Innovation Center of South China Sea Studies, established by the government in 2012 as one of 14 national research projects for the study of maritime issues, and the National Institute for South China Sea Studies, founded in 1996 and affiliated with China's Foreign Ministry and State Oceanic Administration, to push its claims in the South China Sea. The purportedly unaffiliated South China Sea Strategic Situation Probing Initiative, formed in April 2019, seeks to provide an 'objective perspective and accurately observe the area [of the South China Sea] within the parameters of its military, political, economic and environmental contexts'.[21] The efforts of centres and initiatives focused on legitimising China's South China Sea claims have been complemented by Chinese think tanks, including the China Institute of International Studies and the Chinese Academy of Social Sciences.[22]

China has also relied on domestic laws and regulations in seeking to increase its control over the South China Sea. Since 1999, China has imposed an annual moratorium on fishing in the waters between 12°N and 26°30′N in the South China and East China seas. It justifies this restriction based on a desire to 'strengthen the protection of marine fishery resources and promote the harmonious coexistence of human and nature'.[23] But by covering essentially all of the South China Sea, which includes the EEZs of other coastal states, China is effectively claiming extra-jurisdictional control. In 2021, Beijing enacted the Coast Guard Law, permitting China's coastguard to use force to defend China's 'jurisdictional waters' and empowering it to remove structures built by other countries on features claimed by China. Given Beijing's expansive interpretation of 'jurisdictional waters' – a term not mentioned in UNCLOS – an application by China of the Coast Guard Law could pose the risk of military escalation. In addition, China has revised its 1984 Maritime Traffic Safety Law to require foreign vessels to 'report their detailed information' when entering Chinese territorial seas. UNCLOS imposes no such requirement for ships exercising innocent passage, and the requirement contravenes the duty of the coastal state not to interfere with innocent passage in territorial seas.

The Taiwan Strait

The Taiwan Strait has been a major flashpoint in US–China relations, especially since the Trump administration initiated a trade and technology war with China and enhanced relations with Taiwan. China has objected to routine navigation by the US and other countries' navies. In some cases, its response has been aggressive and dangerous. In June 2023, a Chinese warship cut across the bow of a US guided-missile destroyer and sailed within 137 metres of the US destroyer conducting a transit with a Canadian frigate.[24]

Beijing has asserted 'sovereignty, sovereign rights and jurisdiction over the Taiwan Strait' and denied that it constitutes international waters.[25] The first claim is consistent with UNCLOS as long as claims to sovereignty and to sovereign rights and jurisdiction over the Taiwan Strait are over a territorial sea and EEZ, respectively, and sovereign rights and jurisdiction over the EEZ are limited to the sovereign rights to explore, exploit, conserve and manage natural resources, and jurisdiction to establish and use artificial islands, installations and structures, conduct marine scientific research, and protect and preserve the marine environment.[26] The second assertion is technically correct insofar as the term 'international waters' does not appear in UNCLOS. This does not, however, mean that non-Chinese vessels and aircraft, particularly military ones, have no rights to operate in the Taiwan Strait. As noted, such craft enjoy the same 'freedoms … of navigation and overflight … and other internationally lawful uses of the sea' in EEZs as they do on the high seas, subject only to the obligation to pay 'due regard' to the rights and duties of the coastal state.[27]

Beijing's assertions have produced concerns that China is claiming sovereignty over the Taiwan Strait. US officials are worried that China's denial that the Taiwan Strait constitutes 'international waters' may be intended to deter the US from sailing through the strait.[28] China has not clarified its statements, which it has probably kept vague to discourage risk-averse countries from asserting passage and freedoms of the seas.[29]

In the domestic sphere, Article 13 of China's 1998 Law on the Territorial Sea and the Contiguous Zone of the Republic of China appears to adopt Article 42 of UNCLOS, which permits states bordering straits to impose laws and regulations regulating transit through straits. But Article 13 of the domestic statute contravenes UNCLOS insofar as the latter provides that Article 42 'does not apply to a strait used for international navigation if there exists through the strait a route through the high seas or through an exclusive economic zone of similar convenience with respect to navigation and hydrographical characteristics'. In such routes, Article 36 stipulates, 'the other relevant Parts of this Convention, including the provisions regarding the freedoms of navigation and overflight, apply'. The Taiwan Strait, which is roughly 96 nautical miles at its widest and 70 nautical miles at its narrowest, includes an EEZ beyond the 12-nautical-mile territorial sea measured from the baselines of both the Chinese mainland and Taiwan. In this EEZ band, freedoms of the seas apply. Article 58(1) of the Convention provides that all states enjoy, in areas beyond the territorial sea, the high-seas 'freedoms ... of navigation and overflight ... and other internationally lawful uses of the sea related to these freedoms'.

Effectiveness of China's legal diplomacy

The effectiveness of China's legal diplomacy must be assessed against its ability to advance Beijing's goals. For China, as for many countries, international law is a means rather than an end, instrumentalised to advance national interests. The 'Science of Military Strategy', issued by China's National Defence University, states that 'when international law conflicts with national interests ... national interests are above all else'.[30] In the context of legal diplomacy, China's goals include the successful persuasion of third parties of the legitimacy of the country's position and imposing constraints on third-party action in China's favour. A notable attempt at influencing public opinion to accept the legitimacy of China's claims was the screening of a 'documentary' on the South China Sea in New York City's Times Square by its state media outlet, Xinhua.[31] The video aired from 23 July to 3 August 2016 at considerable expense.[32] While summer tourists in New York may not have been the best target audience, the effort was nonetheless striking.

China's efforts to reshape international law in the context of the South China Sea might look silly in the West, but they have gained traction in other parts of the world, including Asia. It is true that Indonesia, Malaysia and Vietnam have come to explicitly or implicitly endorse the international-tribunal ruling in the Philippines' case against China.[33] Malaysia, the Philippines and Vietnam have also rejected, and Brunei and Indonesia have questioned, China's latest map of the South China Sea.[34] But some of these states still subscribe to restrictive legal interpretations of maritime passage and freedoms of the seas similar to China's. Vietnam's domestic legislation, for instance, mandates that warships must provide prior notification before exercising innocent passage in a country's territorial sea, even though UNCLOS mandates no such thing. Malaysia, like China, objects to military activities in its EEZ.[35]

Moreover, even if formally opposed to China's territorial and maritime claims, Southeast Asian claimant states in practice sometimes overlook Chinese incursions.[36] For instance, in 2020, Hishammuddin Hussein, then Malaysia's foreign minister, stated publicly that in his 100 days of helming the Ministry of Foreign Affairs, 'Chinese vessels have not been seen in our waters'.[37] He soon had to walk this statement back when it emerged that a Chinese survey vessel, the Chinese Coast Guard and Chinese fishing militia were present in Malaysia's EEZ in April and May. Governments often turn a blind eye to China's incursions to avoid what would likely be a futile confrontation with a militarily powerful neighbour. They also do not wish to jeopardise economic ties: China continues to be regarded as by far the most influential economic power in the region.[38]

In addition, China's legal arguments help justify pro-China stances on the part of governments, senior officials, business communities and ethnic Chinese communities. This author had an extensive email exchange with a senior Southeast Asian former diplomat who essentially reiterated China's points on the South China Sea, denying that the international tribunal had jurisdiction to hear the Philippines' case and asserting that it was politically motivated in doing so. In making China's case, he cited an *amicus curiae* (literally, 'friend of court') brief submitted to the UN tribunal by the Asia Pacific Institute of International Law (APIIL) on 6 June 2016. The APIIL, which had been established less than two months prior, described itself as 'an independent, non-profit, non-governmental organization … governed by the laws of Hong Kong comprising by way of membership academics and legal practitioners'.[39] Barristers and legal experts from Australia, Hong Kong and the United Kingdom signed off on the brief.

China's arguments have also found some support in the broader Global South, and even among some Western intellectuals.[40] Such support has been reported in Chinese state media and highlighted in opinion pieces.[41] This author has also personally noted support for China's legal arguments on its position in the South China Sea among prominent Western experts on the international law of the sea, though they are in the minority. One argument raised is that it was 'difficult' for the tribunal to pronounce on the dashed line as there was 'no indication' that the convention was intended to do away with historic title (over which the tribunal would have no jurisdiction).[42] Beyond anecdotal evidence, of course, it is difficult to measure popular support for China's position in the South China Sea. But concern about its strength, particularly among Singapore's majority ethnic-Chinese community, led the prime minister of Singapore to raise the UN tribunal's award in his 2016 National Day Rally, at the risk of incurring China's ire.[43]

Building legal capacity

Beijing is boosting legal capacity in the broader maritime and non-maritime domains, no doubt encouraged by its (qualified) success in the South China Sea. As Cai notes, China in recent years has made more efforts

> to improve the legal capability of government officials, enhanced public–private partnership (PPP) including frequently inviting international lawyers to participate in treaty negotiations, financing international

lawyers to conduct background researches, and encouraging international lawyers to defend Chinese international legal policies and practices, and has encouraged Chinese law firms to develop international legal service.[44]

Quantitative data is scarce, but China's decisions to recommend or fund legal research into specific areas is an important indicator of its strategic priorities.

With invaluable research assistance, I conducted a study of state-supported 'Recommended Research Topics' and 'Funded Research Proposals' on international law during the period 2015–22, relying on data from the National Social Science Fund of China, which provides the only publicly accessible data for academic-research funding in China. The study was loosely modelled on an earlier 2009–14 study by Anthea Roberts, a professor of international law at the Australian National University.[45] While the information is limited to the number of projects recommended and funded, and does not include monetary amounts granted, several notable points did emerge. International economic law was the most recommended and funded topic, and international environmental law the second-most recommended and fourth-most funded topic. The Law of the Sea remains important, having fallen only marginally to the third-most recommended topic and second-most funded topic after being the second-most recommended and funded topic in 2009–14. China recommended and funded new topics during the period of the study, such as the Belt and Road Initiative (BRI), unveiled in 2013, and international health, and attention to existing areas such as outer-space law increased. The BRI is the second-most recommended subject, alongside international environmental law, and the third-most funded subject.

The broad trajectory of its legal diplomacy is clear: Beijing is investing resources into developing its ability to shape and reshape international law in areas of strategic interest. Its legal diplomacy is most advanced in the South China Sea and to a lesser extent the Taiwan Strait, although China appears to also be laying the foundations for it in other areas. While there was a drop in the number of research projects on the Arctic and Antarctic funded from the first to the second period, China is likely to invest more in research into these topics as climate change opens new sea routes in the Arctic, Beijing increases its presence in both areas amid intensifying geopolitical competition, and concerns mount over China's actions and intentions there. For instance, in August 2022, NATO Secretary General Jens Stoltenberg warned that China was expanding its reach, declaring itself a 'near-Arctic state', planning a 'Polar Silk Road' linking China to Europe via the Arctic, rapidly strengthening its navy, building the world's biggest icebreaker vessel, and investing tens of billions of dollars in energy, infrastructure and research projects in the region. He underlined Beijing and Moscow's pledge earlier in the year to intensify practical cooperation in the Arctic as part of a deepening strategic partnership that challenges NATO's 'values and interests'.[46]

No comprehensive treaty system applies specifically to Arctic affairs, and China does not claim sovereignty there. Moreover, the rights it asserts do not exceed those provided for under UNCLOS or the Svalbard Treaty, which recognises Norway's 'full and absolute sovereignty' over the Spitsbergen Archipelago (later renamed Svalbard) while conferring certain rights upon other High Contracting Parties (which includes some non-Arctic states, including China).[47] Nevertheless, China's claim that it is a 'near-Arctic state' has raised eyebrows, and Arctic states have, on national-security grounds, blocked or rescinded agreements that would have increased Chinese presence in the Arctic.[48] Although the PLA does not appear to be engaging in military activities in the Arctic,[49] concerns have arisen about its presence and ultimate intentions there.[50] The worsening geopolitical environment and the race to access more of the Arctic's resources mean that change in China's legal position cannot be ruled out. In a 2019 paper, Ma Xinmin, then deputy director-general at the Department of Treaty and Law at China's Ministry of Foreign Affairs, argued that while the international governance mechanisms on the Arctic 'should be maintained and respected, they should be also developed so as to meet the changing needs over time'.[51] China, which gained observer status on the Arctic Council in 2013, now has opportunity and strategic reasons to cooperate with Russia in the Arctic, particularly in light of calls in the US National Strategy for the Arctic Region released in October 2022 for an enhanced US military presence there.[52]

China's presence and involvement in the Antarctic has rapidly increased in the past 30 years, though Chinese scholars maintain that it remains a 'medium power' there.[53] Its presence in the Antarctic was not always viewed with the same wariness it is regarded with in some quarters today. It had, from 1985 to 2014, built up four research stations in the Antarctic and is building a fifth near the western shore of the Ross Sea, where bases owned and operated by Italy, New Zealand, South Korea and the US are already located.[54] Three of the four Antarctic research stations, three of its airfields and two of its field camps are located within the Australian Antarctic Territory – part of East Antarctica claimed by Australia.[55] Further, during President Xi's visit to Hobart in November 2014, China and Australia signed a Memorandum of Understanding on China–Australia Antarctic Cooperation agreeing to strengthen Antarctic cooperation.[56] Present concerns about China in the Antarctic include alleged sovereignty claims[57] – though China does not appear to ever have made such claims; possible exploitation of resources beyond what is permissible under UNCLOS; environmental impact; and strategic intent. Liu Huaqing, commander of the People's Liberation Army Navy (PLAN), has stated that the PLAN's expeditionary foray into the Antarctic would open new routes and enable the PLAN to move past the First Island Chain.[58] Compounding suspicions, China has failed to report military personnel and equipment it has introduced into the Antarctic, which the Antarctic Treaty requires when such assets are used 'for scientific research or for any other peaceful purpose'. The treaty further mandates that Antarctica be used 'for peaceful purposes only' and prohibits 'any measures of a military nature'.[59]

* * *

There is less evidence of a comparably systematic, sustained and integrated approach among other major powers, notwithstanding their recognition of the importance of the rule of law and their attempts to defend and promote it. In practice, the US has focused primarily on hard security, though it has lately mustered an economic response to China's growing influence in the form of the US Indo-Pacific Economic Framework. Washington did not recognise international law as an instrument of national power in its National Security Strategy. The strategy, issued in October 2022, states that the US approach 'encompasses all elements of national power – diplomacy, development cooperation, industrial strategy, economic statecraft, intelligence, and defense'.[60] While it underscores the importance of complying with and upholding international law, the US does not hold it up as a tool of statecraft. Consideration of international law as a strategic tool is similarly omitted from the 'Indo-Pacific Strategy of the United States', launched in February 2022.

Washington has also failed to fully grasp how Beijing is employing international law as an important foreign-policy tool, and to craft an appropriate response. The Indo-Pacific Strategy of the United States observes merely that 'the PRC [People's Republic of China] is combining its economic, diplomatic, military, and technological might as it pursues a sphere of influence in the Indo-Pacific and seeks to become the world's most influential power', overlooking China's increasing international legal arsenal.[61] Similarly, the US National Security Strategy states: 'The PRC is the only competitor with both the intent to reshape the international order and, increasingly, the economic, diplomatic, military, and technological power to do it.'[62]

Although Washington ultimately aligned the US position with the international tribunal's 2016 ruling, it took four years to do so, purportedly because the US claims EEZs and attendant sovereign rights and jurisdiction around features in the Pacific that would likely not meet the criteria laid down by the tribunal for what constitutes an island entitled to an EEZ. More prompt action would have reassured important Southeast Asian allies and partners that the US was interested in upholding the economic rights of coastal states, as well as passage and freedoms of the seas asserted by what the US refers to as 'freedom of navigation' operations or 'FONOPS'. While the US Department of State issued its report, 'People's Republic of China: Maritime Claims in the South China Sea', in January 2022, it was not integrated into a broader, whole-of-government effort to condemn China's expansive maritime claims and deny them legitimacy, and garnered little attention beyond a niche legal community. The US Indo-Pacific Command issues legal despatches which are targeted at the specialist community, but the messages in these despatches could be amplified if expressed less technically and adopted across government. More broadly, it would make strategic sense for the US to accede to UNCLOS, since its failure to do so allows China and other detractors to accuse it of double standards. The US should not underestimate how perceptions of double standards on issues from the South China Sea to Russia's war on Ukraine and now the conflict raging in the Middle East have undermined its position around the world. A professor of international law at the US Naval War College recently noted how, in declining to ratify UNCLOS, the US 'gave up an opportunity to exercise leadership over the development of the global oceans regime from inside its institutions'.[63]

In an age of great-power competition, countries are drawing on a diverse range of tools to gain strategic advantage. Among the major powers, China has stood out in its systematic development and deployment of legal capabilities as part of its broader national-security strategy. Countries that fail to bolster their own legal capabilities and integrate legal diplomacy into their national-security strategies may surrender the power of legitimacy to China, even if, particularly in the South China Sea, Chinese actions have indubitably contravened international law.

Acknowledgements

The author would like to express her thanks to Bryan Chang and Winston Wee for their invaluable research assistance.

Notes

1   See Congyan Cai, *The Rise of China and International Law: Taking Chinese Exceptionalism Seriously* (Oxford: Oxford University Press, 2019), ch. 5 and its references.

2   *Ibid.*, pp. 152–3.

3   This was five years before US Air Force Colonel Charles Dunlap, Jr, popularised the term 'lawfare' in English in 2001 in an essay on law and military interventions. See Charles J. Dunlap, Jr, 'Law and Military Interventions: Preserving Humanitarian Values in 21st Conflicts', prepared for the Humanitarian Challenges in Military Intervention Conference, Carr Center for Human Rights Policy, Kennedy School of Government, Harvard University, 29 November 2001. I do not use the term 'lawfare' in this piece to avoid terminological debates. In particular, the term 'lawfare' is in some cases narrowly defined to refer to the use of international law in a military context to achieve operational objectives. See, for example, Katherine French, *Law and Disorder: Lessons on Legal Diplomacy from Status of Forces Agreement Negotiations Between the United States and Iraq*, senior thesis, Princeton University, 2022.

French writes that 'lawfare' refers to 'how laws may be manipulated to directly impact operational objectives during combat'. See also a report by authors from China's National Defence University, in which they highlight that 'legal warfare' (or 'lawfare') is 'an important form of cooperating with the country's political, diplomatic, and military conflicts, and is an integral part of modern warfare operations. The legal struggle in war operations revolves around military operations as the main line, and is carried out with military strength as the backing. In the process of legal struggle, the pursuit of legal victory is not the fundamental goal, but to achieve victory in the war or create the necessary for victory.' See the translation prepared by the China Aerospace Studies Institute, 'In Their Own Words: Science of Military Strategy 2020', January 2022, p. 241, https://www.airuniversity.af.edu/Portals/10/CASI/documents/Translations/2022-01-26%20 2020%20Science%20of%20Military%20 Strategy.pdf.

4 Jiang Zemin speech as reported in the *People's Daily*, 10 December 1996, available at https://cn.govopendata.com/renminribao/1996/12/10/1/#1042267.

5 Quoted in Orde F. Kittrie, *Lawfare: Law as a Weapon of War* (Oxford: Oxford University Press, 2016), p. 5.

6 Quoted in Cai, *The Rise of China and International Law*, p. 293.

7 Guo, 郭琛, 'Hujintao wenxuan shuzhai: zhengqu taiwan minxin bushi xude ershi shide' 《胡锦涛文选》书摘④：争取台湾民心不是虚的，而是实的 [Excerpts from Hu Jintao: winning hearts and minds of the people of Taiwan is not imaginary but real], 澎湃新闻 (*The Paper*), 2016, https://www.thepaper.cn/newsDetail_forward_1531835.

8 Xi Jinping, 'Speech on the Five Principles of Peaceful Coexistence', 28 June 2014, excerpts available at http://cpc.people.com.cn/n/2014/0628/c164113-25213211-2.html.

9 At the Boao Forum for Asia Annual Conference 2021, Xi stated, 'we need to safeguard the UN-centered international system, preserve the international order underpinned by international law, and uphold the multilateral trading system with the World Trade Organization at its core'. See 'Keynote Speech by President Xi at Boao Forum for Asia Annual Conference 2021', Xinhua, 20 April 2021, https://www.chinadaily.com.cn/a/202104/20/WS607e62d4a31024ad0bab6ba7.html.

10 Cai, *The Rise of China and International Law*, pp. 152–3.

11 Permanent Mission of the People's Republic of China to the United Nations, 'Note Verbale in Response to the Joint Submission by Malaysia and the Socialist Republic of Vietnam to the Commission on the Limits of the Continental Shelf', United Nations, 7 May 2009, https://www.un.org/depts/los/clcs_new/submissions_files/mysvnm33_09/chn_2009re_mys_vnm_e.pdf.

12 See Permanent Court of Arbitration, 'In the Matter of the South China Sea Arbitration Between The Republic of Philippines and The People's Republic of China', PCA Case no. 2013–19, 12 July 2016, https://pcacases.com/web/sendAttach/2086.

13 See Ministry of Foreign Affairs of the People's Republic of China, 'Statement of the Government of the People's Republic of China on China's Territorial Sovereignty and Maritime Rights and Interests in the South China Sea', 12 July 2016, https://www.fmprc.gov.cn/mfa_eng/wjdt_665385/2649_665393/201607/t20160712_679472.html.

14 See 'United Nations Convention on the Law of the Sea' (UNCLOS), Article 47.

15 See 'Law on the Territorial Sea and the Contiguous Zone of the Republic of China', 25 February 1992, Article 7, https://www.un.org/depts/los/LEGISLATIONANDTREATIES/PDFFILES/CHN_1992_Law.pdf.

16 UNCLOS, Articles 58(1), 58(3) and 87.

17 UNCLOS, Article 56. See also Raul (Pete) Pedrozo, 'Military Activities in the Exclusive Economic Zone: East Asia Focus', *International Law Studies*, vol. 90, 2014, pp. 514–43.

18 China's official declaration states: 'The Government of the People's Republic of China will announce the remaining baselines of the territorial sea of the People's Republic of China at another time.' Government of the People's Republic of China, 'Declaration of the Government of the People's Republic of China on the Baselines of the Territorial Sea of the People's Republic of China', May 1996, https://www.un.org/depts/los/LEGISLATIONANDTREATIES/PDFFILES/CHN_1996_Declaration.pdf.

19 See Chinese Society of International Law, 'The South China Sea Arbitration Awards: A Critical Study', *Chinese Journal of International Law*, vol.

17, no. 2, June 2018, pp. 207–748, https://academic.oup.com/chinesejil/article/17/2/207/4995682.

20 See Ministry of Foreign Affairs of the People's Republic of China, 'Position Paper of the Government of the People's Republic of China on the Matter of Jurisdiction in the South China Sea Arbitration Initiated by the Republic of the Philippines', 7 December 2014, https://www.fmprc.gov.cn/mfa_eng/wjdt_665385/2649_665393/201412/t20141207_679387.html.

21 South China Sea Probing Initiative, 'About SCSPI', http://www.scspi.org/en/gywm.

22 See Wu Jiao and Zhang Yunbi, 'Think Tank Examines South China Sea', *China Daily*, 24 February 2014, http://usa.chinadaily.com.cn/2014-02/24/content_17300029.htm; and Shannon Tiezzi, 'China's Academic Battle for the South China Sea', *Diplomat*, 25 February 2014, https://thediplomat.com/2014/02/chinas-academic-battle-for-the-south-china-sea/.

23 'Chinese Authorities Issued Revised Fishing Ban Periods in China', *Oasis P&I*, 21 March 2023, http://www.oasis-pandi.com/index.php?id=98.

24 See Sam LaGrone, 'VIDEO: Chinese Warship Harasses U.S. Destroyer in Taiwan Strait Transit', USNI News, 3 June 2023 (updated on 4 June 2023), https://news.usni.org/2023/06/03/u-s-canadian-warships-transit-taiwan-strait.

25 Ministry of Foreign Affairs of the People's Republic of China, 'Foreign Ministry Spokesperson Wang Wenbin's Regular Press Conference', 13 June 2022,

https://www.fmprc.gov.cn/mfa_eng/
xwfw_665399/s2510_665401/202206/
t20220613_10702460.html.

26 UNCLOS, Article 56.

27 UNCLOS, Articles 58(1), 87.

28 Isabel Reynolds and Krystal Chia,
'China's Claims on Taiwan Strait Could
Raise Tensions with US', Bloomberg,
13 June 2022, https://www.bloomberg.
com/news/articles/2022-06-13/
china-s-claims-on-taiwan-strait-could-
raise-tensions-with-us?sref=zJo4jZBU.

29 See Lynn Kuok, 'Narrowing the
Differences Between China and the
US over the Taiwan Strait', IISS, 13
July 2022, https://www.iiss.org/blogs/
analysis/2022/07/narrowing-the-
differences-between-china-and-the-us-
over-the-taiwan-strait.

30 See China Aerospace Studies Institute,
'In Their Own Words', p. 120.

31 'The South China Sea', VideoChinaTV,
YouTube.com, https://www.youtube.
com/watch?v=XI2s-2vjr70.

32 See Stuart Elliott, 'Sign of Arrival,
for Xinhua, Is 60 Feet Tall', New York
Times, 25 July 2011, https://www.
nytimes.com/2011/07/26/business/
media/xinhuas-giant-sign-to-blink-on-
in-times-square.html.

33 See 'Submissions to the Commission:
Partial Submission by Malaysia in the
South China Sea', Commission on the
Limits of the Continental Shelf, United
Nations, 12 December 2019, https://
www.un.org/depts/los/clcs_new/
submissions_files/submission_
mys_12_12_2019.html.

34 See Amir Yusof, 'Analysis: China's
New Map a Timed Move to Reassert
Its Territorial Claims, Flex Muscles
Ahead of Regional Summits', Channel
NewsAsia, 31 August 2023, https://

www.channelnewsasia.com/asia/
china-new-map-territory-g20-asean-
summit-india-malaysia-russia-
indonesia-protest-3737366.

35 See '6. United Nations Convention
on the Law of the Sea, Montego
Bay, 10 December 1982', Depository
Notifications, United Nations
Treaty Collection, https://treaties.
un.org/pages/ViewDetailsIII.
aspx?src=TREATY&mtdsg_no=XXI-
6&chapter=21&
Temp=mtdsg3&clang=_en.

36 The Philippines recently pushed back
against China's attempts to prevent
resupply of the BRP Sierra Madre,
a Philippine Navy transport ship,
which the Philippines deliberately
grounded in 1999 on Second Thomas
Shoal, a low-tide elevation within the
Philippines' EEZ, to prevent China
from occupying it.

37 See 'Malaysian Foreign Minister Says
No Chinese Vessel Intrusions in Last
100 Days, but Ex-minister Rebuts
Him', Straits Times, 16 July 2020,
https://www.straitstimes.com/asia/
se-asia/malaysian-minister-says-no-
chinese-coast-guard-or-navy-vessel-
intrusions-in-last-100.

38 See Sharon Seah et al., 'The State of
Southeast Asia: 2023 Survey Report',
ASEAN Studies Centre at the ISEAS-
Yusof Ishak Institute, 9 February 2023,
https://www.iseas.edu.sg/wp-content/
uploads/2025/07/The-State-of-SEA-
2023-Final-Digital-V4-09-Feb-2023.pdf.

39 See 'Amicus Curiae Submission by the
Asia Pacific Institute of International
Law (APIIL)', PCA Case no 2013-
19 between the Republic of the
Philippines and the People's Republic
of China, 6 June 2016, p. 2, available

at https://acrobat.adobe.com/link/
review?uri=urn:aaid:scds:US:819f
fda3-d890-38d9-a911-b5afe424125b.

40 See 'Manila's South China Sea
Arbitration Request to Hit Nowhere:
European Experts', Xinhua, 17 August
2015, https://www.globaltimes.cn/con-
tent/937478.shtml; and Wang Wen and
Chen Xiaochen, 'Who Supports China in
the South China Sea and Why', *Diplomat*,
27 July 2016, https://thediplomat.
com/2016/07/who-supports-china-in-the-
south-china-sea-and-why/.

41 See Wang and Chen, 'Who Supports
China in the South China Sea and Why'.

42 This point was made during a lecture
at the Rhodes Academy of Oceans
Law and Policy in 2015.

43 Prime Minister's Office Singapore,
'PM Lee Hsien Loong Delivered His
National Day Rally Speech on 21
August 2016 at the ITE College Central',
21 August 2016, https://www.pmo.gov.
sg/Newsroom/national-day-rally-2016.

44 Cai, *The Rise of China and International
Law*, p. 112; and White House,
'National Security Strategy for the
Arctic Region', October 2022, https://
www.whitehouse.gov/wp-content/
uploads/2022/10/National-Strategy-
for-the-Arctic-Region.pdf.

45 Anthea Roberts, *Is International
Law International?* (Oxford: Oxford
University Press, 2017), p. 227.

46 See Jens Stoltenberg, 'In the Face
of Russian Aggression, NATO Is
Beefing Up Arctic Security', *Globe and
Mail*, 24 August 2022, https://www.
theglobeandmail.com/opinion/article-
in-the-face-of-russian-aggression-
nato-is-beefing-up-arctic-security/.

47 See State Council Information Office
of the People's Republic of China,

'China's Arctic Policy', 26 January
2018, https://english.www.gov.cn/
archive/white_paper/2018/01/26/
content_281476026660336.htm; and
'Treaty Between Norway, the United
States of America, Denmark, France,
Italy, Japan, the Netherlands, Great
Britain and Ireland and the British
Overseas Dominions and Sweden
Concerning Spitsbergen signed in
Paris 9th February 1920', available
from the Arctic Portal Library, http://
library.arcticportal.org/1909/1/The_
Svalbard_Treaty_9ssFy.pdf.

48 Matthew P. Funaiole et al., 'Frozen
Frontiers: China's Great Power
Ambitions in the Polar Regions',
Center for Strategic and International
Studies, 18 April 2023, https://
features.csis.org/hiddenreach/
china-polar-research-facility/.

49 See, for example, Rush Doshi, Alexis
Dale-Huang and Gao Qi Zhang,
'Northern Expedition: China's Arctic
Activities and Ambitions', Brookings
Institution, April 2021, https://
www.brookings.edu/wp-content/
uploads/2021/04/FP_20210412_china_
arctic.pdf.

50 See White House, 'National Strategy
for the Arctic Region'; and Office of
the Secretary of Defense, 'Annual
Report to Congress: Military and
Security Developments Involving
the People's Republic of China
2019', US Department of Defense,
2 May 2019, https://media.defense.
gov/2019/May/02/2002127082/-
1/-1/1/2019_CHINA_MILITARY_
POWER_REPORT.pdf. See also
Funaiole et al., 'Frozen Frontiers:
China's Great Power Ambitions in
the Polar Regions'.

51 Ma Xinmin, 'China's Arctic Policy on the Basis of International Law: Identification, Goals, Principles and Positions', *Marine Policy*, vol. 100, 2019, p. 268.

52 See Funaiole et al., 'Frozen Frontiers'.

53 Nong Hong, 'China and the Antarctic: Presence, Policy, Perception, and Public Diplomacy', *Marine Policy*, vol. 134, December 2021, p. 6.

54 See Gianni Varetto, '5th Chinese Base in Antarctica', W.A.P. Worldwide Antarctic Program, 27 January 2020, http://www.waponline.it/5th-chinese-base-in-antarctica.

55 See Hong, 'China and the Antarctic', pp. 4–5; and Ann-Marie Brady, 'China's Expanding Antarctic Interests: Implications for New Zealand', Research Project Policy Brief no. 2, Small States and the New Security Environment, 3 June 2017, p. 9, https://www.canterbury.ac.nz/media/documents/research/China's-expanding-Antarctic-interests.pdf.

56 Hong, 'China and the Antarctic', p. 45.

57 Brady, 'China's Expanding Antarctic Interests', pp. 2, 7.

58 See Wu Dianqing, 'Zhong guo hai jun yu nan ji po bing zhi lü' 中国海军与南极破冰之旅 [China's navy and its journey into the Antarctic], 百年潮 (*Hundred Year Tide*), 2021, p. 35.

59 'The Antarctic Treaty', available at https://documents.ats.aq/recatt/att005_e.pdf.

60 White House, 'National Security Strategy', October 2022, p. 11, https://www.whitehouse.gov/wp-content/uploads/2022/10/Biden-Harris-Administrations-National-Security-Strategy-10.2022.pdf.

61 White House, 'Indo-Pacific Strategy of the United States', February 2022, p. 5, https://www.whitehouse.gov/wp-content/uploads/2022/02/U.S.-Indo-Pacific-Strategy.pdf.

62 White House, 'National Security Strategy', p. 23.

63 Peter A. Dutton, 'China Is Rewriting the Law of the Sea', *Foreign Policy*, 10 June 2023, https://foreignpolicy.com/2023/06/10/china-sea-south-east-maritime-claims-law-oceans-us-disputes/.

Military Allies and Economic Conflict

Ethan B. Kapstein

Countries form military alliances to deter or defeat a common adversary. Yet numerous obstacles stand in the way of alliance cohesion and strategic alignment. Governments may differ over their respective roles and responsibilities, and over the most effective strategies for dealing with an adversary. The adversary will naturally seek to exploit these divisions to undermine the alliance as a vehicle for collective action. Robert Osgood contemplated these tensions many years ago when he wrote: 'Every viable defensive alliance must reconcile the requirements of external security with those of internal cohesion. Since allies, even under the pressure of war, seldom see the requirements of security in the same way, an alliance must permit concessions to the needs of cohesion in order to reap the benefits of collective security – but without, of course, undermining security in the process.'[1]

Issues of alliance cohesion are coming into sharp relief as Western allies endeavour to forge a common strategy for dealing with a rising and more aggressive China. The allies (including those in NATO, as well as such Asian allies as Australia, Japan, the Philippines and South Korea) appear to be converging in their views towards Beijing's global ambitions.[2] But significant policy differences among them remain, as demonstrated by the European Union's recent discussions of 'strategic autonomy'.[3] As Lindsey Ford and

Ethan B. Kapstein is Executive Director of the Empirical Studies of Conflict Project at Princeton University.

Survival | vol. 65 no. 6 | December 2023–January 2024 | pp. 179–192 https://doi.org/10.1080/00396338.2023.2285609

James Goldgeier have noted: 'Unfortunately, US allies are not of one mind regarding their relationships with China, nor in many cases are they united with Washington about the best way to manage China's behavior. Beijing has exploited these fissures within and between allies repeatedly.'[4] One reason for these continued fissures is economic. Facing US pressure on South Korea to halt semiconductor sales to China, Seoul must decide to what extent it is prepared to sacrifice its commercial interests to maintain strong relations with the United States.[5] Likewise, for Germany to economically decouple from China 'would amount to economic vivisection for Germany and indeed the rest of Europe', as Constanze Stelzenmüller has put it.[6]

Economic disputes over a wide range of issues go back to the beginning of the Western alliance. Allies have often feared that they would undermine collective military capability and political resolve. In recognition of these challenges, Article 2 of the North Atlantic Treaty calls upon the member states to 'eliminate conflict in their … economic policies and … encourage economic collaboration between any or all of them'.

Examining efforts to do so and understanding the circumstances under which they have succeeded or failed could yield useful insights. In essence, allies calculate the costs and benefits of their economic relations with one another and with non-allies, and their cohesion or strategic alignment depends upon that calculation. When the costs of disrupting an economic relationship are high, an ally is less likely to do so in the interest of strategic alignment. It follows that the ally must receive a 'side-payment' (or a coercive sanction) from other members equal or greater to the forgone income if it is to fall in line.

A concrete example of a side-payment is Washington's willingness to export energy to Western Europe during the Russia–Ukraine war to compensate its European allies for the loss of Russian oil and gas supplies. Strategic alignment among the allies on Ukraine would have proved more difficult in the absence of this side-payment. Indeed, it has not been enough for at least one NATO ally, as Turkiye has continued to trade with Russia.[7] More broadly, the United States' imposition of tough export controls in the 1950s and 1960s (including during the Korean War) did not keep its Western allies from continuing trade with Communist China.

Strategic consequences of alliance economic relations

The idea that allies may have sharp policy differences over an array of issues is hardly a novel insight. That said, the Russia–Ukraine war has produced the greatest degree of NATO cohesion since the end of the Cold War. Naturally, differences remain among member states over such issues as the quantity and quality of military aid, the design and enforcement of economic-sanctions regimes, and Ukraine's eventual NATO membership.[8] But, as George Liska wrote, 'cooperation in alliances is in large part the consequence of conflicts with adversaries and may submerge only temporarily the conflicts among allies'.[9] In fact, at least in the case of the Western alliance, conflicts among allies have rarely been submerged for long. From the post-war integration of Germany into NATO, to America's abandonment of its allies at Suez in 1956, to France's 1966 exit from NATO's integrated military command, to the proposed deployment of neutron bombs into Western Europe in the late 1970s, to the management of such 'out-of-area' challenges as Iraq after 9/11, Alliance policy schisms have emerged repeatedly. Yet the Alliance has endured.[10]

Nevertheless, how allies have managed their economically centred conflicts has received relatively little attention.[11] What Phillip Taylor once wrote of NATO conflicts with respect to arms exports could be generalised to other sectors: 'It is not in any of the member-states' self-interest to surrender a profitable dominant position or yield any degree of national sovereignty at the expense of domestic economic harm.'[12] In the early years of NATO, the Eisenhower administration wrestled with this very problem within the US itself. An internal State Department document noted that 'we face the practical dilemma posed by the conflict between the special and often short-run interest of particular domestic economic groups and the more general longer-run national interest in free world strength and solidarity'.[13] This passage contemplates mainly how to shape trade patterns so as to satisfy both economic and national-security interests. But two other strategic issues also arise: how to build an efficient military coalition, and how to prevent harmful scrambles for critical minerals and natural resources.

Firstly, with respect to trade policy, domestic interest groups may pressure a government into trading with adversaries, which stands to undermine the country's relative military power if that trade strengthens the enemy.[14] The idea is captured in a quote commonly attributed to Vladimir Lenin: 'The capitalists will sell us the rope with which to hang them.'[15]

Joanne Gowa and Edward Mansfield observe that allies will trade more with one another than they will with non-allies, since they are wont to generate these externalities and inclined to engage in economic behaviour that makes their allies stronger militarily. They add that the effect is more pronounced when the international security environment is bipolar than when it is multipolar. In a bipolar system, the allies have fewer opportunities to opt for other trading partners than they do in a world with multiple great powers. Thus, allies will be more dependent on one another under bipolarity than under multipolarity; this is reflected in trade policy and patterns. One thing this analysis overlooks, however, is that the allies might act as free riders in any defence-oriented trade regime, continuing to trade with the enemy so long as the dominant ally provides a security umbrella, as some European states did with communist countries during the Cold War despite American objections. Conversely, while the United States undoubtedly wished to strengthen its allies economically and militarily for decades after the Second World War via the Marshall Plan and European rearmament, this policy came under question during the Trump administration, if not earlier. That administration, for example, imposed tariffs on steel and aluminium imports from the EU as well as China, claiming that these imports threatened national security.[16] The 'Buy American' provisions of the Biden administration's Inflation Reduction Act also have generated considerable ire in Europe.[17]

Secondly, inefficient defence spending among allies can also undermine strategic alignment and military capability. While monopolistic defence industries or 'pork barrel' politics often contribute to this problem, the deeper structural cause is the refusal of the allies to allocate defence projects to one another on the basis of comparative advantage. Policymakers tend to defend such conduct as being in the interests of 'autonomy'. Whatever the justification, it leads to the duplication of resources, often to an egregious degree. This problem most clearly arises in the area of weapons procurement. NATO allies collectively produce 17 types of main battle tanks, 13 types of air-to-air missiles and 29 types of naval frigates.[18] France, Sweden, the United States and a consortium of European countries also produce bespoke jet fighters.

The third issue is how to secure needed but scarce defence-related inputs, such as energy and raw materials, without engaging in zero-sum competition with other allies. A prominent example is the Arab oil embargo of 1973–74, when the Arab members of the Organization of the Petroleum Exporting Countries (OPEC) penalised countries that supported Israel during the Yom Kippur War by cutting off their oil supplies. Today, there are concerns that the allies may end up scrambling for the minerals needed to supply the 'green' transition.[19]

In sum, economics matter strategically to military allies for at least three key reasons: their international trade generates security externalities that may bolster enemy capabilities; inefficiencies in weapons procurement lead to wasteful spending; and markets for some goods may generate zero-sum competition that raises costs and threatens strategic alignment.

The Chinese example

In January 1950, the US and its allies established a 'Coordinating Committee for Multilateral Export Controls' (COCOM), based in Paris, aimed at restricting exports to the Soviet Union and Eastern bloc nations.[20] Six months later, with the start of the Korean War, China and North Korea were brought into the fold. When China entered the war in December 1950, the US imposed a complete embargo on Beijing. A United Nations General Assembly resolution was passed in May 1951 that recommended a trade embargo against Beijing, by which time some 30 countries had bilaterally restricted their exports to China. By May 1952, a China committee (CHINCOM) was formed within COCOM; notably, however, only the US continued a complete cessation of trade with China. In a 1955 assessment, the CIA found that CHINCOM controls had been 'subject to frequent circumvention' and that since 1950 China had increased its foreign trade. Among the Western allies, Japan, which was still occupied by US forces, increased its trade with China, as did the United Kingdom from 1951 onward. The CIA also found that Beijing had evaded sanctions by having goods rerouted through such ports as Hong Kong and Macao.[21]

Following the end of the Korean War, it became even more difficult for the US to persuade its allies to maintain stringent trade controls. In particular, the UK, which still ruled Hong Kong and had extended diplomatic recognition to Beijing in 1950, lobbied for a 'drastic cut' in the sanctions regime, causing extreme consternation in Washington.[22] Further, the US believed that European pressure to increase trade with the Soviet bloc would only serve to strengthen communist China as Moscow would arrange for the trans-shipment of Chinese goods.

By the 1960s, the United States' ability to enforce an embargo against China had weakened considerably. As the CIA noted in an intelligence report, 'China is already receiving from Japan and Western Europe substantial quantities of machinery and equipment directly related to its military effort', some of it assisting China in the development of advanced weapons.[23]

Thus, early in the Cold War, China's immense economic pull led several Western allies to trade with it even at the risk of endangering Pacific security. This trade enabled China to channel economic gains into military resources that supported its efforts against the West (and the US in particular) in such conflict zones as Korea and later Vietnam. The US recognised, however, that the European economies needed export markets in order to grow.[24] Washington faces similar dilemmas today in dealing with a more economically and militarily powerful China.

Autonomy vs collective defence

Following the Second World War, the Western alliance was formed in recognition of the communist threat. Yet even once the Alliance was created, the member states still had to ask themselves how much they could count on it for their security. Even if the Alliance could be relied upon in certain instances – like a Soviet attack on Western Europe – it was unclear what its role would be in other cases, such as conflicts involving the allies with countries beyond the North Atlantic. These questions meant that the allies wanted to retain some autonomous capacity for military action.

The impulse towards autonomy sometimes created impediments to cooperation among the Europeans themselves, which has always been more limited – despite important exceptions like the *Eurofighter* – than would be optimal given the size of each European military force. For its part, the United States has consistently sought to 'divide and conquer' the European defence market through various production-sharing schemes, such as those involving the F-16 fighter and now the F-35 fighter. But some countries, France among them, have vigorously protected their independence in the aviation sector.[25] The economic rewards of arms exports have also blunted allies' incentives to buy American.

From both an economic and a strategic perspective, however, the multiplicity of weapons programmes and platforms across the Alliance is hardly efficient. A 1978 US General Accounting Office report noted that 'if NATO were to achieve greater standardization, it would not only increase its military operating efficiency but could reduce weapon systems costs, and possibly free funds to buy additional quantities of needed weapons'.[26] This elusive drive for 'rationalization, standardization, and interoperability' (RSI) goes back nearly to the Alliance's earliest days.[27]

NATO's failure to make greater advances in these areas gets to the heart of the 'arms versus allies' trade-off illuminated by James Morrow.[28] According to Morrow, 'arming (neorealists call arming a form of "internal balancing") produces a more reliable improvement in security ... at the political cost of diverting resources to the military. Alliances (neorealists call this "external balancing") produce additional security quickly but with less reliability.' Complicating this trade-off is the role of the arms market, in which at least some allies may play an active role. Few NATO member states have been willing to sacrifice their domestic defence industries in the interest of greater coalition efficiency.[29] Autonomy – every nation's dominant preference – tends to prevail over both allies and efficiency. Efforts aimed at achieving autonomy may be economically inefficient and may therefore even erode security. Achieving security through allies may be more efficient, but it erodes autonomy.

Resource scrambles

A recent report from the Center for European Policy Analysis presents a grim view of future competition for raw materials needed to support the transition to a green economy demanded by climate change. 'Demand for critical minerals is soaring', writes the author. 'There won't be sufficient supply for stakeholders wishing to carry out net zero policies. While the EU and US should be applauded for starting to cooperate, the two will end up fighting over limited supplies.'[30] The scramble among allies, of course, affords China, which also seeks to secure key minerals, a potential lever to divide and conquer them.

This sort of thing has happened before. With the 1973–74 Arab oil embargo, which followed the Yom Kippur War, Arab members of OPEC split the allies on the basis on their degree of support for Israel. Limited oil supplies due to OPEC price hikes and production cuts led to long lines at petrol stations and economic recession. King Faisal bin Abdulaziz Al Saud – then also serving as prime minister of Saudi Arabia, the largest of the OPEC producers – saw several political and economic benefits to supporting the war, including a show of pan-Arab solidarity and the fact that wars generally lead to higher oil prices and thus revenues. But he understood that the United States was the ultimate guarantor of Saudi security and feared causing a major rupture in that strategic relationship. He also knew that the US had become dependent on foreign-oil imports, had little spare oil-production capacity, and therefore would be incapable of acting as supplier of last resort to countries that backed Israel. In short, the US was in no position to offer side-payments to allies to keep them strategically aligned.

The Europeans got the message loud and clear. The UK agreed to ship arms to Arab states but not to Israel, while France engaged in a similar arms-export strategy (for much of Israel's history France had been its major arms supplier). European members of NATO – except Portugal – refused landing rights to American transport planes bound for Israel, while Turkiye allowed the Soviet Union, which backed the Arab states, use of its airspace. The Arab oil producers then allocated oil supplies on the basis of how 'friendly' states were towards their cause. As states scrambled for supply, oil prices tripled.[31]

The Arab oil embargo precipitated the sharpest conflict in Western alliance relations since the Suez Crisis of 1956. While then-secretary of state Henry Kissinger led the Western allies in establishing what he called a 'consumers' cartel' – it eventually became the International Energy Agency, which provides research on energy markets but does not actively confront oil producers – tensions over Middle East policy became an enduring feature of Alliance politics.[32] Indeed, Richard Nixon, then the US president, observed that 'security and economic considerations are inevitably linked' and warned that European actions had eroded support for the Alliance in the US Congress.[33] France and Britain saw the Yom Kippur War as an opportunity to carve out an independent role in the Middle East, one that would be of great benefit to their domestic arms industries.

Dynamics similar to those of the Arab oil embargo could take hold again with respect to the green transition. Some of the essential minerals are highly concentrated in parts of Latin America and Africa, and enter a supply chain largely controlled by China, which is the world's major processor of these resources. As a recent report by the Brookings Institution puts it, this dependence on China poses 'major geopolitical risks' and could lead to future beggar-thy-neighbour scrambles.[34]

On balance, allies have proven willing to trade with enemies, engage in inefficient defence production and compete against one another for scarce resources, even at the expense of their diplomatic allegiances. The US has been unwilling to provide, or incapable of providing, the side-payments that might have kept the allies in strategic alignment. In some cases, it has even undermined allies to maintain dominance. These considerations bear on Alliance strategy vis-à-vis China.

De-risking China?

By trading with and investing in China, the allies have helped to enrich it, generating security externalities that have bolstered Beijing's military power and global influence. By insisting on some degree of autarky in weapons manufacture, they have become competitors on export markets, creating further conflicts while hindering progress towards standardisation and rationalisation. New defence spending among the allies prompted by China's rise as well as Russia's revanchism may be duplicative, while they continue to engage in trade and investment that bolsters Beijing's economic and military capacity. China's huge importance in the global economy – not least with respect to green supply chains, from raw materials through final production – gives it tremendous leverage that can be used to pit allies against one another, potentially creating a 'scramble' for needed resources.

Given its size and reach, no single ally could possibly contain Beijing unilaterally. In that respect, autonomy seems a mirage. It is daunting to forgo a market with a billion consumers. Furthermore, the allies remain sharp economic competitors, even with respect to building and exporting defence technologies needed to counter Chinese expansion. In facing China, each ally faces sharp trade-offs in balancing strategic alignment and economic gain. In inducing Australia to scupper a deal with France to purchase diesel submarines in favour of buying nuclear subs from America and Britain, for instance, Washington essentially sought to enforce strategic alignment at France's expense and to the UK's benefit.

Against this backdrop, the allies have nonetheless drawn closer on China strategy.[35] But deep divisions among them remain, even though some efforts at side-payments have been made. In the wake of the AUKUS kerfuffle, both the US and Australia offered France some compensation for the lost sale.[36] But the extent to which the US is prepared to compensate its allies for the loss of the China market is a different matter entirely. In an important speech in April 2023, European Commission President Ursula von der Leyen sought to distinguish the EU's position from that of the US, emphasising that 'decoupling' from China is not 'viable, desirable or even practical' for Europe.[37] Decoupling from China now also appears infeasible to the Biden administration.[38]

The new transatlantic approach is called 'de-risking'. It emphasises the separation of commercial and military-related trade and investment. Despite efforts to coordinate through bodies like the Trade and Technology Council, however, wide gaps remain.[39] Some are due to intra-European differences over such things as export controls and investment screening; Germany and the Netherlands, for instance, have adopted different approaches to export controls on semiconductor-related technology. Others stem from transatlantic differences; the US Inflation Reduction Act, which in part is designed to wean the US off dependence on China for certain green technologies, continues to annoy Washington's military allies with its 'Buy America' provisions.[40]

* * *

Economics and security are inextricably linked, and policymakers need to bring these two streams together in crafting strategic doctrine. In Washington and likely in most Alliance capitals, economic and security decision-making tend to be stovepiped. They generally treat different sets of issues, with experts who have very different skill sets and stakeholders. Bridging these worlds remains an ongoing challenge for every administration. Policymakers also need to confront stark economic and security trade-offs more analytically. Many of those described here can be measured with some degree of accuracy and assigned numerical and monetary values. It is not that difficult, for example, to calculate the costs of forgone trade. Better analysis, in turn, could help policymakers to understand the scale of side-payments that might be needed to achieve strategic alignment, and whether they are economically and politically feasible. Finally, NATO should play a more active role in these economic and security debates, honouring and building upon the sentiments found in Article 2 of the North Atlantic Treaty.

Notes

1   Robert Osgood, 'NATO: Problems of Security and Collaboration', *American Political Science Review*, vol. 54, no. 1, March 1960, pp. 106–29.

2   See NATO, 'NATO 2022: Strategic Concept', 29 June 2022, https://www.nato.int/nato_static_fl2014/assets/pdf/2022/6/pdf/290622-strategic-concept.pdf.

3   See European Parliament, 'EU Strategic Autonomy, 2013–2023: From Concept to Clarity', EU Strategic Autonomy Monitor, July 2022, https://www.europarl.europa.eu/RegData/etudes/BRIE/2022/733589/EPRS_BRI(2022)733589_EN.pdf.

4   Lindsey Ford and James Goldgeier, 'Retooling America's Alliances to Manage the China Challenge', Brookings Institution, 25 January 2021, https://www.brookings.edu/articles/retooling-americas-alliances-to-manage-the-china-challenge/.

5   See Alan Beattie, 'South Korea Ponders the High Cost of Being America's Friend', *Financial Times*, 27 April 2023, https://www.ft.com/content/d5a05da6-860e-44d9-a42a-99f57ad190e2.

6   Constanze Stelzenmüller, 'Germany's China Dilemma Takes on a New Urgency', *Financial Times*, 28 April 2023, https://www.ft.com/

content/03851aaa-409d-43b9-81df-729c98b39224.

7   See Nathaniel Taplin, 'Turkey Epitomizes the West's Russia Sanctions Dilemma', *Wall Street Journal*, 30 March 2023, https://www.wsj.com/articles/turkey-epitomizes-the-wests-russia-sanctions-dilemma-5b20a451.

8   See Steven Erlanger, 'Despite Successes at NATO Summit, Divisions Remain', *New York Times*, 12 July 2023, https://www.nytimes.com/2023/07/12/world/europe/nato-summit-ukraine-biden.html.

9   George Liska, *Resurrecting a Discipline: Enduring Scholarship for Evolving World Politics* (Lanham, MD: Lexington Press, 1999), p. 58.

10 See Alexanders Lanoszka, *Military Alliances in the Twenty-first Century* (Cambridge: Polity Press, 2022).

11 On Alliance differences over economic sanctions towards the Soviet Union, see Michael Mastanduno, *Economic Containment: CoCom and the Politics of East–West Trade* (Ithaca, NY: Cornell University Press, 1992).

12 Phillip Taylor, 'Weapons Standardization in NATO: Collaborative Security or Economic Competition?', *International Organization*, vol. 36, no. 1, Winter 1982, pp. 95–112.

13 US Department of State, 'Foreign Economic Relations of the United States', in *Foreign Economic Relations of the United States, 1952–1954*, vol. 1 (Washington DC: United States Government Printing Office, 1982), p. 68.

14 See Joanne Gowa and Edward Mansfield, 'Power Politics and International Trade', *American Political Science Review*, vol. 87, no. 2, June 1993, pp. 408–20.

15 See 'Lenin 1870–1924, Russian Revolutionary', in *Oxford Essential Quotations*, 5th ed. (Oxford: Oxford University Press, 2017), no. 10, https://www.oxfordreference.com/display/10.1093/acref/9780191843730.001.0001/q-oro-ed5-00006613.

16 See Maria Demertzis and Gustav Fredriksson, 'The EU Response to US Trade Tariffs', *Intereconomics*, vol. 53, no. 5, 2018, pp. 261–8.

17 See Christian Scheinert, 'EU's Response to the Inflation Reduction Act', Briefing Requested by the ECON Committee, European Parliament, June 2023, https://www.europarl.europa.eu/RegData/etudes/IDAN/2023/740087/IPOL_IDA(2023)740087_EN.pdf. For a measured analysis of the act's trans-atlantic strategic impact, see Nicholas Crawford, 'The Energy Transition, Protectionism and Transatlantic Relations', *Survival*, vol. 65, no. 2, April–May 2023, pp. 75–102.

18 Max Bergmann et al., 'Transforming European Defense', Center for Strategic and International Studies, August 2022, https://www.csis.org/analysis/transforming-european-defense.

19 See Maciej Bukowski, 'The Scramble for Critical Minerals Heats Up', Center for European Policy Analysis, 4 April 2023, https://cepa.org/article/the-scramble-for-critical-minerals-heats-up/.

20 For the history of COCOM, see Mastanduno, *Economic Containment*.

21 See CIA, 'Controls on Trade with Communist China', 11 January 1955, FOIA Reading Room, https://www.

cia.gov/readingroom/document/
cia-rdp79r01012a006200030012-9.

22 See 'Memorandum of Discussion at the
188th Meeting of the National Security
Council on Thursday, March 11, 1954',
in *Foreign Economic Relations of the
United States, 1952–1954*, vol. 1, p. 1,108.

23 CIA, 'Intelligence Report: The Effects
of the Vietnam War on the Economics
of the Communist Countries', July
1968, FOIA Reading Room, https://
www.cia.gov/readingroom/docs/
DOC_0000309820.pdf. More recently,
despite declaring an 'arms embargo'
on China following the Tiananmen
Square massacre of 1989, several EU
countries have continued to sell 'non-
lethal' defence technologies to Beijing.
See Oliver Bräuner, 'Beyond the Arms
Embargo: EU Transfers of Defense and
Dual-use Technologies in China', *Journal
of East Asian Studies*, vol. 13, no. 3,
September–December 2013, pp. 457–82.

24 See 'Memorandum of Discussion at
the 188th Meeting of the National
Security Council'.

25 Taylor, 'Weapons Standardization in
NATO'. See also Ethan B. Kapstein,
'International Collaboration in
Armaments Production: A Second-
best Solution', *Political Science
Quarterly*, vol. 106, no. 4, Winter
1991/1992, pp. 657–75.

26 US General Accounting Office,
'Improving the Effectiveness and
Economy of Mutual Defense', PSAD-
78-2, 19 January 1978.

27 See Kapstein, 'International Collaboration
in Armaments Production'.

28 James Morrow, 'Arms Versus Allies:
Trade-offs in the Search for Security',
International Organization, vol. 47, no.
2, Spring 1993, pp. 207–33.

29 See Taylor, 'Weapons Standardization
in NATO'.

30 Bukowski, 'The Scramble for Critical
Minerals Heats Up'.

31 For an excellent account of the oil
crisis, see Raymond Vernon (ed.), *The
Oil Crisis* (New York: W. W. Norton &
Co., 1976).

32 See Henry Kissinger, *Years of Upheaval*
(New York: Little, Brown, 1982), p. 905.

33 *Ibid.*, p. 916.

34 See Rodrigo Castillo and Caitlin Purdy,
'China's Role in Supplying Critical
Minerals for the Energy Transition',
Brookings Institution, 1 August 2022,
https://www.brookings.edu/articles/
chinas-role-in-supplying-critical-
minerals-for-the-global-energy-
transition-what-could-the-future-hold/.

35 See, for example, NATO, 'NATO 2022:
Strategic Concept'.

36 See 'Australia Announces Compensation
Deal with France for Scrapped
Submarine Contract', France 24, 11 June
2022, https://www.france24.com/en/asia-
pacific/20220611-australia-announces-
compensation-deal-with-france-over-
scrapped-submarine-contract/.

37 European Commission, 'Speech
by President von der Leyen at the
European Parliament Plenary on the
Need for a Coherent Strategy for
EU–China Relations', 18 April 2023,
https://ec.europa.eu/commission/
presscorner/detail/en/speech_23_2333.

38 See, for example, Damien Cave, 'How
"Decoupling" from China Became
"De-risking"', *New York Times*, 20 May
2023 (updated 22 May 2023), https://
www.nytimes.com/2023/05/20/world/
decoupling-china-de-risking.html; and
Ana Swanson and Keith Bradsher,
'U.S. Does Not Want to "Decouple"

from China, Commerce Chief Says',
New York Times, 29 August 2023,
https://www.nytimes.com/2023/08/29/
business/us-china-raimondo-
decouple-he-lifeng.html.

[39] See Eric Meyers and William Alan
Reinsch, 'The Push for U.S.–EU
Convergence on Economic Security
Policy', Center for Strategic and
International Studies, 7 July 2023, https://
www.csis.org/analysis/push-us-eu-
convergence-economic-security-policy.

[40] See Scheinert, 'EU's Response to the
Inflation Reduction Act'.

The Ambivalence of Soft Power

David W. Ellwood

Soft Power and the Future of US Foreign Policy
Hendrik W. Ohnesorge, ed. Manchester: Manchester University
Press, 2023. £90.00. 256 pp.

On 27 September 2023 – ten days before Hamas's devastating attack on Israel would present the Biden administration with perhaps its greatest diplomatic challenge to date – the US Department of State launched the 'Global Music Diplomacy Initiative'. The press release noted

> a worldwide effort to elevate music as a diplomatic tool to promote peace and democracy and support the United States' broader foreign policy goals. The Initiative aims to leverage public–private partnerships to create a music ecosystem that expands economic equity and the creative economy, ensures societal opportunity and inclusion, and increases access to education. It will build on current public diplomacy music programs.[1]

The GZERO news website, which publicised the event, spoke of 'hoochie coochie diplomacy', as the launch was accompanied by Secretary of State Antony Blinken's performance of Muddy Waters's Delta Blues classic

David W. Ellwood is a senior adjunct professor at the Johns Hopkins School of Advanced International Studies (SAIS–Europe) in Bologna, Italy.

Survival | vol. 65 no. 6 | December 2023–January 2024 | pp. 193–200 https://doi.org/10.1080/00396338.2023.2285611

'Hoochie Coochie Man' on an electric guitar, fronting a professional band brought in for the occasion.[2]

A new volume of essays edited by Hendrik W. Ohnesorge includes one on music diplomacy by Carla Dirlikov Canales, a professional opera singer who is also an arts envoy for the State Department and director of the Future of Cultural Diplomacy initiative at Harvard University. She comments that cultural diplomacy has a 'distinguished history ... in actively changing minds in support of foreign policy objectives'. But, as she also points out, in the United States, 'cultural diplomacy efforts have typically been relegated to the "children's table" of foreign policy discussions along with much of the work of public diplomacy more broadly. This has led to spotty success and many missed opportunities' (p. 180). Her job at Harvard is to promote the reorganisation and relaunching of official American activities in this area.

SOFT POWER AND THE FUTURE OF US FOREIGN POLICY

Edited by Hendrik W. Ohnesorge

Key Studies in Diplomacy

What is soft power?

Discussions of soft power invariably begin with definitions. In the edited volume *Soft Power and US Foreign Policy* – published in 2010, some 33 years after Joseph Nye originated the term 'soft power' – Nye himself emphasises in the foreword the non-official, cultural resources the US should count on, listing Hollywood, philanthropic foundations, universities, corporations, churches and even protest movements.[3] Blinken would doubtless include musical performers and other artists. In his editorial introduction, Ohnesorge – author of an authoritative book exploring all aspects of the soft-power concept[4] – adds values, policies and personalities. Given the considerable impact of US tycoons like Elon Musk on the conduct of world affairs, corporate leaders in particular would belong on the list.

These resources contribute critically to a nation's standing, credibility and authority in the world, and to its reputation and influence. In the end, however, soft power is about the relationship between a country's hard-power heritage – political, military, economic – and its less tangible sources of influence. Today, many governments and other institutions are looking for ways to organise and manage that relationship.

Several of Ohnesorge's contributors describe and deplore the wreckage inflicted on America's influence by the Trump presidency. But in one of the book's most thoughtful chapters, Michael F. Oppenheimer observes that problems afflicting America's reputation today also come from other sources, including the declining quality of life for many sectors of American society; the 'shambolic response to COVID-19' (p. 34); recent foreign-policy disasters and the problems of competence underlying them; and the 'coercive' use of soft power by way of imposing market fundamentalism on developing countries under the so-called 'Washington Consensus'. 'The good news', concludes Oppenheimer, echoing what Nye has often said, 'is that we possess the capacity to fix what ails us' (p. 27). Prescriptions follow.

Applying soft power

In his chapter, Nicholas J. Cull advises that US officials should avoid hectoring 'putative allies' on media freedom in such places as the Persian Gulf, where problems such as corruption can be endemic. Yet his advice itself sounds a bit sanctimonious: 'Leaders who struggle to rein in corruption should be especially supported and leaders who turn a blind eye held to account' (p. 113). It may also be unrealistic. In June 2023, in a *Financial Times* op-ed, Alan Beattie recounted a comment by a senior politician from a developing country to former US secretary of the Treasury Lawrence Summers, who was visiting his country: 'When we're engaged with the Chinese, we get an airport. And when we're engaged with you guys, we get a lecture.'[5]

None of the authors closely examines the actual performance of those responsible for official projection of US soft power – in particular, the under secretary of state for public diplomacy and public affairs, and the separate US Agency for Global Media. The latter sprang into action following the Hamas attack on Israel of 7 October, mobilising its extensive collection of digital networks.[6] Meanwhile, Under Secretary of State Liz Allen was set to visit Fiji, Vanuatu, Australia and Chile.[7]

Neither do Ohnesorge's authors scrutinise the gap between promise and performance in US public diplomacy elaborated in the 'Comprehensive

Annual Report on Public Diplomacy and International Broadcasting', supplied since 1948 by the bipartisan US Advisory Commission on Public Diplomacy. The 2022 report indicates that 'overall [public-diplomacy] spending in fiscal year (FY) 2021 was $2.1 billion, a $106 million decrease (4.7 percent) from FY 2020'. The report describes, with long lists of programmes and projects, what the taxpayer gets for the expenditure. But the accompanying assessment is frank and downbeat:

> This year, as in previous years, spending on public diplomacy activities has fallen far short. [Public-diplomacy] budgets in real dollars have not matched the need for resources … The rise of authoritarian influence, the widespread increase in extremist and foreign government disinformation and propaganda campaigns, the need to remain competitive in the contemporary media ecosystem, and the persistent fall-out effects of the global pandemic have created challenges to national security and economic interests that public diplomacy programs are uniquely able to address. And yet the U.S. government fails to prioritize resources for its public diplomacy programs.
>
> This resource gap makes no sense … Successful public diplomacy initiatives … require cutting-edge expertise in content creation, audience and market analysis, technological systems, emerging and established social media platforms, and local media industries, in addition to the deep knowledge of U.S. policies and values that inform every public diplomacy effort. These skills and experiences are crucial for building and strengthening relationships in the field, which form the basis for the protection and promotion of national security and economic interests.[8]

Daniel Runde highlights another dimension of the relationship between soft power and foreign policy in *The American Imperative: Reclaiming Global Leadership Through Soft Power*. Runde is a Republican veteran of Washington's foreign-aid community. His argument is that foreign aid is a significant soft-power resource, that it has been neglected by successive administrations, and that the expanding global presence of China on this front, especially through its Belt and Road Initiative, is a challenge that the US cannot and must not ignore. 'The United States must rebuild its capacity, its primacy, as a driver of global progress', asserts Runde.[9] In this effort, he says, ideas and values will be more important than military kit or digital technology. The US Agency for International Development's website proclaims that 'democracy delivers'.[10] Yet in 2022, the Biden administration gave $1.3bn in military assistance to Egypt, compared to $126.8m in economic aid, with 10% of the total held back to penalise Cairo for its abysmal human-rights record.[11] The White House hoped Congress would allocate $29.4bn to the agency this year, but the debt-ceiling deal froze all discretionary federal spending at pre-existing levels.[12] By contrast, the European Union will spend over €50bn in the current year.[13]

Relevant in this context is conservative scholar Christopher Layne's withering assessment of the very notion of soft power, and development aid's role in it, in *Soft Power and US Foreign Policy*. Layne laid the blame for the long list of development failures and the collapse of America's 1950s 'modernisation theory' in the Third World firmly at the door of those who argued that American convictions about the connection between liberal democracy and capitalist growth must be exported by way of some 'smart' combination of technical, political, economic and cultural means. Such efforts had failed in Vietnam, he said, and were just as likely to fail in Afghanistan, Iraq and Pakistan 'because experts really don't know what it takes for outsiders to "cause" development in other countries'.[14]

* * *

Many practitioners of US foreign policy recognise, of course, that nothing can be imposed, that foreign-aid efforts must be interactive and that – as US President Joe Biden and former president Barack Obama have often stressed – the force of America's example must be left to do its own work. This is a proposition with deep historical roots, directly echoing the moral and ideological dimensions of Nye's original formulation. In his view, a nation's soft power is derived from its culture 'when it is attractive to others', but also from 'its political values (when it lives up to them at home and abroad), and its foreign policies (when they are seen as legitimate and having moral authority)'.[15] This definition captures the force of example. But when Biden dispatches carrier strike groups to the eastern Mediterranean, the example he has in mind is that of hard power. It is the ability to call upon a uniquely abundant variety of means to project power that still distinguishes the United States from all its competitors.

Notes

1   US Department of State, 'U.S. Secretary of State Antony J. Blinken Launches Global Music Diplomacy Initiative, Music Icon and Former U.S. Jazz Ambassador Music Director Quincy Jones Receives Inaugural Peace Through Music Award', 27 September 2023, https://www.state. gov/u-s-secretary-of-state-antony-j-blinken-launches-global-music-diplomacy-initiative-music-icon-and-former-u-s-jazz-ambassador-music-director-quincy-jones-receives-inaugu-ral-peace-through-music-awar/.

2   See Alex Kliment, 'What We're Listening To: US Tries Out Hoochie Coochie Diplomacy', GZERO, 28 September 2023, https://www.gzeromedia.com/what-were-listening-to-us-tries-out-hoochie-coochie-diplomacy.

3   See Inderjeet Parmar and Michael Cox (eds), *Soft Power and US Foreign Policy: Theoretical, Historical and Contemporary Perspectives* (London: Routledge, 2010).

4   Hendrik W. Ohnesorge, *Soft Power: The Forces of Attraction in International Relations* (Cham: Springer International Publishing AG, 2019).

5   See Alan Beattie, 'How the US and Europe Can Beat China's Belt and Road', *Financial Times*, 29 June 2023, https://www.ft.com/content/2a0814cb-afdd-4c9a-8f5e-09f07ceb3d64. Of course, disasters can ensue when China endows a less-developed country with an airport. See Daisuke Wakabayashi, Bhadra Sharma and Claire Fu, 'China Got a Big Contract. Nepal Got Debt and a Pricey Airport', *New York Times*, 16 October 2023, https://www.nytimes.com/2023/10/16/business/nepal-pokhara-airport-china.html.

6   See US Agency for Global Media, 'Statement from CEO Amanda Bennett on Hamas Attack on Israel', 11 October 2023, https://www.usagm.gov/2023/10/11/statement-from-ceo-amanda-bennett-on-hamas-attack-on-israel/. The agency also runs Radio Liberty and Radio Free Europe, as well as networks for Asia, Cuba and the Middle East.

7   See US Department of State, 'Under Secretary of State for Public Diplomacy and Public Affairs Allen Travels to Fiji, Vanuatu, Australia, and Chile', 11 October 2023, https://www.state.gov/under-secretary-of-state-for-public-diplomacy-and-public-affairs-allen-travels-to-fiji-vanuatu-australia-and-chile/.

8   US Department of State, '2022 Comprehensive Annual Report on Public Diplomacy and International Broadcasting', 9 December 2022,

https://www.state.gov/wp-content/uploads/2022/12/FINAL_2022_ACPD_AnnualReport_508Ready.pdf.

9 Daniel F. Runde, *The American Imperative: Reclaiming Global Leadership Through Soft Power* (New York and Brentwood, TN: Bombardier Books, 2023), p. 209.

10 United States Agency for International Development, 'Democracy Delivers', https://www.usaid.gov/.

11 See American Chamber of Commerce in Egypt, 'U.S. Foreign Assistance to Egypt', 2023, https://www.amcham.org.eg/information-resources/trade-resources/egypt-us-relations/us-foreign-assistance-to-egypt.

12 United States Agency for International Development, 'FY 2023 Budget Justification', https://www.usaid.gov/cj/fy-2023. See also Carl Hulse and Catie Edmondson, 'House G.O.P. Prepares to Slash Federal Programs in Coming Budget Showdown', *New York Times*, 8 March 2023, https://www.nytimes.com/2023/03/08/us/politics/house-republicans-deficit-budget-biden.html.

13 See European Commission, 'Recipients and Results of EU Aid', https://commission.europa.eu/aid-development-cooperation-fundamental-rights/human-rights-non-eu-countries/recipients-and-results-eu-aid_en.

14 Christopher Layne, 'The Unbearable Lightness of Soft Power', in Parmar and Cox (eds), *Soft Power and US Foreign Policy*, pp. 70–1.

15 Joseph S. Nye, Jr, *Soft Power: The Means to Success in World Politics* (New York: PublicAffairs, 2004), p. 11.

Book Reviews

Europe
Hanns W. Maull

Homelands: A Personal History of Europe
Timothy Garton Ash. New Haven, CT: Yale University Press,
2023. $28.00. 384 pp.

**Democracy Erodes from the Top: Leaders, Citizens, and
the Challenge of Populism in Europe**
Larry M. Bartels. Princeton, NJ: Princeton University Press,
2023. £25.00/$29.95. 280 pp.

Timothy Garton Ash and Larry M. Bartels provide two pertinent yet very different takes on what is happening in Europe today. Garton Ash's *Homelands* is
exactly what the subtitle promises: a history of contemporary Europe since the
mid-1970s told by one of its eminent witnesses and activists. Beautifully written
and full of perceptive detail and personal observations, it brings to life the rise
of Europe from the hell of war, continues through the triumphant unification
of Germany and Europe, and concludes with the onslaught of crises since the
2010s. The leitmotiv of this history is the struggle for freedom – never entirely
won, afflicted by setbacks, yet never quite defeated either. In his astute reflec-
tions on the arc of European history since the Second World War through to the
return of major war in Ukraine in 2022, Garton Ash does not let his aspirations
for Europe obscure the enormous challenges it faces today, such as the Russia–
Ukraine war, immigration, terrorism, a faltering economy and socio-economic
inequalities. Nor does he mince his words about its flaws: 'We linked our dream
of spreading individual freedom much too closely to one particular model of
capitalism', he notes, adding that, while paying attention to the world's poor

as good internationalists, '[we] neglected the other half of our own societies' (p. 238). He summarises the cause of Europe's failings in a single word: hubris. Yet he does not give up hope for the freedom, peace and prosperity offered by his cherished European project, and in a moving epilogue he finally manages to persuade, on the beaches of Normandy where his father fought in June 1944, a French supporter of Brexit and 'Frexit' to drink to the future of 'l'Europe'.

Is there a crisis of democracy in Europe? If so, what are its origins? Bartels, the author of the refreshingly contrarian *Democracy Erodes from the Top*, is not so sure. For Bartels, the real issue is the chronic vulnerabilities of democratic systems. He does not deny the realities of right-wing populism and the dangers it poses, but he challenges much of the conventional wisdom about it. Leaders are to blame for the failures of democracy rather than the people, he argues. Right-wing populist views are entertained by significant but fairly stable minorities across Europe: 'European public opinion has long provided a reservoir of right-wing populist sentiment that political entrepreneurs have drawn on', Bartels writes (p. 14). In his view, the principal culprit for misguided views about the state of democracy in Europe is obsessive concern with the elusive phenomenon of public opinion. Quoting Walter Lippmann writing in 1925, Bartels proposes 'to think of public opinion as it is, and not as the fictitious power we have assumed it to be' (p. v). To do so, he closely analyses data from 23 European countries from 2002 to 2019 provided by the European Social Survey, probably the most extensive and detailed pool of information about political and social attitudes across Europe.

Taking the financial and economic crisis of 2008–09 as a major watershed, the author assesses social and political attitudes before, during and after the crisis on a wide range of issues relevant for the state of European democracy, such as support for European integration, assessments of the welfare state, trust in democratic institutions and attitudes towards immigration. On all these issues and across the 23 countries surveyed, he finds surprisingly limited fluctuations in a remarkably robust support for democracy. The overall pattern Bartels establishes is a modest decline of pro-democracy attitudes during the crisis followed by a rapid return to high and stable pre-crisis levels of satisfaction. There are, of course, differences between countries, but the link between the prevalence of right-wing populist attitudes and politics is tenuous: among the nine countries with the highest levels of right-wing populism, right-wing parties played a significant role in only three (Hungary, Italy and Slovenia). In a detailed analysis of Hungary under Viktor Orbán and Poland under the Law and Justice (PiS) party, Bartels also shows that in these countries – now notorious for efforts to dismantle democratic checks and balances – electoral success became possible only because parties toned down their right-wing populist rhetoric during the campaigns that brought them to power, presenting themselves as moderates. In other countries, surges in support for right-wing populist forces were effectively countered by established parties, and the support ebbed.

Overall, Bartels builds a powerful case for taking public-opinion surveys with a hefty pinch of salt. Yet his data does not include political behaviour, such as verbal abuse on social media and physical violence. Moreover, since 2019 further major shocks have shaken Europe: the COVID-19 pandemic, war in Ukraine and a new surge in immigration. In Italy, the right-wing Brothers of Italy (Fratelli d'Italia) now lead the government, and right-wing parties continue to attract significant parts of the electorates in other countries. Support for European democracy may well be deeper than we often assume – but will it also be determined enough to keep right-wing extremism at bay, and will it find the right people to organise that support? Ultimately, the key 'is not the institutions themselves, but the character and values of the political leaders operating within and upon them' (p. 230).

Trading Power: West Germany's Rise to Global Influence, 1963–1975
William Glenn Gray. Cambridge: Cambridge University Press, 2022. £34.99. 498 pp.

Energy and Power: Germany in the Age of Oil, Atoms, and Climate Change
Stephen G. Gross. Oxford: Oxford University Press, 2023. £35.99. 408 pp.

These excellent volumes demonstrate that understanding West Germany's past can provide useful insights into contemporary Germany's economic and political predicament, and its eventual choices for the future. William Glenn Gray's *Trading Power* looks at the rise of West Germany from the mid-1960s to the mid-1970s. 'Germany in 1965 was rich but vulnerable', Gray observes (p. 1), something that holds true for Germany today. During the 12 years the author dissects, West Germany learned to conceive of and pursue a grand strategy that served the country well: by 1975, it had become a highly respected and influential member of the Western alliance and the United Nations. It did so by learning to stay away from military entanglements beyond its immediate NATO obligations; to embed itself in diverse multilateral arrangements, from NATO and European integration to the General Agreement on Tariffs and Trade (GATT), the IMF and the UN; to navigate between the divergent expectations of its key allies in Washington and Paris; and to wield its economic and financial power in ways that helped to enhance international stability. Gray's comprehensive analysis covers West Germany's foreign relations in this formative period, taking on foreign economic relations and foreign policy in roughly equal measure, while giving defence-policy issues shorter shrift.

Drawing exhaustively on official and private documents from archives in several countries, this richly detailed, analytically astute study delineates how West Germany 'acquired a striking degree of influence in a globalizing economy' by 'trad[ing] in many conventional trappings of military power' (p. 3). Yet Gray also shows how much the success of West Germany as a 'civilian power' and a 'trading power' (pp. 462–3) depended on European and global factors too: on the United States underwriting West Germany's security and providing the capital and the markets for the European post-war miracle; on West European neighbours that quickly allowed a symbiotic economic and political relationship to develop with the former aggressor; and on a Soviet Union that had become a status quo power troubled by its own bureaucratic inertia and systemic weaknesses. Today, Germany faces an entirely different, rather less favourable context, with an aggressively revisionist Russia bent on undermining the present European order, an America riveted by domestic political polarisation and focused on its rivalry with China in the Indo-Pacific, and a neighbourhood rife with political uncertainties and socio-economic tensions. In this rather more complicated world, the new Germany will have to relearn the art of grand-strategic design and implementation, and rediscover the sources of the economic strength that fuelled the West German economic miracle.

Gray does not explore the reasons for this miracle, but rather starts with its results: West Germany's economic strength. *Energy and Power* by Stephen G. Gross, which looks at Germany's multiple energy transitions from the mid-1950s to the present, helps us to understand how Germany became the economic power it is today. Gross does this through the prism of (West) Germany's evolving energy system. The book identifies five major energy transitions. From 1950 to 1970, West Germany shifted from coal to oil as its primary energy source faster than any other industrialised country. During the 1960s and 1970s, it also tried to build an internationally competitive nuclear industry to diversify its energy sources. The oil crises of the 1970s triggered a third transition, this one towards greater energy efficiency. In Gross's view, Germany was the first country to recognise the need to separate economic growth and energy demand, which had come to be considered axiomatic, but it also saw this as an opportunity to strengthen its industrial prowess. While that separation did not occur in France, the United Kingdom or the US, West Germany showed that economic growth was achievable with drastically lower specific energy inputs. Thus, the energy efficiency of the German economy grew by 19% from 1973 to 1978 while it declined in other major industrial countries. Accepting higher prices for energy was the key to this transition.

From 1998 to 2005, the first coalition government after German unification bringing the Social Democrats and the Greens to power built on the conceptual seeds and practical successes of the 1970s by shifting the economy towards renewable energy. Between these shifts, another energy transition took shape: the 'energy entanglement of Germany and Russia' (p. 238) through natural gas, sold – against the facts – as a clean source of energy amid growing anti-nuclear sentiment in German society. The fifth, most recent energy transition, starting in the 2010s, aimed to make the German economy compatible with the imperative of containing global warming, yet ended up making it heavily dependent on Russian natural gas. These transitions were marked by repeated energy crises – shortages and constraints in energy supply that catalysed and accelerated change and contributed to the intensely politicised nature of energy policymaking.

Political–economic visions about future energy, social actors and the coalitions they built, and policy linkages were therefore as important as the costs and prices of energy in shaping Germany's energy-policy choices and the trajectories of its energy transitions. By demonstrating the pervasive role of an activist state that heavily intervened in energy markets, Gross's analysis effectively demolishes the myth of West Germany's post-war recovery as the product of faithful adherence to free-market principles. The author quotes Ludwig Erhard, West Germany's first minister of economics and generally considered to be the architect of West Germany's post-war economic miracle: 'Even if one wants to grant a market price, one must still have the right to influence the market' (p. 32).

Gross uncovers two sets of competing paradigms at the heart of Germany's energy policies. The first sets cheap energy to support Germany's manufacturing prowess against the need to make energy expensive to encourage its efficient use and to contain climate change. The second contrasts the corporatist traditions and practices of modern industrial Germany with a postmodern vision of a decentralised, democratic, small-is-beautiful energy system. The struggles of coalitions adhering to these divergent philosophies repeatedly produced inherently contradictory policies. As Gross has it, Germany was 'profoundly shaped by the tense interplay between these two systems and two ways of thinking about energy, in everything from its foreign policy and domestic economy, to the nature of its democracy' (p. 295).

Germany's most recent energy transition, which began around 2010 and aims to reduce its CO_2 emissions in line with the 1.5°C target for limiting global warming, effectively showcases those contradictions. On the one hand, there has been a strong push for renewables, inspired by a vision for a Germany that champions sustainable-development technologies. On the other hand, pressed by Germany's corporate sector, the economy has shifted to domestic brown coal and natural-gas imports from Russia, which are supposedly intended as 'bridges' to a sustainable energy future but are in fact incompatible with containing global warming.

Europe Alone: Small State Security Without the United States
David Schultz, Aurelija Pūraitė and Vidmantė Giedraitytė,
eds. Lanham, MD: Rowman & Littlefield, 2022.
£100.00/$130.00. 451 pp.

Small states are sometimes the canaries in the coalmine of a dangerous international order. The fate of the Baltic states has shown this repeatedly, and as this book demonstrates they were thoroughly alarmed by the Russian invasion and annexation of Crimea in 2014. Since then, Latvia and Lithuania have more than doubled their defence expenditure from less than 1% to more than 2% of GDP. (Estonia had already been close to that level, and has since further expanded its defence spending.) The principal value of this wide-ranging collection lies in educating the reader about the way security issues are viewed and studied in the Baltic states. The editors have assembled an impressive cast of (mostly) Lithuanian experts, and the book tackles security-policy issues with an exhaustively comprehensive approach. No fewer than 11 chapters map the whole spectrum of possible security threats, ranging from traditional issues of defence through pandemics, energy, ecology, terrorism, organised crime, artificial intelligence and natural disasters to human rights and sustainable development. The only major lacuna concerns cyber security. After all, Estonia experienced significant cyber attacks – most likely as part of Russia's hybrid warfare against NATO – in 2007, and since 2008 it has been home to the NATO Cooperative Cyber Defence Centre of Excellence.

It is hard to think of any other aspect of human, public, national or international security that is not covered here. Nor does the collection confine itself to analysis: three chapters focus on possible policy responses and recommendations for enhancing small-state security, with two of them emphasising the potential for leadership of small states in international collaborative efforts. Two chapters assess where European security efforts stand and where they may be headed, as future European security frameworks will have to operate with much less support from across the Atlantic than Europeans have been used to. Unsurprisingly, the tone is somewhat sceptical, but not completely without hope. The traditional military means of defending against Russia are covered, but accorded less prominence than one might expect. Instead, the emphasis is on the domestic preconditions of security. In the authors' view, what matters most are individual freedom and human rights, democracy, civil-society cooperation and social resilience. Small states' security inevitably relies on deterrence by making them hard to digest for any potential aggressor.

While the analyses presented here make it clear that the Baltic states are extremely difficult to defend, they are certainly mobilising for resistance. As one contributor points out, this could involve close to half a million Lithuanian citizens, as about 22% of the population expressed a willingness to participate in the armed defence of their country (p. 77). The other method of deterring aggression is collective defence through international collaboration, notably within NATO and the European Union.

The conclusion of *Europe Alone* ambitiously pleads for the establishment of security and safety studies as a separate discipline that can holistically deal with the entire range of issues – from waste management and nuclear strikes to organised crime and sustainable development – that are ably discussed in this collection.

Counter-terrorism and Intelligence
Jonathan Stevenson

The Pigeon Tunnel (film)
Errol Morris, director and writer. Distributed by Apple TV+, 2023.

John le Carré, who died in 2020 at 89, was more than just the world's reigning spy novelist. He lifted the genre to the level of literary fiction and perforce became a ranking moral authority on the Cold War and the activity of espionage. Errol Morris, in his documentary *The Pigeon Tunnel* – also the title of le Carré's memoir, referring to a conduit through which pigeons bred as game are sent so that rich men who fancy themselves sportsmen can shoot them – seeks to remove some of the self-styled mystery from le Carré's persona. Whether Morris's reputation as a probing and perspicacious interrogator is fully deserved is an open question. But here the point seems moot, as le Carré himself is a charming interlocutor who welcomes the opportunity to hold forth candidly in light of his 'great age'. With a tight, knowing smile of seductive reassurance, he is serious and forthcoming within the boundaries he sets; it is clearly he who controls the conversation. These features confirm preconceptions that he is a master of the game as well as a sage observer of human nature, and make the film thoroughly satisfying on the level of fandom.

It also holds deeper rewards. Born David Cornwell to an amoral and disreputable grifter of a father and a despairing mother who abandoned them both when the boy was five, le Carré approvingly quotes Graham Greene, his literary and existential progenitor, as saying 'childhood is the credit balance of the writer'. Thus, he connects the child with the man. Le Carré's father, Ronnie Cornwell, trafficked in duplicity, but for all his decadence and fecklessness, for all the instability and heartache he visited on his son and others, le Carré notes that in some ways his childhood was 'romantic' and 'exciting'. It helped him fit the desired profile for post-war British intelligence: separated early from conventional family, sent off to boarding school, enamoured of sport, cast as one of the boys but never feeling like one, and 'looking for institutional embrace'. Life then proceeded as a 'succession of embraces and escapes'. After graduating from Oxford, where he was a covert MI5 asset, and teaching at Eton, he worked for MI5 and then MI6 as a junior officer, latterly in West Germany. Dismayed by what he saw as the 'enforced forgetting' of the Cold War manifested by the West's exculpatory instrumentalisation of ex-Nazis and the tragic plight of the East Germans, he discovered empathy for the first time. The secret world seemed

Survival | vol. 65 no. 6 | December 2023–January 2024 | pp. 208–215 https://doi.org/10.1080/00396338.2023.2285614

too small. He needed a more expansive one that he could populate himself to tell a full story.

Writing fiction was the answer – 'a journey of self-discovery'. Yet, like those haplessly duped pigeons, he never really left the old world, and in his dotage he claims still not to know what love is. Le Carré retained a lifelong fascination with betrayal, and never forgot his father's most vivid and concrete message: that what mattered most was neither truth nor honesty, but rather 'the imprint of personality'. Superficially, this mindset might seem in line with the James Bond stereotype which le Carré famously repudiated with more complex and downbeat characters such as Alec Leamas, Magnus Pym, Jerry Westerby and of course George Smiley – the father he wished he'd had, he confesses. But what le Carré means by personality in the context of espionage is the will to deceive. In his view, the complete spy is one who does not choose to betray but is compelled to do so by instinct and what he calls 'addiction', which overwhelm ideology and psychologically place the spy 'at the hub of the universe'.

The notorious British mole Kim Philby, whose 'murky light lit [the author's] path' for *Tinker Tailor Soldier Spy*, was the crowning embodiment of these stealthily megalomaniacal qualities and, to le Carré, 'evil' in his lethal service to Josef Stalin and Soviet communism. Notwithstanding such penetrating insights, le Carré owns up to an adjacent myopia in his consistent portrayal of Western intelligence services, despite their undeniable faults, as 'brilliant' and 'effective' because they were ultimately in the hands of singularly wise and rational people such as Smiley. At the end of a long life of examining the clandestine side of humanity, which he considered pervasive if not encompassing, he concludes that 'the inmost room is bare'. It's a daunting verdict but, at least as a net assessment, an increasingly credible one.

Killers of the Flower Moon (film)
Martin Scorsese, director and co-writer (with Eric Roth).
Distributed by Paramount Pictures and Apple Original Films, 2023.

Domestic white Christian extremism now poses a greater terrorist threat to the United States' security and stability than transnational jihadism. While there are many causes – including immigration, the economic struggles of the white working class and emotive social issues like abortion – the factors that have made white militancy so powerful are its deep roots in American history and its consequently toxic latency in American culture. The phenomenon most often cited is the gauzy southern myth of the 'Lost Cause': a genteel agrarian way of life guided by an honour code and a noble aristocracy that treated its slaves well and was defeated by a soulless, uncultured mongrel society. Florida's requirement that public middle schools teach students that slavery benefitted African Americans by giving them skills and Governor Ron DeSantis's vociferous defence of this edict are examples of that wilful delusion.

Martin Scorsese's film *Killers of the Flower Moon*, based on David Grann's acclaimed 2017 book of the same title, mercilessly illuminates America's other main shrouded and sanitised abomination: its near-genocidal brutality towards Native Americans. His lens is a comprehensively duplicitous white family's systematic intermarriage with and subsequent murder of Osage people who had become wealthy by virtue of oil discovered on their reservation, to secure their oil headrights by inheritance in the early 1920s. At three and a half hours, it's a slow-burning masterpiece of topical melodrama, revisionist western, and neo-noir sensibility, impelled by seamlessly woven characters and immersive atmospherics.

The Oklahoma town where the story begins is a calamity of unregulated cars, traumatised horses, incongruously well-heeled and flamboyant Native Americans, and seething whites openly carrying pistols, shotguns and rifles. Osages are being murdered by the dozen. If that seems suspiciously like a MAGA daydream, it is probably supposed to be. Ernest Burkhart – Leonardo DiCaprio, effective in a freighted and benighted role – returns from service in the First World War a suggestible naif eager for money and in thrall to his uncle William 'King' Hale, Robert De Niro in insidious trim, a rich cattleman who has cast himself as the singularly sympathetic white patron of the Osage nation. He dominates the local political and social order, which teems with smug assumptions of Native Americans' mental and genetic inferiority used to justify the abuses visited on them.

Ernest falls for Mollie Kyle, a winsome but sussed Osage woman. In this encapsulating role, Lily Gladstone is simply brilliant – restrained yet expressive and exuding fatalistic dignity. Burkhart marries Mollie with the encouragement of Hale, who then enlists him in his homicidal designs. What is most disturbing here is that Burkhart genuinely loves Mollie but cannot overcome his fealty to a vaunted white father figure who subverts that love. Like generations of Americans, this man is too ignorant and lazy to deal effectively with ethical quandaries, so dumb bigotry defeats complex humanity. Even after he has confessed his complicity in the murders of Mollie's relatives, he can't admit to himself or his wife that he knowingly poisoned her.

As Tom White, the straight-laced, purposefully quizzical G-man and former Texas Ranger who eventually works a measure of justice, Jesse Plemons nicely projects the kind of stolid institutional decency in which admirers of the United States' system of government have placed their faith, at least before Donald

Trump raised the prospect of its evisceration. Scorsese winds up the story by way of a true-crime radio play, stepping in as the on-air narrator to note that in Mollie's 1937 obituary the murders of members of her family were never mentioned. Some critics have found this epilogue gratuitous and even, per Anthony Lane, 'cheesy'. That's harsh. In fact, it artfully illustrates just how Americans have compartmentalised and sealed off ignominious history, consigning it to the realm of novelty entertainment. This searingly clever film means to break that mould.

Wind of Change (podcast)
Patrick Radden Keefe. Pineapple Street Studios, Crooked Media and Spotify, 2020.

In 1990, when the Berlin Wall had come down and the Soviet Union was about to collapse, the West German heavy-metal band Scorpions came out with the power ballad 'Wind of Change'. It's a song about political liberation that became the anthem of peaceful revolution in Europe, and one of the most popular singles of all time. Some fans call it the song that ended the Cold War. Some 20 years later, the eminent journalist and New Yorker staff writer Patrick Radden Keefe heard from a US intelligence-community contact that espionage circles believed the CIA to have written the song and orchestrated its implementation as propaganda to destabilise the Soviet Union. It was a tantalising notion that Keefe couldn't shake. Hence the podcast.

Keefe – who with his book Empire of Pain (2021) and reporting in the New Yorker arguably did more than anyone else to take down Oxycontin manufacturer Purdue Pharma and hold the Sackler family who ran it accountable, and who shed new light on the Northern Irish Troubles in his prize-winning book Say Nothing (2018) – is a top-notch journalist who knows his craft. He gets the tonal balance between whimsical speculation and hard reporting just right; the background he provides on non-official-cover operatives, codeword clearance and other inside intelligence matters is unusually clear and sound; and he duly recounts the CIA's rather abundant record of enlisting artists. Being a fine storyteller, he withholds final judgement as long as is credible to maintain suspense. As a highly professional journalist, however, he doggedly runs down every lead, and assiduously resists the temptation to reach the juiciest conclusion without sufficient evidence. At least passively, of course, that integrity serves to perpetuate the rumour. The archness of Keefe's subjects also contributes. Though Klaus Meine, Scorpions' frontman and putative author of 'Wind of Change', denies being a CIA asset, he seems more gratified than outraged to be suspected of being one.

Keefe's investigation relates to more than the substance of the central claim about the authorship of 'Wind of Change'. It also tellingly reflects the process and mindset of investigative reporters and their salience in the intelligence eco-system. The persistent classification of long-past operations relevant mainly to old news – presumably on grounds of concealing sources and methods that may continue to be useful – helps keep rumours about them alive, and journalists by their nature and calling inevitably are moved to look into them, and in doing so amplify their public presence. If the CIA actually did pen a song that vouchsafed the end of the Cold War, it pulled off a psychological operation that rivalled and may have surpassed its audacious printing of *Doctor Zhivago* and distribution of the copies behind the Iron Curtain. Even if it didn't, the tale's apparent plausi-bility, deservedly or not, still stands to buoy the agency's reputation and legend.

Saints and Soldiers: Inside Internet-age Terrorism, from Syria to the Capitol Siege
Rita Katz. New York: Columbia University Press, 2022.
£25.00/$30.00. 368 pp.

General news reports frequently touch on the importance of the internet to ter-rorist recruitment, indoctrination, training and even operations. Precisely how it facilitates these functions, however, can be opaque. In *Saints and Soldiers*, Rita Katz – founder and executive director of the oft-cited SITE Intelligence Group, which she began in 2002 as a source of information on terrorist threats for gov-ernment agencies and private companies – provides needed clarity, background and analysis. An Iraqi-born Jew who emigrated to the United States from Israel, Katz found it relatively easy to wrap her head around jihadism. But the bur-geoning of domestic neo-Nazism, anti-Semitism and white supremacism, as well as incel and misogynistic communities in the United States, which she had regarded as the world's bastion of liberalism, has truly shocked her.

Written in an urgent, sometimes breathless, but agreeably conversational first person, Katz's book provides nicely detailed, thematically grouped accounts of terrorist events in digital context, including illustrative screenshots, charts and graphs. A key theme running through the book is the 'screw your optics' stance that jihadists and far-right extremists share, and have adopted and energetically advertised online, whereby they eschew winning over relatively mainstream adherents through moderation in favour of fomenting accelerationist uprisings through expressively violent mass-casualty attacks without caring how crazy they look. This empirically observed phenomenon connects far-right and jihad-ist terrorists insofar as both, unlike ethno-nationalist extremists, are overtly and self-consciously uninterested in plausibly negotiable political ends. It has also given rise to what Katz calls 'siege groups': a rising species of accelerationist outfit that signifies 'a new phase of far-right terrorism' (p. 181) in seeking to optimise the balance between flat, leaderless resistance and focused direction through online memes and other forms of branding.

Katz occasionally discusses the stresses of professionally monitoring political violence. Referring to her research team's apprehension of online celebrants of Brenton Tarrant's murder of 51 Muslims in Christchurch, New Zealand, in March 2019, she writes: 'As much I hate to grant these sycophants any satisfaction, their callousness and relentless sadism was affecting us' (p. 97). She goes on to recount an employee's nightmares and his decision to take extended leave. At first blush, this may seem self-indulgently tangential and a bit sentimental. But it does highlight the insidious daily grind of the practice of counter-terrorism in a world in which it has become a necessity and has required a large number of people to witness extreme brutality on their computer screens. SITE itself has been a Telegram target of the neo-Nazi extremist group Moonkrieg Division. Emotionally taxing as the work is, Katz points out that it has paid dividends in cohering the efforts of government agencies and private companies, especially to diminish the Islamic State's online presence.

The US government assesses that far-right extremists now pose a greater danger to US security and stability than jihadist ones. Katz notes that many of them harbour bizarre conspiracy theories as 'foundational premises' – QAnon's purported conviction that a cabal of satanic Democrats is running a global paedophile ring is only the most prominent – and that these 'are what separates the far right from your average bigots and racists' (p. 216). What she sardonically calls 'tinfoil hat terrorism' would be funny if it wasn't real. Internet communications stimulate and turbocharge the terrorist impulse, and Katz believes disempowering them requires a joint effort by government agencies and an informed and incentivised tech sector to stifle extremist propaganda. To her way of thinking, there is no real first-amendment or state police-power issue here:

> If someone causes a disturbance at a movie theater, restaurant, or bar, they will be kicked out – not by any particular law tailored to address this specific behavior, but by the rules of the private venue they're in. Internet-based services must say the same: *this is our establishment; if you don't like our rules, get out.* (p. 265, emphasis in original)

That seems a matter of common sense. But the very spread of conspiracy theories and their political exploitation suggest that lawmakers and captains of industry may have too little of it.

Terror in Transition: Leadership and Succession in Terrorist Organizations

Tricia L. Bacon and Elizabeth Grimm. New York: Columbia University Press, 2022. £28.00/$32.00. 312 pp.

Eradicating the leaders of terrorist organisations has been considered one of the most effective means of weakening them, and it is clear from the flattened transnational trajectories of al-Qaeda and the Islamic State that 'decapitation' can disrupt and constrain terrorist groups' ability to conduct effective operations. At the same time, the overall persistence of such groups indicates that leadership targeting is hardly a counter-terrorism panacea. By way of admirably clear exposition, four tidy, well-conceived case studies and a deftly derived analytic framework, Tricia L. Bacon and Elizabeth Grimm – associate professors at American University and the Edmund A. Walsh School of Foreign Service at Georgetown University, respectively – show that the effectiveness of transitions in terrorist groups is subtle and contingent. Setting a baseline, they note that 'what is not debated is that the loss of a founder is the most significant leadership loss a group can experience. Indeed, some groups cannot survive it. Others do, however, especially contemporary religious terrorist organizations' (p. 9).

The effectiveness of a transition, they assess, depends to a considerable extent on whether a terrorist leader's successor is one of five types: a 'caretaker', who incrementally changes both framing and operations; a 'signaller', who changes framing dramatically (their term is the somewhat opaque 'discontinuously') but operations incrementally; a 'fixer', who changes framing incrementally but operations dramatically; a 'visionary', who dramatically changes both framing and operations; or a 'figurehead', who is not really a functional leader and has little effect on either framing or operations (p. 41). In the authors' view, Egyptian Islamic Jihad's long path from founders to figureheads, fixer and then visionary in the form of Ayman al-Zawahiri, culminated in its factionalisation and absorption into al-Qaeda – an ambiguous result from an organisational standpoint. The progression from founder to signallers in al-Qaeda in Iraq appears to have been quite efficacious insofar as the latter facilitated the reframing of the organisation into the Islamic State in Iraq, which significantly enlarged its operations and remit. Al-Shabaab has endured in incrementally moving from founder to fixer to figurehead. Perhaps because it has lacked a signaller or visionary that would prompt dramatic change, its path has not been as expansive as the Islamic State's, but it also has not attracted comparable counter-terrorism attention, and its current leader's status as a mere figurehead suggests that decapitation 'would not meaningfully change al-Shabaab's mission or methods' (p. 192).

The case study of the Second Ku Klux Klan – founded in 1915, when D.W. Griffith's *The Birth of a Nation* appeared, lionising the original Klan – should be of particular interest to analysts of contemporary far-right extremist movements in the United States. Founder William Joseph Simmons had exploited nineteenth-century nativism, later trends in immigration, xenophobia and fraternalism, and a highly permissive counter-terrorism environment to refashion the clandestine Protestant white-supremacist organisations that arose during Reconstruction into a superficially destigmatised and largely overt national community, downplaying its modus operandi of 'extralegal violence, lynchings, floggings, and night rides' (p. 49). Arguably, present-day groups such as the Oath Keepers, the Proud Boys and the Three Percenters are similarly trying to revive the Second Klan. Hiram Wesley Evans, who ousted Simmons, was a fixer, embracing Simmons's vision but looking to advance the Klan's national political standing and power. This involved plausibly denying culpability for the violence it advocated and encouraged. While a loose command structure was useful in this regard, 'it also weakened the organization and undermined Evans's attempt to assert top-down leadership' (p. 71). Corruption and moral hypocrisy were also major problems. Although the Second Klan had dissipated by the end of the 1920s, 'it is significant that the *why* that motivated so much Klan intimidation and violence did not fade' (p. 187, emphasis in original). One current lesson may be that, while arresting and imprisoning the leaders and players of white-supremacist groups could function as a deterrent on several levels, firmly containing them requires addressing the social and political conditions that have produced them and afforded them a degree of impunity. Though hardly a revelation, the point is still worth stressing.

While the authors' dutifully academic approach and their study's correspondingly rigid architecture and habitual qualification can impede the flow of their argument, it rewards unpacking owing to its analytic soundness, practical utility and, lamentably, its ongoing relevance. Especially as Hamas appears to have created a watershed transitional moment for itself, this book should have staying power.

United States
David C. Unger

Realigners: Partisan Hacks, Political Visionaries, and the Struggle to Rule American Democracy
Timothy Shenk. New York: Farrar, Straus and Giroux, 2022.
$30.00. 464 pp.

In this fascinating and original book, Timothy Shenk reorganises the familiar narrative of American political history. Instead of chronicling great presidents or ideological turning points, he spotlights a succession of political figures he calls 'realigners'. Some are well known, such as James Madison, Theodore Roosevelt and Barack Obama; others less so, such as Martin Van Buren, Ruth Hanna McCormick and Phyllis Schlafly. What distinguishes them all is their role in creating new majority-governing coalitions. Some, like Madison and Van Buren, succeeded. Others, including the Reconstruction-era senator Charles Sumner and the early-twentieth-century African-American luminary W.E.B. Du Bois, fell short, by greater or lesser degrees. By focusing on these men and women and their times, Shenk shines new light on broader dynamics of American history.

Shenk, a history professor at George Washington University and a former co-editor of *Dissent*, is an engaging and lucid writer, able to convey complexity with clarity. His main thesis is that, given America's size and diversity, those who aspire to govern, or the political operatives behind them, need to work long and hard to put together wide-ranging and sometimes unlikely electoral coalitions, which they then need to hold together through changing economic times and social climates. To succeed, such realigners also need a talent for seeing the political scene as a whole, and the good luck of launching their efforts at a time when older coalitions are fragmenting.

One realignment effort that triumphed was Madison's late-eighteenth-century coalition of southern planters and northern political machines, built around their shared demands for expanded (white male) suffrage and greater (white male) popular sovereignty. Another was Mark Hanna's late-nineteenth-century uniting of manufacturers and workers around policies of protectionism, sound money and federally driven economic development. A third was Franklin D. Roosevelt's 1930s lining up of northern Progressives and southern segregationists around a platform of federally financed relief from Great Depression miseries.

Du Bois, however, repeatedly saw his efforts to secure and advance African-American rights stymied by white racism. Schlafly won limited victories by successfully navigating the Republican right's passage from Barry Goldwater's leadership to Donald Trump's. Obama's once-promising coalition now appears to have ended with his presidency, though it is still too soon to know what its ultimate fate may be. And what of Trump's realignment of America First nationalists, the religious right and the self-perceived victims of immigration, globalisation and affirmative action?

Realigners leaves us to ponder interesting questions about the limits imposed by America's two-party duopoly on prospects for far-reaching change, but also the potential incentives it offers for seeking areas of common ground between otherwise diverse constituencies.

The Project-state and Its Rivals: A New History of the Twentieth and Twenty-first Centuries
Charles S. Maier. Cambridge, MA: Harvard University Press, 2023. £39.95/$45.00. 528 pp.

Through his decades of scholarship and teaching on both sides of the Atlantic, Charles S. Maier has focused on one basic question, formulating and refining his answers with each successive book and monograph. His goal has been to understand and explain the ways in which advanced capitalist states evolved over the past century in response to world war, colonial war, cold war and economic globalisation. His findings do not always comfortably fit into traditional geographical, terminological or disciplinary confines. Maier has learned to go where his subject matter takes him. He was a pioneer of global history and has not hesitated to cross the disciplinary boundaries that separate history, political economy and sociology, if these stand in the way of more unified thought. This fascinating book provides a summation and updating of Maier's lifelong work.

The 'project-state' of the title refers to regimes that aim to mobilise and transform their own societies, and sometimes neighbouring societies as well. Examples include the Turkish state created by Mustafa Kemal Atatürk, the New Deal state created by Franklin D. Roosevelt in the United States, and the national communist states created by Josef Stalin in Russia and Mao Zedong in China. Their chief rivals over the past century, according to Maier, have been 'resource empires', a category that includes not just the formal political empires of old, but also the neocolonial patterns of resource exploitation that have often succeeded decolonisation.

These two categories of states are not the only actors in Maier's self-described 'new history of the twentieth and twenty-first centuries'. He systematically analyses the many subnational and supernational forms of sovereignty – non-governmental organisations; public–private partnerships; the International

Monetary Fund and World Bank; the League of Nations and the United Nations; NATO; the Marshall Plan; OPEC; and the European Union – that have taken on governance functions since 1918.

Maier illustrates his arguments with examples drawn from Argentina, France, Germany, Italy, Japan, Poland, the United Kingdom, the United States and elsewhere. He also analyses transnational processes such as depressions and decolonisation, along with the evolution of the EU, which affected many states but played out somewhat differently in each of them. His lens is ever shifting between successive trends in economics and politics, and in the distributional class struggles that result.

It is not a flaw in his analysis, but to Maier's credit, that the final picture he leaves us sometimes seems blurry and incomplete. That is the trade-off for breaking out of the traditional narrative frame of state-by-state, year-by-year history. Reality itself is blurry, and no history of one's own times can be considered fully complete.

My only real quibble is with the surprising number of minor errors that made it into the published text. For example, James Callaghan became Britain's foreign secretary, not prime minister, in spring 1974 (p. 261). No such error has the slightest bearing on Maier's arguments, but they distract the knowledgeable reader. Harvard University Press owed this important book more careful copy-editing.

The Rise of Common-sense Conservatism: The American
Right and the Reinvention of the Scottish Enlightenment
Antti Lepistö. Chicago, IL: University of Chicago Press, 2021.
$40.00. 261 pp.

Conventional wisdom sees little in common between the writings of neoconservative public intellectuals such as Irving Kristol, Gertrude Himmelfarb, James Q. Wilson (and, for a time, Francis Fukuyama) and the platform oratory of politicians like Donald Trump. Antti Lepistö, a lecturer in the History of Science and Ideas at Finland's University of Oulu, tells a different story.

In this well-researched history of contemporary political ideas and their philosophical forebears, Lepistö shows that first-generation neoconservatives like Kristol, Himmelfarb and Wilson, who had once dismissed with elitist disdain what they condemned as the destructive moral choices made by most Americans, had, by the late 1980s, fundamentally altered the tone and substance of their arguments. Their writings from this later period adopted what Lepistö characterises as a species of populism, reflecting Kristol's 1983 summons to fellow neoconservatives 'to explain to the American people why they are right, and to the intellectuals why they are wrong' (quoted on p. 15).

This later neoconservative argument, Lepistö demonstrates, derived from a selective reading and recasting of two leading philosophers of the Scottish Enlightenment: Adam Smith and David Hume. Smith and Hume wrote of an innate human capacity for moral judgements that they called 'common sense', but whereas Smith and Hume thought this capacity needed to be cultivated to produce reliable moral judgements, neoconservatives implied that common sense was inborn. The very basis of Kristol's call to explain to the people 'why they are right' rests on this politically expedient elision of the need for cultivation and education.

Lepistö explains that in the context of the eighteenth-century Scottish Enlightenment, both Smith and Hume belonged to a particular philosophical school known as 'sentimentalists' (as in the title of Smith's major philosophical work, *The Theory of Moral Sentiments*). Both argued, as Lepistö puts it, that 'moral sentiments are not reliable in the absence of proper education' (p. 38).

Kristol was a restless political thinker and a skilled polemicist with a talent for intellectual leadership. His ideological evolution unfolded over nearly seven decades, from his days as a student Trotskyist at New York's City College in the 1930s through his receipt of the Presidential Medal of Freedom from George W. Bush in 2002. Himmelfarb, who met Kristol at a meeting of the Trotskyist Young People's Socialist League in 1941 and married him the following year, was a distinguished academic historian specialising in Victorian England. Wilson was a widely renowned social scientist, who evolved from a Kennedy-era liberal into a neoconservative later in his career. (Fukuyama, being a generation and a half younger, has continued to evolve in his own neoconservative thinking.) All three, by virtue of their credentials and skills, brought presumed intellectual authority to their common-sense conservatism. As Lepistö shows, that authority was more apparent than real.

The Republican Evolution: From Governing Party to Antigovernment Party, 1860–2020
Kenneth Janda. New York: Columbia University Press, 2022.
£25.00/$30.00. 326 pp.

The US Republican Party was founded shortly before the American Civil War. Over the intervening decades, according to political scientist Kenneth Janda, it has swapped its core founding principles – racial equality, economic development and inclusive, strong-state nationalism – for their opposites: white-nationalist ethnocentrism, states'-rights federalism and divisive cultural warfare. Janda supports his argument with an extensive statistical analysis based on evidence drawn from 14 decades of Republican presidential platforms.

Reversals of founding party principles are not unique to the Republicans in American politics. The Democrats also pivoted from the states'-rights agrarianism of their slave-owning Jeffersonian founders to the multicultural, big-government party they are today. What most interests Janda, a lifelong scholar of political parties, is the 'Republican evolution' from being a 'governing party' to an 'antigovernment party'.

While it is commonly believed that platforms are discarded once the electoral votes have been counted, Janda finds that, on the contrary, their planks are more reliable indicators of changing party positions than, say, the presidential speeches much used by other scholars.

Janda evaluates 1,666 of 2,722 planks adopted over 14 decades. He sorts them into broad categories including freedom, order, equality, public goods, government, military, foreign policy and symbolic. The resulting tables provide what he considers objective grounding for his central claim that around the year 1928, the Republicans changed from the party of nationalism to the party of neoliberalism. He then traces their further twenty-first-century evolution into the party of ethnocentrism. In measurable stages, what had once been the party of the eastern and midwestern business establishment became the party of a southern, western and evangelical counter-establishment.

Janda traces an accompanying evolution in the nature of the Republican Party itself, from a nineteenth- and twentieth-century party whose direction was largely shaped by successive successful electoral teams to a twenty-first-century party shaped by what he describes as loyalty to a political tribe and social identity, and finally, in the Trump era, to a personality cult.

That today's Republican Party fundamentally differs from the party of old is something that few would venture to dispute. In this well-written, carefully researched book, Janda uses social-science tools to shed new light on the political history that nurtured that epochal change.

Pandemic Politics: The Deadly Toll of Partisanship in the Age of COVID
Shana Kushner Gadarian, Sara Wallace Goodman and Thomas B. Pepinsky. Princeton, NJ: Princeton University Press, 2022. £30.00/$35.00. 383 pp.

Why did the United States, despite all its economic and scientific resources, fail so badly in its response to the COVID-19 pandemic? Under Joe Biden as under Donald Trump, the US has consistently reported the highest COVID death rate per capita of any of the 38 developed countries belonging to the Organisation for Economic Co-operation and Development (OECD).

In seeking to explain this, Shana Kushner Gadarian, Sara Wallace Goodman and Thomas B. Pepinsky, all three trained as political scientists, conducted six waves of surveys between March 2020 and April 2021. These divided the American population into subsets sorted by traits such as race, gender, party preference, income and education levels. Participants were asked questions about how serious a danger they felt the epidemic posed, how well they felt national and local officials were responding to it, and what health precautions they personally did and did not take.

The authors tested several possible hypotheses to account for America's outlier result – invoking, for example, the country's comparatively weak public-health infrastructure; its high healthcare costs; the poor coordination between national and state-level responses; and deeper racial and economic inequalities. All of these, they report, contributed to some degree to the larger national failure. But, based on their survey findings, they conclude that the most important cause of America's poor showing was political partisanship, deliberately stoked by Trump.

As the authors define it, political partisanship in present-day America goes well beyond electoral alignment with one party or the other. For Trump's supporters and opponents alike, it has become the basis of their very social identity. Instead of thinking 'I vote red' (Republican) or 'I vote blue' (Democrat), the authors report that people now think 'I am red' or 'I am blue', where being blue connotes seeing COVID as a serious threat and being red connotes minimising its dangers (p. 8).

It is not the authors' fault that their surveys were concluded before the massive surge of infections and deaths associated with the Omicron variant of the SARS-CoV-2 virus, which they discuss in an epilogue. The premature end date to their survey research led the authors to form expectations about Biden administration policies and vaccine effectiveness that proved incorrect, weakening their case that Trump-induced partisanship was the key factor in producing a high death rate. But another problem derives from the methodology of the surveys themselves. Designed to measure attitudes of sample populations at preset intervals of time, the surveys did not necessarily coincide with decisive instances of partisan political messaging, meaning the book ultimately fails to clinch the authors' case that attitudes were correlated with key moments of partisan political messaging.

Applying History: Gaza and the Twentieth Century

Dana H. Allin

I

An underlying premise of 'applied history' is that our understanding of the past will shape – whether consciously or unconsciously – our approach to the policy choices of the present. So, we should try to get it right. This means understanding what is different as well as what may look similar.[1]

Hamas launched its shocking infiltration of Israel and massacre of Israelis exactly a half century after the surprise attack by Egyptian and Syrian forces on Yom Kippur in 1973. It appears that the historical resonance was intended. The parallels are also beguiling, if potentially misleading, with respect to the role of the American superpower. In 1973, the Arab armies threatened Israel's very existence and a massive airlift of American military supplies helped turn the tide. The 1973 war was also the fire-and-blood prologue to a sequence of immense diplomatic achievements. In the following months, US secretary of state Henry Kissinger's shuttle diplomacy enabled the disengagement of armies on both fronts; in 1977 Egyptian president Anwar Sadat travelled to Jerusalem to address the Israeli Knesset; in 1978 US president Jimmy Carter hosted Sadat and Israeli prime minister Menachem Begin for historic negotiations at Camp David; and the following year Israel and Egypt signed their peace agreement.

Dana H. Allin is an IISS Senior Fellow and Editor of *Survival*, and adjunct professor at the Johns Hopkins School of Advanced International Studies (SAIS–Europe) in Bologna, Italy. He is co-author, with Steven N. Simon, of *Our Separate Ways: The Struggle for the Future of the U.S.–Israel Alliance* (New York: PublicAffairs, 2016).

Survival | vol. 65 no. 6 | December 2023–January 2024 | pp. 223–230 https://doi.org/10.1080/00396338.2023.2285616

Meanwhile, Egypt moved decisively from the Soviet to the American strategic orbit.

In this issue of *Survival*, Steven Simon and Jonathan Stevenson observe a key difference between that era and this one: 'Back then, Egyptian president Anwar Sadat and his Israeli counterparts were already open to some kind of accommodation. [Israeli Prime Minister Benjamin] Netanyahu and the Hamas leadership are not.'[2] In his memoirs, Kissinger himself lauded Sadat in particular as the rare model of a statesman who fought a war 'to lay the basis for moderation in its aftermath'.[3] In my own book, I summarised Kissinger's assessment that Sadat

> had gone to war not to win back territory, but to create a psychological shock that would make both Arabs and Israelis more serious about seeking peace. The Israelis needed to be shocked out of their complacent sense of military invincibility. The Egyptians needed to be liberated from their burning sense of national humiliation, a humiliation that rendered them incapable of diplomatic flexibility.[4]

The videos of Hamas's performative sadism in southern Israel are evidence enough that the group does not conceive of a universe in which it coexists with Israel. 'The attack settled the debate about Hamas's identity: resistance prevailed over governance', as Emile Hokayem writes, also in this issue.[5] And while many Israelis were sceptical about the current government's long-term project to render a two-state solution unviable, and while they are likely to demand a reckoning for Netanyahu's role in presiding over this disaster, the horrors of 7 October are unlikely to create a more accommodating mood. 'The genocidal character of Hamas's attack on Israel was the living embodiment of the latter's deepest national nightmare: that its enemies' true objective was the annihilation of Jews, as Jews, and ultimately the destruction of the state of Israel', writes Chuck Freilich, a former Israeli deputy national security advisor, in *Survival*. Significantly, Freilich, long a harsh critic of Netanyahu and strong promoter of peace with the Palestinians, says the consequence is probably the death of a two-state solution, although he also writes that the Biden administration's efforts to revive it are 'wise'.[6]

The Biden administration has indeed tried to summon the creative political imagination and diplomatic patience for conjuring a better future, including progress towards a Palestinian state, from the current disaster. Joe Biden flew to Israel and hugged Netanyahu to express genuine anguish and support, but also to restrain Israel, as he said pointedly, from committing the kind of grand strategic blunders the United States itself committed after the 9/11 terrorist attacks.[7]

Yet the analogy suggests a kind of tragic inevitability. Washington will support Israel in a war presumably intended to destroy Hamas for good. Biden stated that the Israeli government has a right, 'indeed a duty', to try.[8] And yet, as all four of the *Survival* authors cited above suggest, the task may be impossible at an acceptable cost.

II

The cost of trying to destroy Hamas is already evident in harrowing scenes of Palestinian suffering and death in Gaza. Inevitably, this suffering and death has caused a backlash around the world, including in the United States, where it weighs on Biden's – and, arguably, American democracy's – prospects in the 2024 election.

This political threat to Biden comes partly from disaffected Arab Americans in key swing states including Michigan, and partly from a progressive Left that has been impatient with decades of Israeli governments that prioritised expanding settlements over making peace. This impatience is justified. However, in addition to eliding the fact that at least a couple of these Israeli governments did make a serious effort to negotiate peace, the reaction from some on the Left to recent events has a sinister aspect that is worth dwelling on. Having scrutinised some of the initial reactions to the 7 October massacres in southern Israel, the centre-left American journalist Josh Marshall reproduced on his blog a day-after statement from the National Students for Justice in Palestine, a main organiser of anti-Israel demonstrations on American campuses. It reads:

> Today, we witness a historic win for the Palestinian resistance: across
> land, air, and sea, our people have broken down the artificial barriers

of the Zionist entity, taking with it the facade of an impenetrable settler colony and reminding each of us that total return and liberation to Palestine is near. Catching the enemy completely by surprise, the Palestinian resistance has captured over a dozen settlements surrounding Gaza along with many occupation soldiers and military vehicles. This is what it means to Free Palestine: not just slogans and rallies, but armed confrontation with the oppressors.[9]

A few days later the group released an organisational 'toolkit' that explained their logic more explicitly:

On the 50th anniversary of the 1973 war, the resistance in Gaza launched a surprise operation against the Zionist enemy which disrupted the very foundation of Zionist settler society. On the morning of October 8th [sic], the Palestinian resistance stormed the illegitimate border fence, gaining control of the Gaza checkpoint at Erez, and re-entering 1948 Palestine.[10]

The pernicious logic, repeated ad nauseum in anti-Zionist rhetoric, is that the civilian victims of 7 October are not really civilians; rather, they are 'settlers'. And 'settlers are not "civilians" in the sense of international law, because they are military assets used to ensure continued control over stolen Palestinian land. Responsibility for every single death falls solely on the zionist entity.'[11] And thus, as the prominent Jewish and pro-Palestinian writer Peter Beinart has noted, the fashionable cant of decolonisation serves to mask unspeakable evil in just the way that George Orwell saw thoughtless rhetoric and bad writing masking the totalitarian evils of Left and Right.[12]

Such thinking is not only monstrous on its face, but also historically illiterate. An important reality and context to the creation of Israel was well understood, indeed impossible to ignore, at the time, but is too often forgotten today. Jews had inhabited Palestine for millennia, and those who came after the Second World War were hardly the 'colonists' of the extreme Left's imagination. And the boatloads of weary and desperate European Jews disembarking on the beaches of Tel Aviv and Haifa and Ashkelon were far from the only Europeans on the move. Moreover, the

Arabs of Palestine fleeing their own genuine *Nakba* (catastrophe) in the war of 1948–49 were themselves among the countless waves of refugees on an ocean of movement after the world war. While the Holocaust of its own uniquely evil force impelled Jews' exodus from Europe, the mass movement of people from their homelands was more broadly the consequence of an international consensus and plan, however inchoate. In *Postwar*, his great work of history, Tony Judt was precise about an important difference between this post-war settlement and previous ones:

> At the conclusion of the First World War it was borders that were invented and adjusted, while people were on the whole left in place. After 1945 what happened was rather the opposite: with one major exception [Poland] boundaries stayed broadly intact and people were moved instead. There was a feeling among Western policymakers that the League of Nations, and the minority clauses in the Versailles Treaties, had failed and that it would be a mistake even to try and resurrect them. For this reason they acquiesced readily enough in the population transfers. If the surviving minorities of central and eastern Europe could not be afforded effective protection, then it was as well that they be dispatched to more accommodating locations. The term 'ethnic cleansing' did not yet exist, but the reality did – and it was far from arousing wholesale disapproval or embarrassment.[13]

This does not mean that the human consequences were not understood. *New York Times* correspondent Anne O'Hare McCormick wrote on 23 October 1946: 'The scale of this resettlement, and the conditions in which it takes place, are without precedent in history. No one seeing its horrors first hand can doubt that it is a crime against humanity for which history will exact a terrible retribution.'[14] As Judt commented, 'history has exacted no such retribution'.[15] It is difficult to deny, however unpalatable the implications, that the population transfers helped advance the relative stability of post-war Europe. The arguable exception was the spillover of European refugees into Palestine, for it would be difficult to argue that they fostered stability in the Middle East.

But we are where we are. And leftist posturing about justice for Palestinians 'from the River to the Sea' offers a prospect at least as morally repugnant as the mirror image of the Israeli settler movement and its right-wing promoters in the United States, who are also historically oblivious to the legitimate rights and dignity of long-suffering Palestinians.[16] As Marshall also observes, '[from the River to the Sea] and similar phrases have been used for decades on both sides of the conflict as defenses of and statements of maximalism. It doesn't "mean" expulsion or genocide. It's intentionally not that specific. It's how both sides of the conflict say, "we get everything."'[17]

III

It is true, of course, that Israel is the far stronger party, and Palestinians the underdogs. This power imbalance makes the conflict polarising in the United States – especially for young Americans without living memory of the Zionist imperative – and internationally. As false as the Israel-colonialism equation may be in historical terms, it is perhaps inevitable that since much of the world comprises former colonies of European powers, many will perceive Israel as a bully supported in its oppression by those same powers, from which the United States historically has struggled in vain to differentiate itself.

And so it is that Russia, as it prosecutes a war of empire against Ukraine, can gain support or at least neutrality from an anti-colonial Global South. This is among the complications that Biden's fractured America faces as it tries to defend a fracturing international system. Simon and Stevenson suggest that the jury is out on how much America's steadfast support for Israel will damage its strategic diplomacy in much of the rest of the world. But, clearly, the longer this war continues and the more civilians it kills, the greater the reputational damage.

In any event, diplomacy has in large measure given way to deterrence. The idea of a US–Israeli–Saudi grand bargain must be moribund for the foreseeable future. US suggestions that major Arab states provide post-war security to Gaza have been rebuffed by those states as well as Israel. With Israel's security establishment looking nervously at Hizbullah missiles and the risk of a second front opening to its north, the United States sent two carrier strike groups to the Eastern Mediterranean. One purpose was to reassure traumatised Israelis, but another was to signal to Iran that America would not stand aloof in the event of full-scale attack from another direction.

The organic connection of crises, foreign and domestic, is another echo from half a century ago. In October 1973, after Israel had pushed the Arab armies back and threatened the survival of Egypt's Third Army, indications of a Soviet airlift to save the Egyptians prompted the United States to place its nuclear forces on alert. Today, after Russia's invasion of Ukraine, Washington and Moscow are again fierce adversaries under the shadow of nuclear risk. In 1973, while dealing with the Arab–Israeli war, the Nixon administration was also in the throes of the Watergate crisis that would bring it down; in 2023, the once and perhaps future president Donald Trump faces criminal charges in four different courtrooms in four different cities.

Richard Nixon's underlying domestic crisis was the Vietnam War and his criminal reaction to the anti-war opposition. Biden's is a far more serious threat to democracy itself. In 1970s America, the political centre held and, in fact, after the disastrous extension of the war in Vietnam and before being forced from office, Nixon and his administration had put the US in a stronger position to prevail in the Cold War. I concur with Simon and Stevenson that the Biden administration has done as well as could reasonably be hoped for in navigating the current coil of crises. Whether it is enough to leave the US and its allies, including Israel, in a stronger position is a question at which history can only hint.

Notes

1   See Charlie Laderman, 'Time Is Short: Ukraine, Taiwan and the Echoes of 1941', *Survival*, vol. 65, no. 6, December 2023–January 2024, pp. 77–90; and Benjamin Rhode, 'Historical Imagination and the Unspoken Assumptions of Our Age', *Survival*, vol. 65, no. 2, April–May 2023, pp. 213–28.

2   Steven Simon and Jonathan Stevenson, 'The Gaza Horror and US Policy', *Survival*, vol. 65, no. 6, December 2023–January 2024, pp. 47–8.

3   Henry Kissinger, *Years of Upheaval* (Boston, MA: Little, Brown, 1982), p. 460.

4   Dana H. Allin, *Cold War Illusions: America, Europe, and Soviet Power,*

1969–1989 (New York: St. Martin's Press, 1994), p. 48.

5 Emile Hokayem, 'The Gaza War and the Region', *Survival*, vol. 65, no. 6, December 2023–January 2024, p. 58.

6 Chuck Freilich, 'Israel and the Palestinians: The Day After', *Survival*, vol. 65, no. 6, December 2023–January 2024, p. 68.

7 See John Reed et al., 'Joe Biden Warns Israel to Avoid 9/11 "Mistakes"', *Financial Times*, 18 October 2023, https://www.ft.com/content/3168166a-4d0b-429f-88b4-be8d6dd36db9.

8 Quoted in Peter Baker, 'In Unforgiving Terms, Biden Condemns "Evil" and "Abhorrent" Attack on Israel', *New York Times*, 10 October 2023, https://www.nytimes.com/2023/10/10/us/politics/biden-israel-hamas.html.

9 Quoted in Josh Marshall, 'History from the River to the Sea and Across the Ocean', Talking Points Memo, 14 November 2023, https://talkingpointsmemo.com/edblog/history-from-the-river-to-the-sea-and-across-the-ocean.

10 National Students for Justice in Palestine, 'Day of Resistance Toolkit',

12 October 2023, https://docs.google.com/document/d/12IuQt1usUsyHWoHIcFYdAbpYK2H3bHJocPCrVyYTo8s/edit.

11 *Ibid.*

12 See interview with Peter Beinart on the Ezra Klein Show (podcast), 'The Jewish Left Is Trying to Hold Two Thoughts at Once', *New York Times*, 24 October 2023, https://www.nytimes.com/2023/10/24/opinion/ezra-klein-podcast-spencer-ackerman-peter-beinart.html.

13 Tony Judt, *Postwar: A History of Europe Since 1945* (London: Vintage Books, 2010), p. 27.

14 Cited in *ibid.*, p. 26.

15 *Ibid*, p. 27.

16 As Marshall also observes, it is 'precisely that river to the sea maximalism' – applied by a settlers' movement and governments beholden to it – 'that has been eating away at Israel from the inside since 1967'. Marshall, 'History from the River to the Sea and Across the Ocean'.

17 *Ibid.*

Correction

Article title: One Cold War Among Many?
Author: Pierre Hassner
Journal: *Survival*
Bibliometrics: Volume 65, Number 5, pages 203–212
DOI: https://doi.org/10.1080/00396338.2023.2261273

This article was republished in a 'From the Archives' section in the October–November 2023 issue of *Survival* (volume 65, number 5) with incorrect endnotes.

Notes 6–24 have now been removed and the correct Notes section for the article is as follows:

1   Paul Goble, 'Window on Eurasia: What the Georgian Events Demonstrate', http://windowoneurasia.blogspot.com/2008/08/window-on-eurasia-what-georgian-events.html. For Putin's nostalgia for the Soviet Union and wish to revive it in a different form, see his statement in *Komsomotskaya Pravda*, 2 February 2000.
2   Fyodor Lukyanov, 'Georgian Crisis Is a Trap for US Leadership', *Moscow Times*, 21 August 2008; Kishore Mahbubani, 'The West Is Strategically Wrong in Georgia', *Financial Times*, 21 August 2008.
3   George Friedman, 'The Russia–Georgian War and the Balance of Power', *Stratfor.com*, 12 August 2008, and 'Russia and Rotating the U.S. Focus', 1 April 2008.
4   Ronald Steel, 'A Superpower Is Reborn', *New York Times*, 24 August 2008.
5   See the five points outlined by Dmitri Medvedev on 1 September 2008 as guiding Russian foreign policy, especially the fourth, about protecting its foreign nationals everywhere, and the fifth about the right to 'historically special relations with its spheres of privileged interests'. See also Paul Reynolds, 'New Russian World Order, the Five Principles', BBC News, 1 September 2008, and the vigorous critique by Gareth Evans, 'Putin Twists U.N. Policy', *The Australian*, 2 September 2008.

This correction has been made to the online article.

Printed in the United States
by Baker & Taylor Publisher Services